# Arthur Fiedler

# Papa, the Pops and Me

## JOHANNA FIEDLER

# Arthur Fiedler

D O U B L E D A Y

New York   London   Toronto   Sydney   Auckland

PUBLISHED BY DOUBLEDAY
a division of Bantam Doubleday Dell Publishing Group, Inc.
1540 Broadway, New York, New York 10036

DOUBLEDAY and the portrayal of an anchor with a dolphin are
trademarks of Doubleday, a division of Bantam Doubleday Dell
Publishing Group, Inc.

Library of Congress Cataloging-in-Publication Data
Fiedler, Johanna.
Arthur Fiedler: Papa, the Pops and me / Johanna Fiedler.—1st ed.
p.   cm.
Includes bibliographical references (p.) and index.
1. Fiedler, Arthur, 1894–1979.   2. Conductors (Music)—United
States—Biography.   3. Boston Pops Orchestra.   I. Title.
ML422.F53F5   1994
784.2′092—dc20
[B]   94-7676
CIP   MN

ISBN 0-385-42391-8

1   3   5   7   9   10   8   6   4   2

For Peter Conrad

# Acknowledgments

I AM VERY GRATEFUL to the many people who shared their memories of my father with me, especially his close friends Pasquale Cardillo, William Cosel, Harry Ellis Dickson, Thomas Morris, David Mugar, and William Shisler, as well as Everett Firth, Angel Romero, and Roger Voisin.

His colleagues at the Boston Symphony Orchestra who took the time to talk to me included Victor Alpert, Carol Greene, William Moyer, Fredy Ostrovsky, Sheldon Rotenberg, and Harry Shapiro. His former professional associates who helped me included Harry Beall, David Foster, Harry Kraut, David Levinson, Margo Miller, Richard Mohr, Thomas Mowrey, Andrew Raeburn, Marvin Schofer, Mary Smith, and Max Wilcox. I would also like to thank William Berenberg, M.D., for his reminiscences.

I am indebted to the kindness of several institutions. At the Boston Symphony Orchestra, I would like to thank Kenneth Haas, Executive Director; Caroline Smedvig, Director of Public Relations; and, especially, Bridget Carr, Archivist. Materials preserved in the Boston Symphony Archives are used by permission of the Boston Symphony Orchestra, Inc.

My father's papers are kept at Boston University. The Arthur Fiedler Papers are preserved as part of Special Collections, Dr. Howard B. Gotlieb, Director. In addition to Dr. Gotlieb, I would like to thank Karen Mix and Charles Niles, Manuscript Technicians; Margaret Goostray, Assistant Director; Rhona Swartz, Executive Secretary; and Vita Paladino, Assistant to the Director.

I discovered an unexpected treasure trove of my father's newspaper clippings and miscellaneous letters and photographs at the Boston Public Library, and I am grateful for the patience and kindness of many people there: Laura Monti, Keeper of Rare Books and Manuscripts; Diane Ota, Curator of Music; Giuseppe Bisaccia, Curator of Manuscripts; Maryann Katsiane, Receptionist; Stuart Walker, Book Conservator; R. Eugene Zepp, Reference Librarian; and Roberta Zonghi, Curator of Rare Books.

I found many of the newspaper and magazine articles, reviews, and interviews with my father in the Fiedler Collection at the Boston Public Library. My father assembled these clippings himself, and did so in a haphazard fashion. He frequently clipped articles with no periodical reference and no dateline. I was usually able to ascertain the year and often even the month of the clipping, but was unable to be more specific in most cases as to the actual date or even the writer.

Part of this book was written at The Writers Room in New York City, and I am grateful to this organization for peace and sanctuary hard to find anywhere else in Manhattan.

Members of my family offered support, photographs, and reminiscences without ever asking to read the manuscript. I especially want to thank May Kenney Bottomley, Lydia Fuller Bottomley, James and Mary Bottomley, Anita and Axel Hoffer, Deborah Fiedler Stiles, and Anna Marie Svedrofsky. Up to the time of her death, in 1993, Cécile Gervais was a constant source of comfort and strength in the gestation of this book, as she was throughout my entire life.

Several people were helpful by reading all or part of the manuscript in its various manifestations, and I will always appreciate their support, criticisms, and honesty, including Peter Conrad, Richard Dyer, Nancy Malitz, Tim Page, and David M. Reuben.

For unceasing, generous kindness, I also thank the friends without whose patience and understanding I would never have been able to finish the manuscript.

My most profound thanks go to my editor, Jesse Cohen, and my agent, Cynthia Robbins. At Doubleday, I would also like to thank Jacqueline Onassis and Stephen E. Rubin for their faith in this book.

# Contents

INTRODUCTION
A Long-Distance Goodbye
15

ONE
"You're a *Fiedler*"
19

TWO
The House on Hyslop Road
35

THREE
Papa
71

FOUR
Mummy
106

FIVE

Sinfonia Domestica

120


SIX

Backstage at Symphony Hall

146


SEVEN

Papa and the Other Men in My Life

172


EIGHT

Part of Papa's World

193


NINE

The Last Concert

213


TEN

After Papa

240


Notes

255


Selected Discography

259


Index

261

Arthur Fiedler

?

# INTRODUCTION

---

# A Long-Distance Goodbye

---

I T'S BEEN A LONG TIME now, but sometimes I still hear my father's footsteps in the mornings, his eager steps as he hurries past my room on his way to Symphony Hall. I hear his whistle—the first four notes of Beethoven's Fifth, the Boston Symphony whistle—outside my windows, calling the dogs in from their walks. I hear the clink of the ice cubes in the pantry as he pours a drink before lunch; I hear him tossing bits of salami to the dogs, ripping open the day's mail. While we don't live in the big brick house in Brookline anymore—I have never even driven by it since the day we left, a few months after my father died—I still hear all these things.

Every time I went home to Boston while my father was alive, the routine was unchanged. I could set my watch by the unvarying schedule of his days; it's been years now, and I could fall back into the comfort of that schedule without thinking. The rest of life was often chaos but the routine went on. Every time I went home, I was reassured.

I didn't go home to Boston for the Fourth of July in 1976. Of course I knew my father was conducting a Bicentennial Concert at the Esplanade Shell on the banks of the Charles River, and that the free Independence Day concert was a special tradition in a city not much given to festivity. I had been living in New York for four years and wanted to spend the holiday with my friends, watching the Tall Ships and the fireworks from apartments high over the Hudson. Besides, I thought, why go home for another Independence Day concert? For me, it was just one more element of the routine. Papa conducted that concert almost every year, and every year the crowds got larger.

No, there was no reason to go home then, so I spent the long day in Manhattan, going from one party to another, watching the Tall Ships, eating and drinking, until, in the evening, it was time for the fireworks. We began to watch the display from someone's rooftop, but it was crowded, too hard to see, so we all went downstairs to a friend's apartment to watch on television. The immediacy wasn't quite the same, but it was a lot more comfortable.

"Look," someone said to me, pointing to the television set, "there's your father." I glanced at the screen, not particularly interested; after all, my father was on television all the time. CBS was broadcasting bicentennial celebrations from all over the United States, and although I was pleased that they included Papa's Esplanade Concert, I wasn't surprised. By then, I was used to extensive press coverage of almost everything Papa did.

Everyone else in the room was watching, though, so I began to concentrate—and soon realized that something different was going on. Papa was conducting Tchaikovsky's *1812 Overture*, but his audience wasn't listening in rapt silence. They were jumping up and down. I looked at the faces on the screen; the audience was young and energetic, not the kind of audience that usually went to classical music concerts.

And the crowd was huge. I had gone to my first Esplanade Concert—my first concert ever—when I was nine months old, and had been to innumerable others since. One of my first paying jobs had been distributing programs at the Esplanade. By this time, I could estimate the audience as accurately as the Metropolitan District Commission police in Boston.

From the overhead shots taken by panning cameras on the roofs of neighboring apartment buildings, I could tell this was the largest crowd I had ever seen. People filled the Esplanade and the adjacent highway, crammed boats on the Charles River Basin, and stretched back as far as the television cameras were able to show. Later I found out that the crowd had been just as dense on the Cambridge side of the river, where the music must have been almost inaudible. *The Guinness Book of Records* was to list this as the largest mass of people ever to attend a classical music performance.

As CBS stayed with the Esplanade Concert, I watched my father, wearing his usual Esplanade outfit of white shirt and white pants, conduct as vigorously as I had ever seen him. The orchestra was playing with more than customary spirit. The audience continued to dance and jump and gyrate in time with the music. And then came the fireworks as the *1812 Overture* reached its climax.

On the Upper West Side of New York City, I sat, mesmerized. It was as if the performance had crystallized that whole day of patriotic fervor. I felt an exuberance, a sense of occasion, and it wasn't just because I was watching my father conduct his orchestra; I was seeing him share with the entire country at once the happiness and pride he had always felt in being an American.

The concert was coming to an end. The fireworks exploded, the *1812 Overture* crashed to its conclusion, and Papa and the orchestra swung into their trademark concert closer, "The Stars and Stripes Forever." The audience went wild. People were clapping and shouting and singing, and Papa turned around on the podium and began conducting the audience, too. I loved seeing the joy on his face, even though I knew that there would be dark moments for him after the concert.

Almost half a million people were on hand to help my father and the Boston Pops celebrate the country's two hundredth anniversary, and I missed it. Although Papa was eighty-one years old, I thought the performances would never end. There would always be another Fourth of July, another opening of the Pops, another Carnegie Hall concert, another guest-conducting trip where I could join my father in a different city.

Of course I was wrong. I think now that Papa's career and, in fact, his life peaked at that Fourth of July concert. I wasn't there, and playing a video of it now doesn't diminish my regret. There should be a tutorial for children of famous people in choosing between those events involving your parents that you can miss because you have to get on with your own life, and those you can't miss because you'll regret it for the rest of your life. I never found the solution while Papa was alive.

Almost three years after the Bicentennial Concert, my father died, two months and five days after his last concert ever. I missed that concert, too.

After he collapsed at the end of that last performance, Papa knew there would be no more concerts. "When are you coming home?" he had asked me over the phone a few days before his death.

"I'll be home at the end of the week," I said.

I was too late. I never said goodbye to him in person. Like so much else in my relationship with my father, our goodbye took place long distance.

# ONE

---

## "You're a *Fiedler*"

---

Boston—The widely known director of the Boston Pops Concerts, Arthur Fiedler, has become a father. Fiedler announces the birth of a first child, a daughter, to Mrs. Fiedler, formerly Ellen Bottomley, a daughter of the late Dr. John Bottomley, prominent Boston surgeon.

IN THE FAMILY of a famous man, birth is the opportunity for a news story: this was how the Associated Press announcement read only hours after I was born. Too late to be included was the decision to name me Johanna, after my father's mother.

A reporter once asked my father why he had had children. "Mrs. Fiedler is a Roman Catholic, you know," he replied, "and they love big families. I suppose everyone does. At first I told her I didn't marry her to have children. I told her I married her so we could have wonderful times together, so she could go with me on my trips, so we could share our lives together. But she wanted children. My wife is twenty years younger than I, you know."

My mother had wanted children from the beginning of her marriage, but he had steadfastly refused to consider the idea. He was almost fifty when he married, and considered himself much too old and settled in his ways to become a father. After all, he had not even been able to imagine sharing a bedroom with his wife. My mother pleaded, but he was adamant.

When my parents had been married about four years, a series of events in my father's life changed his mind. He suffered a serious career reversal; his own father died at the age of eighty-four; and he himself almost died. Papa was stricken in his early fifties with a heart attack so serious that when he was brought to the hospital, the admitting doctors assumed he was going to die.

He too thought he was dying. In the ambulance on the way to the hospital, he told my mother that if he survived, he would grant her wish for children. Knowing my mother's tendency to dramatize history, I didn't believe this story until one of Papa's friends told it to me and said he had heard it from my father himself. "He was afraid that he was going to die without leaving anything behind," the friend said. "He wanted to leave a mark on the world." Children, he apparently thought, were more durable than recordings or broadcasts.

My father, as always, was a man of his word, and within a reasonable period of time, my mother was pregnant with me.

Often I wonder if things in our family were amiss from the beginning. My mother would make me cry when she described the paradise that was her marriage before I was born. "When I told your father I was pregnant," she said to me once—I was eight or nine—"do you know what he said to me?"

I cringed; I didn't want to hear the answer. "What did he say, Mummy?" I asked dutifully.

My mother assumed her most persecuted expression. "He said, 'Damn it all, Ellen, we were having so much fun.' "

The August before I was born, my father and his close friend John Cahill went on vacation together. My mother, eight and a half months pregnant, may have been happy to stay at home, but I can't imagine she was pleased when Papa set off for a leisurely three-week exploration of Canada. He did get back in time for my birth on September 17; that was also the solemn Jewish holiday of Yom Kippur, as my Jewish father delighted in reminding my Catholic mother. Because of this, he began to call me "Yom-Yom," which evolved to "Yum-Yum" before resolving into "Yummy," much to my dismay. Quite recently, a famous conductor who had known my father well died at an advanced age; a friend remarked, "At least now there's one less person in the world who calls you Yummy."

Years after my father died, I reminisced about him with the man who had been my pediatrician. "I was a young doctor," he told me, "and I always looked forward to spending my Saturday evenings with my wife and children. But, inevitably, on Saturday night I would get a call from your father."

Every Sunday afternoon at that time, Papa conducted members of the Boston Symphony in a live national radio broadcast from the Boston Opera House. By Saturday evening, he would be nervous about the next day's concert, and what he considered an out-of-control situation at home would drive him over the edge. He would call the young doctor, who, reluctantly but faithfully, would go over to the Brookline apartment where we were then living.

My father, his luxuriant hair in disarray, would open the door and demand that the doctor "do something!" The housekeeper, Louise, an elderly German woman who had been with my father during most of his bachelor years and who did not get on with my mother, would be sulking in the kitchen. My mother would be sobbing hysterically in her bedroom. And I would be all by myself in the dining room, which served as my bedroom, crying inconsolably. There was never anything wrong with me, the doctor reported; it was the unbearable tension in the apartment that was upsetting me. As there was no way to medicate the atmosphere, he would advise my mother and father to calm down, and he'd go back to his own family, delighted to get out of the Fiedler household.

Although Papa decided that, aside from these moments, I was cute and interesting as a newly living creature, he quickly returned to his life of rehearsals, concerts, broadcasts, and recording sessions, pausing only to complain when my unhappiness intruded on his concentration. But my mother had achieved her often-proclaimed life's goal, and there was no escape for her.

Mummy was overwhelmed by a real baby. The daughter of wealthy Irish-Catholic parents, she had never experienced a moment of responsibility up to the day she married, at the age of twenty-eight. Then, by marrying an older man with an established household, she postponed having to make any arrangements or decisions for herself.

When I arrived, she was confronted with a helpless creature who cried constantly, was colicky, broke out in hives, and was frequently sick. This wasn't the beautifully dressed little doll she had been expecting when she begged my father for a child; this was a noisy, dirty, smelly little animal that she had never imagined she could produce. After a few weeks, my mother, an immaculate woman horrified by natural functions, could no longer bear direct contact with vomit and diapers, and she hired a nurse. For the first two years of my life, I was taken care of by a series of unreliable nannies, and, in extreme emergencies, by my own mother, the most unreliable of all. "Your mother never got out of her nightgown for the first six months of your life," my Aunt May has often said to me.

Despite all of this, my mother kept up the façade and called me her "heaven-sent" baby. Of course, she was to call my sister and brother exactly the same thing, but after I was born she religiously wrote her reminiscences of my babyhood in a powder-pink volume entitled *Our Baby's First Seven Years*. Her entries didn't extend much beyond my second year, when my sister was born, but Debbie's baby book is even emptier, and I don't think there is a single word written in Peter's.

After a full page of newspaper clippings announcing my birth, there is an account of my first ten days, noted by the baby nurse who came home from the hospital with my mother. I heard only one story from my mother about the very beginning of my life. My father came to visit her in the hospital every evening of her ten-day stay, and he always brought a bottle of champagne. One evening when he had a rehearsal and couldn't come, she had no champagne. That was the night I refused to nurse.

There are lots of pictures in the baby book. Several of the early ones show me at concerts on the Esplanade, a serious child dressed impeccably, often sitting on a blanket at my mother's feet. With my favorite stuffed animal safely at my side, I am staring at the stage and my father's back, my fat little arms raised in the air as though copying Papa's gestures.

According to my mother's notes, I was an unusually musical child. At eight months, I was sitting on my father's bed while he had breakfast, and my mother wrote, "She always swayed to music on the radio, and if the radio was not on, swayed to indicate she would like to hear music. Beamed as the music came on! One could very definitely understand her singing the first few measures of 'The Bowery' at ten months. Before two would go around playing, singing very much in tune and absolutely on pitch. At two years showed a definite sense of rhythm. Loved to dance to any music heard."

When I was a baby, perhaps during a chorus of "The Bowery," which my family obviously considered preferable to "Mary Had a Little Lamb," Papa discovered by accident that I had inherited his perfect sense of pitch. On the rare occasions that he paid attention to me, he would take me to the piano and help me bang away at the keyboard. Sometimes he would strike various notes and have me guess what they were. Apparently I was almost always able to answer correctly. Papa was thrilled; often when he and my mother had guests over for the evening, he would get me out of bed, seat me by the piano, and bang out notes for me to identify. I'm sure I was gratified by the attention, particularly from my father, but evidently I didn't like being awakened out of a sound sleep to perform. I stopped having perfect pitch as one of my earliest acts of rebellion against my own set of family obligations.

There were many obligations for members of our family. The comments in my pink baby book attest to my mother's frustration when I was unable to live up to her expectations in "personal habits." Although I was walking, running, and climbing stairs "with great assurance" by the time I was a year old, my mother remarked, "*Still* unable to pick herself up after falling down. Just lies or sits still until someone gives her a lift up." Fortunately by eighteen months, "she can now pick herself up, but what a struggle!" I also seemed to have trouble learning to hold a glass with two hands unless "she pleases to," or using a spoon "with good control. Lazy about helping herself! Can do if she wants to!" The implication was that I was slothful or, even worse, defiant.

By the time I was four and attending nursery school, I had learned to be an extremely self-controlled little girl. A long evaluation from the Park School in Brookline commented, in part:

Being a most fastidious person, Johanna has found it difficult at first to play with clay despite a great desire to do so. She handled it with as little of her hands as possible . . . Exceptionally well poised and most polite . . . her play has been chiefly solitary. Johanna, possessing an excellent memory and a long attention span, derives much pleasure from story time, being able to listen to four or five books at one time.

I have a vision of a child trying desperately to be perfect. I was already a failure in the eyes of my perfectionist mother and not of much interest to my busy father. At school I would be charming to everyone, just as I saw my mother behaving with people outside the family. I would stay by myself as much as possible, avoid finger painting or outside activities that might make me dirty, enjoy music in my limited way, and, best of all, lose myself in the fantasy world of stories.

Although I had never seen this evaluation before beginning this memoir, I somehow knew that I was doing well at school, even when I was very little. My father frequently expressed his great pride that I was a good student, and he encouraged me to enjoy the process of educating myself. My mother, on the other hand, dismissed my good school reports: "Angel at school, devil at home," she would say to me.

Pictures of me at the time show a perfectly dressed little girl. My mother was mystified by my curly hair—inherited, she pointed out, from the Fiedler side of the family—and experimented with various hair styles before she gave up and decided to hack it all off. But even in photos with my mother and father, I always have a stuffed animal nearby. For years, I would go to bed only if I could take all my stuffed animals under the covers with me.

In the pink baby book, my mother wrote that I "stuttered and stammered badly about two and a half to three. Recovered from it completely, with an occasional reappearance once in a great while." No one seemed to notice that the beginning of my stuttering coincided with the arrival of my new baby sister, Deborah, when I was two years old. Even if my mother had made the connection, she would doubtless have been horrified by this evidence of my resentment. In her imagination, her perfect children would all get along with one another, although she herself had fought constantly with her sister and four brothers. If Debbie and I didn't get along—and we didn't—the reason was clear to Mummy. I was the older and it was my duty to love and welcome a little sister. Since I didn't, there must have been something wrong with me.

When I was grown, I once asked my mother why she had never understood that my temper tantrums and general misbehavior came from jealousy of the new baby. "Why would you mind Debbie being born?" she asked in true bewilderment. "After all, I took you out for an ice cream the day before she arrived."

To make matters worse, there was a great difference in personality between my sister and me. I had been a difficult baby, fussy and inconsolable. As is often the case with second children, when the parents are less nervous, Debbie was more placid. She was also cute—plump and sweet, with huge brown eyes. I was a skinny, nervous little thing, obsessed about being neat, probably in a desperate attempt to please my mother. I wouldn't go to bed unless my shoes were precisely lined up on the closet floor and would stubbornly refuse to continue a walk if a piece of dirt got on my shoes or socks. I imagine I was not a great pleasure to be around.

I was lucky as the first child because I was forgiven by my father for not being a boy. Debbie was much more of a disappointment to him. "Ellen and the baby got home and everything is fine—but how (!) do you get a boy!?!" Papa wrote to one of his friends. Ironically, by the time my brother was born, four years after Debbie, Papa was tired of being a father. Neither Debbie nor I had yet reached the age of carrying on an extended conversation, and all of a sudden my father found himself surrounded by three children who were noisy, demanding, took up most of my mother's time, and weren't interesting or productive.

Shortly after Debbie was born, a most important person came to live with us. Cécile Gervais, a French-Canadian nanny, was in her early thirties when my mother hired her, and from the first few days, my parents realized they had found someone extraordinary. None of my nannies had lasted more than a few weeks, but Celie immediately took charge, bringing order and regularity to the chaotic household. Even our pediatrician, when Celie took Debbie and me for our check-ups, quickly noticed the difference. "Thank God," he said to Celie, specifically pointing out the change in me. I had begun to relax under Celie's calming influence.

But I was already two years old. Debbie was an infant, and Celie regarded her as her own child; they shared a bedroom until Debbie was nearly a teenager. There was no way I could be as important to this new savior as my sister was. Celie was also on hand for Peter's birth, and he became equally dear to her. I felt left out. Although Celie went out of her way not to show favoritism, I felt I wasn't as loved as the others.

My jealousy of my sister continued to eat at me. My parents had moved out of their apartment to a house in Brookline when Debbie was born. The new house was so big that my father had his own suite of rooms, where he could completely shut himself off from the rest of the family. There was less pressure on my mother to keep the new baby from crying, and no one had to hear the unstoppable tantrums I began to produce after Debbie's appearance. My mother would simply lock me in the linen closet.

She also continued to ignore the reason that I was hysterical. I was told years later of an event that rings so true, I can almost remember it happening. One evening, my mother was in bed nursing Debbie—she breast-fed all three of us, oddly enough for her—when I came into her bedroom and ran round and round the bed. "I want some, too!" I am supposed to have cried.

"No," my mother said firmly. "This is only for good babies." If she really did say this, it was the first instance of her voicing her "bad baby" theory about me. She became firmly convinced, as I displayed my jealousy of my sister in more and more vehement ways, that there was something inherently wrong with me. "You're like your father's family; you're bad-tempered and mean," she said to me over and over. "You're a *Fiedler."* She made it sound like the worst fate in the world.

Eventually, being a Fiedler seemed to me a badge of honor. My father never called me a bad baby. He never seemed more interested in the new baby than he was in me, although, to be honest, he wasn't particularly interested in either of us. But I do remember his being a much more loving father than the way my mother later described him. He would take me into bed with him while he ate breakfast and draw me pictures on big sheets of paper. He was a fairly talented caricaturist, and although I never showed any artistic inclinations as I scribbled alongside him, he didn't seem irritated. He would bounce me up and down on his knees, telling me it was like riding a horse, and every once in a while he would open his knees, and I would collapse on top of him, shrieking with glee.

Celie held the family together; she got up in the mornings when we did, ate her meals with us, was available for chats in the evenings when we had finished our homework and before we went to bed. Papa was often away, and Mummy was vaguely unavailable, rarely in the same room as the three of us. "We'll always take care of you, Celie," we would say, probably hoping that if we promised to worry about her future she wouldn't leave us. The other two adults we lived with already had.

I think we all missed our mother, and I certainly missed my father. Mummy's presence became increasingly ghostly as we got older. But we were used to turning to Celie for our practical needs. She created a schedule for us and kept us to it; she laid the foundation for our home life and whatever sense of security we would carry with us. Like my parents, however, she was not an outwardly affectionate person. There were no spontaneous hugs, no quick kisses when we went off to school, no cuddles in the lonely evenings. But there was reliability. Without Celie, there would have been chaos.

WHEN MY MOTHER accusingly described me as "a *Fiedler,"* I had a vague sense of what she meant. "Fiedlers" were definitely different from her own family, the Bottomleys, and probably inferior as well. My Fiedler relatives weren't as affluent as the Bottomleys; they didn't speak English as well, loved animals more, paid more attention to me, squabbled frequently among themselves, and, most obviously, were Jewish, not Catholic. I thought it exotic that my Fiedler relatives were almost all musicians and usually spoke German to one another, but I also knew that my mother didn't think them as good as her own family.

The Fiedlers came originally from Sambor, which in the nineteenth century was part of the Austro-Hungarian Empire. After the First World War, Sambor became a part of Poland and, after the Second World War, part of the Soviet Union. It is now located in Ukraine.

My father never talked about Sambor; he did make a trip there in the 1920s to see the little city where he had spent summers as a child, but left quickly, horrified by its provincial atmosphere. Still, I was able to find out a few things about his family's life in Sambor. The Fiedlers had been musicians for generations. In fact, the family name means "violinist." "After all," Papa once said, "as a tailor came by the name of Schneider in the old country, and a cobbler was a Shumacher, so we fiddlers became Fiedlers."

My father's grandfather, a violinist named Isaac, became conductor of the town orchestra at the age of seventeen. He and the orchestra traveled around the countryside playing at fairs and weddings. Isaac had three boys and three girls. The sons, including my father's father, Emanuel, studied music, just as the Fiedlers had for as far back as anyone could remember. When Emanuel left Sambor and attended the Vienna Conservatory, he was a classmate of Fritz Kreisler and won the school's prestigious Gold Medal, awarded to the best student on graduation. Having decided not to return to Sambor, he began playing for one of the opera orchestras in Vienna.

In the 1880s, American orchestras competed fiercely to recruit the top graduates of the best conservatories in Europe. There were few native-born American musicians at that time because there was no teaching tradition established in the United States. When Wilhelm Gericke, the conductor of the Boston Symphony, approached Emanuel in 1885, the young violinist was twenty-six; spending a few years in the United States must have seemed a great adventure to him. The only thing holding him in Vienna was his romantic involvement with Johanna Bernfeld, whom he had met as a student. Emanuel promised Johanna that as soon as he had established himself and made a home in Boston, he would come back to marry her and bring her to America. In time both of Emanuel's brothers joined the Boston Symphony—Bernhard in 1896 and Gustav in 1918.

When Emanuel arrived in Boston, the symphony was only four years old. (Coincidentally, 1885 was the year the Boston Symphony instituted its Pops concerts.) By 1888, he was secure enough in his position and new home to return to Vienna, marry Johanna, and bring her to Boston. On December 17, 1894, my father was born, the third of four children and the only boy. The birth took place in Emanuel and Johanna's apartment on Norway Street in Boston, just around the corner from Symphony Hall.

My grandfather had never intended to stay in Boston. In 1910, when he was fifty years old, Emanuel retired from the Boston Symphony and brought his family back to Europe. Papa always remained puzzled by his father's actions. "It's funny, but he never became an American citizen. They [the Symphony] kept giving him short-term contracts and he kept signing them. But he never gave a thought to citizenship. He was thoroughly European and always thought he'd be going home. We went back to Vienna and, after about a year, on to Berlin."

Emanuel gave up more than just the Boston Symphony when he returned to Europe. He had been a founding member of the Kneisel Quartet, an ensemble of Boston Symphony musicians and one of the most acclaimed chamber music groups in the United States. It toured extensively throughout the country, and my father became accustomed to Emanuel's long absences on concert trips. When his own career expanded, he saw nothing unusual about leaving his wife and the three children for extended periods.

Emanuel also never got involved in the running of his household. "My father didn't do a damned thing," my father said about the family's return to Europe in the spring of 1910. Johanna packed up the accumulated possessions of twenty-five years in Boston, and the moving men trooped in and out of the house

under her direction while, in the distance, the sounds of Emanuel's violin filtered from his study. In my own life there were many
family upheavals accompanied by the sound of Papa playing the
piano in his own closed-off study—if, by chance, he happened to
be home.

My father was five when he began studying the piano with Johanna and the violin with Emanuel. But music was not all he was
studying. He received lessons in French and German. "I was
brought up in a thoroughly European manner," my father said. He
freely admitted that he hated to practice, "but I did it anyway,
because it was my duty. You see, I was given music lessons, not for
a career, but for discipline. I had to learn German, too. I even
learned to write in German script—which is not at all easy—because it was my duty to write to my grandfather in Europe. I was a
busy lad, and hated all of it."

The little fun my father had as a child came from outside the
strict household.

When I was growing up, I liked to play ball with the other kids, but I
spent most of my time practicing and couldn't get out. So when I had a
little time free, I'd go down the street to the nearby firehouse, play with
the dogs, pat the horses—they had horse-drawn trucks in those days—
and make friends with the firemen. They were all nice fellows and let me
slide down the pole from the room upstairs where they slept or played
cards between calls. Then the alarm would sound and off they'd go.

Unlike his driven father, the men at the firehouse let him be a
little boy. But when they were needed, the fun stopped. "When
that alarm sounded, I always thought, 'Gee, I wish I could go,
too,'" he said. As Papa watched the engines tear down the street,
a determination must have been born in him: when he grew up, he
was never going to be left behind.

Of course, Papa's fascination with fires became his most famous
eccentricity, and he was made an honorary fire chief in more than
three hundred cities around the world. He never tired of receiving
the fire hats and badges that came with these honors; they symbolized his joining the ranks of those mythic men he had idolized as a

boy. To him, being a firefighter was more manly and heroic than being a musician.

In 1969, Papa was at home eating breakfast on the morning of his seventy-fifth birthday when he heard the wail of sirens. Although he had a rehearsal with the Boston Symphony that morning —the best birthday present the orchestra could give him was a rare opportunity to conduct the B.S.O. under its real name—he jumped up and went to the front door. "I kept sniffing the air, trying to smell smoke," he said afterward. A flock of fire engines and hook-and-ladder trucks filled Hyslop Road, and right in the middle of the Boston Fire Department's state-of-the-art equipment was a 1938 pump truck that a friend of mine had located in New Hampshire, and that Mummy, Debbie, Peter, and I had bought Papa for his birthday.

He got into the front seat of the pumper, and a procession of scarlet fire engines rolled through the streets of Boston toward Symphony Hall. Bells rang and sirens howled as the parade sailed through intersections, the traffic halted by beaming policemen who waved at Papa and shouted, "Happy Birthday!" Finally, the procession pulled up at the stage door of Symphony Hall, just in time for the rehearsal.

"Ah, what a beauty she is!" he exclaimed. "I keep my fire engine in the garage and I put my Lincoln out in the street."

FIEDLER GETS BOYHOOD WISH AS HE TURNS 75, the Associated Press story proclaimed.

Because of his well-publicized hobby, my childhood was full of shrieking sirens, panting Dalmatian dogs, and phones ringing in the middle of the night to announce the latest conflagration in the city; my father had a standing arrangement with the Boston Fire Department to be notified of any fire that went above three alarms. Our cars were equipped with police radios, Fire Department license plates, and even sirens, which Papa loved to turn on. All this may have contributed to how unsafe I felt as a child. I lay awake night after night, sure that there was a fire somewhere in our enormous house. Or maybe this was a way of wishing that my father would come home from one of his long tours; if the house were on fire, Papa would have to come back.

I didn't consider my father's interest in fires strange when I was a child, just as I didn't consider his profession unusual, even though none of my schoolmates' fathers went to work at night wearing white tie and tails and carrying a baton, or went away on tour for months at a time. Almost no other children my age had chores at home that included the cataloguing of a seemingly endless collection of miniature scores. And surely few fathers had three hundred fire helmets distributed casually throughout their home or had a siren in the family car.

I got used to my father's sudden departures in the middle of the night after one of the Fire Department phone calls and to his return in the early morning smelling strongly of smoke. Some of my earliest memories are of him shrugging off his overcoat in the front hall as he described the night's blaze, his eyes dancing with excitement. In my scrapbooks are pictures from those fires: of Papa giving artificial respiration to a dog he had rescued from a burning building; of Debbie and me, as little girls, clinging to the back of an enormous fire engine with expressions of sheer terror on our faces. We were scared of going to fires, with the roaring flames, suffocating smoke, gushing hoses, and shouting firemen, but we saw there a side of Papa that made up for the fright. At the fires, he turned back into a child himself, the little boy sneaking away from his violin practice to have some fun.

THE CONVIVIAL WORLD of a firehouse must have been a welcome contrast to Papa's home life while he was growing up. Emanuel kept to his world of music, and Johanna was reserved, strict, and distant. She was not a mother whom her children could run to and hug, and my father grew up to be a person who could not abide impulsive displays of affection. I kissed Papa good morning and good night every day we spent together, just as he had done with his mother and father, but these were ceremonial gestures. When there was any kind of family gathering, my father would open the festivities by announcing, "No kissing!" And he meant it.

Johanna was in charge of all aspects of the four children's upbringing except music, and she ran the household with an iron hand. Although my father's sister Rosa told me she thought Papa had been his mother's favorite—he was the only child Johanna referred to by an affectionate German diminutive, Arturchen—he did not escape her firm discipline.

Papa was a handful. He was a mischievous child who put frogs in his sisters' beds and teased them unmercifully. He sneaked out of the apartment on a regular basis, once for an entire day, and several times for most of the night. On these escapades, he and his friends would go to watch the circus set up for a Boston engagement or roam about the streets shooting off firecrackers and toy guns.

He would come home from these outings to face a powerful scolding from his mother, who confined him to the house for varying lengths of time. Strict as the Fiedler parents were, house arrest was the sternest punishment they meted out. There was never any physical discipline, although Emanuel would occasionally rap the children over the fingers with his violin bow while they were practicing.

But Papa was terrified of his mother's displeasure. As a child, he once fell into the pond in the Boston Public Garden while ice skating. Instead of going home to get out of his wet clothes, he was so afraid of his mother's wrath that he went to the Public Library several blocks away, on Copley Square, and sat there until he was dry.

That story always reminded me that I was terrified of Papa, even when I was in my twenties. I would hurry back from an evening out to make sure I got home before my father, and often barely got into the house before I heard his car returning from that night's concert. I would run into my room, not turning on the light, so that Papa wouldn't see it from the driveway, and jump into bed with all my clothes on. Then I'd pull the covers up to my neck, strip off my earrings, and try to quiet my rapid breathing. Soon, I would hear him coming down the hall and pausing at my door. There would be a peremptory knock; the door would open. "You're home?"

"Yes, Papa."

"Did you have a good evening?" He never asked where I had been, because he often didn't want to know.

"Yes, Papa."

"Well, sleep well and I'll see you in the morning. Let me know if my radio is on too loud." My door would close, his door would close, and I would sigh with relief.

When Papa told me stories about his childhood—the endless practicing, the discipline, the language studies—I would feel untalented, unproductive, lazy. But there was one story he told that inevitably made me cry.

Papa loved any kind of theatrical performance. His mother took him to the circus or a vaudeville show to reward him for a particularly diligent stretch of practicing and good behavior. On one occasion, when he was very small, his mother arranged to take his two older sisters to the circus but did not invite him. When he pleaded to be included, his mother teased him by saying that the circus was not for children with brown eyes. "They don't want children with black, dirty eyes," he remembered her saying to him. Papa, who was as pragmatic a child as he would be an adult, went into the bathroom and began to wash his eyes with soap on a nail brush, certain he could lighten them enough to qualify for the circus trip. He immediately screamed in pain, and his mother had to wash his eyes out with milk. No one went to the circus that day.

When I was a child, I would lie awake and think of that little boy, made to feel unwanted because of the color of his eyes, and I would cry in sympathy. There were plenty of times in my own childhood when I was told I was unlovable because of things about myself that I couldn't change, such as those similarities to my father which my mother pointed out with scorn. I wonder at my grandmother's thoughtless cruelty, yet I'm sure she never meant to hurt her children. All the Fiedlers, though, have the ability to wound with unthinking remarks or actions. My brother and sister and I are no different, and our heritage goes directly back to Johanna.

# TWO

---

# The House on Hyslop Road

---

W E LIVED at 133 Hyslop Road in Brookline from the time I was two until my father's death, in 1979. Our home was referred to in countless stories about my father as "a stately Georgian mansion," "a comic's clone of Symphony Hall." Its size afforded everyone who lived there plenty of room. "Privacy is the secret of a happy home," Papa always said. "Take the word of a converted bachelor."

The house was impressive from the outside, thanks to the combined and unrelenting efforts of our gardeners and us three reluctant children. Joseph Spotts, my father's long-time valet and handyman, also helped; he regularly and thoroughly washed the cars that gleamed by the front door, and he carefully raked the gravel in the driveway.

Inside, the house was different. My mother kept it darkened; she flew through the house every morning, particularly in nice weather, drawing the curtains and lowering the shades of the many windows. "The sun will ruin the rugs and the furniture," she claimed. I would open my curtains as soon as she had moved on, but if I left the house for even a brief errand, my bedroom would be darkened again by the time I got back. The gloom had a forbidding quality that our infrequent guests noticed as soon as they walked in the front door.

The gloom probably served to hide the shabbiness of the interior. Only the wood-paneled library, everyone's favorite room, was kept in good condition. In all the other parts of the house, the paint was peeling, the rugs and upholstery were threadbare, and the appliances were prehistoric. Celie had a green thumb with flowers, and the only note of cheer was provided by the house plants that flourished despite the lack of sunlight.

The dining room, although it opened directly onto the sunny terrace at the back of the house, still managed to be dark and dreary. Part of the problem was the wallpaper, a turgid design of brown flowers on a light brown background, which would have looked more appropriate in my grandmother's Victorian town house. Papa, having grown up in the Victorian era, was unaccountably fond of this wallpaper, but the rest of us were delighted when it began to peel off the walls. Even my mother, who paid little attention to her surroundings, made plans to have the room redecorated.

One morning when I was nearly grown up, I came down to breakfast after waiting to make sure Papa had already headed off to Symphony Hall. Much as I loved him, I found him unbearably critical in the mornings. "Ssh!" Celie warned me as I came into the kitchen before I had even thought about speaking. "Your father's in the dining room."

"Uh-oh" was my instinctive response. Any variation from Papa's established schedule meant something was wrong. I got a cup of coffee and tiptoed into the dining room. There, clad in one of the sleepcoats he always wore to bed, Papa was standing on a shaky ladder, holding a large container of the special adhesive tape he used to repair torn pages in his orchestral scores. To my disbelief, I saw that he was taping the wallpaper back on the walls.

"What are you doing?" I asked.

"I *like* this wallpaper," he said icily. "We'll never find anything like it, so I'm fixing it." Teetering on the unsteady ladder with his equally unsteady legs, he went back to work with his characteristic concentration.

One of the stranger highlights of our home decor was a large hole in the wall at the foot of the front stairs. Mummy had slipped on the stairs one afternoon, and had plunged down the full flight with such force that she knocked a crater in the wall so deep that it cracked the dining room wall on the other side. After making sure she was all right, Papa surveyed the hole and arrived at a solution. For years, he had been collecting scatter rugs from various exotic countries. He went upstairs, got one of the rugs, and tacked it neatly up on the wall, covering the hole. The rug stayed there until we sold the house; the hole was never fixed.

Upstairs were our bedrooms, separated by long corridors. My mother's room and my father's suite were at opposite ends of the house, an arrangement we never thought of as peculiar, especially since their relationship was characterized by formality in many areas. I never heard my father refer to my mother as anything other than "Mrs. Fiedler" in the presence of people outside the family. They kept their financial lives completely separate; neither of them had any real idea of how much the other was worth. When Papa's accountant finally prevailed on him to file a joint income tax return with my mother to lower his tax rate, Papa consented only grudgingly. Each April he would present the tax return to my mother folded in such a way that the only line she could see was the one where she had to sign.

My mother contributed generous amounts to the household expenses from the comfortable income she had inherited. She paid for our clothes, the cleaning ladies' wages, and most of the groceries. Papa, with enormous grumbling, paid the taxes, the heating bills, Celie's and Spotts's salaries, and the general upkeep on the house. But he kept an exceptionally vigilant eye on everything he paid for. "Close the front door!" he would bellow when we opened it to let the dogs out. "What are you trying to do? Heat all of Brookline?"

My father was known throughout Boston for his conservative attitude toward money; he had a definite miserly streak. Boston Symphony musicians who knew him all have stories about his ploys to have them pick up restaurant tabs; he checked his bank statements so carefully that he once caught an error of one penny made by the bank. Papa seemed oblivious of any stigma that could be attached to this behavior. He went to the box office at Symphony Hall one day to ask a favor. "Would you be able to cash a check for me?" he asked. "I'd like to take Mrs. Fiedler out to dinner."

The box office treasurer quickly took stock of the cash on hand. "How much will you be needing, Mr. Fiedler?"

Papa thought for a moment. "Well, it's a special occasion. I'd better make it for twenty dollars."

He considered food an easy area in which to economize. "Most people eat too much," he often said, "and then they waste too much energy digesting." When I was in my middle twenties and living in New York, my father launched a campaign to lure me back home. Since I was lonely during my first years in New York, the idea wasn't totally repugnant to me, which my father sensed. "I'll give you all the freedom in the world," he promised. "I'll even give you your own key to the front door." A few doubts began to fester in me.

I came home for a weekend, and Papa announced that we would be having a festive lunch in my honor. He went down to his fusty wine cellar and dredged up an ancient bottle of champagne. We regularly opened similar bottles of champagne on Thanksgiving and Christmas only to find that the wine had turned to vinegar years before. It then had to be consigned to the salad-dressing ingredients. Papa never understood the concept that some things couldn't be hoarded.

This bottle was passable, as I remember, and Papa said, "We're having your favorite lunch—lobster." I had been a vegetarian for several years by then; my father, customarily unforgiving of other people's eccentric beliefs, had enthusiastically supported me. "The price of beef really *is* shocking," he said when, trembling, I first told him that I didn't eat meat anymore.

We sat down at the table, Papa in an unusually expansive mood, and the main course was brought in. As promised, my plate had a cold lobster on it—a small cold lobster, but a lobster. Everyone else was served two boiled hot dogs. "Why am I the only one who's having lobster?" I asked.

"Do you know how much those things cost?" Papa demanded.

FOR OUR BIRTHDAYS, Papa had decided that the appropriate gift would be a dollar for each year of our age. When I was eighteen, he gave me eighteen dollar bills; when I was away or he was away on my birthday, I would receive a prompt check for twenty-one dollars or twenty-four dollars or whatever was applicable.

On one birthday, however, he broke the tradition. He came to visit my tiny apartment in New York when I first moved there to work for the New York Philharmonic and, instead of being appalled by the impoverished conditions in which I lived, was actually pleased. "Neat as a pin," he reported to my mother, "and quite Bohemian." But he was horrified that I didn't own a television, something I couldn't afford on my minuscule salary as a fledgling in the performing arts. With no TV, there was no way for me to watch his series, "Evening at Pops," which had become one of his proudest achievements.

So, with great fanfare and advance publicity to everyone he knew, he declared he would give me a television set for my birthday in 1976. Unable to procure a free one from RCA or any of his other recording companies, he got in touch with a friend who dealt in wholesale electronics and was able to get a nine-inch color set at what to anyone else would have seemed a good price. But a friend of mine who was working at Symphony Hall told me later that my father had gone to every office in the building, showing the receipt for the television set and the extravagant amount it had cost.

His thrifty nature led to another of his quirks as the head of the household: his insistence that everyone be productive. He believed that children were idle creatures who needed to be forced to work. When we were little, we would freeze as we heard his car scrunching over the pebbles of our driveway. Sometimes I would run up to the rarely used third floor and hide in the closet of the "guest room"—a fanciful name, since we never had overnight guests.

The front door would slam and Papa would whistle hello to

whoever happened to be in the house. The dogs would run to greet him, and we three children would follow, with considerably more reluctance. "What are you kids doing?" he would demand. "Have you done your practicing?"

We would nod, knowing what lay ahead. If it was winter, the next question would be about our homework. My sister and I would suddenly remember that we hadn't finished our French or our algebra, and would escape to our bedrooms. Peter, who was no scholar, would usually declare that he didn't have any, and my father would launch a search for chores. No child of his was going to sit around the house unoccupied.

Summers were worse, because there was no school and therefore no homework. There were, however, dandelions. Our house was surrounded by about an acre of lush lawn—and flourishing dandelions. At some point, Papa had developed an obsession about getting rid of the weeds, and the three of us had been chosen as his agents. If, on arriving home from Symphony Hall, he found us lounging around doing something as shiftless as reading (when he was in a particularly bad mood; the rest of the time reading was fine), he would bluster, "What's happening with the dandelions? The front lawn is full of them." We knew there was no hope of reprieve, so we would put away our books, fetch our little hoes from the pantry, and set to work on the never-ending task of uprooting the dandelions. I hate the sight of those weeds to this day.

But there were the loving moments, too. My father liked to relax by watching boxing matches on television, the "prizefights," as he always called them. Mummy considered boxing the height of barbarism and refused to join him. But I did. Papa would get me out of my bedroom and take me up to his bed, where together we would watch the fights. I wasn't the least bit interested in seeing two men pummeling each other, but I was very interested in spending all this time alone with my father, so I pretended to be fascinated. We lay there companionably while he explained the subtleties of the sport to me, and eventually, feeling as safe as I possibly could, I would fall asleep. My only desire, other than being with my father, was to see a fighter knocked out, but the one time there was a KO, I was fast asleep.

These intimate times came less often as my father traveled more. Peter particularly suffered, because Papa was around the house so little while he was growing up. I know my father loved Peter, but it must have been hard for outsiders to tell. Early one summer evening during the Esplanade season, Peter, about six at the time, was riding his bike up and down Hyslop Road; Debbie and I were sitting on the front lawn; Papa was upstairs getting ready for the concert.

There was a tremendous crash, and Debbie and I rushed down the street to find Peter lying on the pavement. Riding his bike too fast around a curve in the road, he had run into a car coming the other way. Although the car had been going slowly, Peter had a bad cut through his eyelid.

Debbie and I raced back to the house to get help, and in seconds Mummy and Celie were running down the street. Just then the driver coming to take Papa to the concert pulled up at the front steps.

The next few minutes are a confused memory. One of our neighbors carried Peter, bleeding profusely, back to the house. Mummy and Celie were weeping, and Debbie and I hovered nervously nearby. Then Papa came out the front door, dressed from head to toe in white, the outfit he wore for outdoor concerts. He gazed from Peter to my mother to Peter to the neighbor.

"Is he all right?" Papa asked.

"He's fine," the man said. "He has a bad cut and needs stitches, but I don't think anything is broken. Do you want me to drive him to the emergency room?"

Papa nodded his thanks. All of us were mesmerized by the contrast between Peter's dark red blood and Papa's snowy clothing. "I'll call later to make sure he's all right," he said to my mother.

He walked over to my brother, carefully keeping his distance from the blood. "Keep your chin up, Peter," he said, and turned away. He walked purposefully up the front steps to the street. The driver held open the car door, Papa got in, the door closed, and the car drove away. None of us thought that episode unusual, and my mother and Celie went to the hospital with Peter. Later, Papa did call, and we reassured him that Peter was better. He conducted the last section of the concert with a free mind.

WE LEARNED EARLY that part of our duty was to maintain the public image of being a happy family. This was our responsibility twenty-four hours a day. We were instructed never, under any circumstances, to boast or even speak proudly about our father, but at the same time we were to assume that everyone knew. We were supposed to be perfectly behaved, perfectly dressed, and perfect in our schoolwork and musical activities. Otherwise, "it would reflect badly on Papa," I can hear my mother's words echoing in my head. Papa would never have said anything so specific, although it was clear he concurred in his expectations of us. Even now, I weigh what I do lest it "reflect badly on Papa."

Debbie and I were trotted out on various ceremonial occasions such as the twenty-fifth anniversary of the Esplanade Concerts. "Among the tributes was a large Paul Revere–style silver bowl from the members of the Esplanade Concert Committee. Little Johanna and Deborah presented the bowl to their father, who held it aloft and then returned it to the two girls in gray frocks, who, walking as if on eggs, bore it carefully offstage." I can only imagine what the reprisals at home would have been if we had dropped the bowl. On another anniversary, the two of us actually rode out into the middle of the Boston Pops Orchestra on a Vespa motor scooter that was being presented to Papa by a local radio station.

Even my first concert at the age of nine months became an extended photo opportunity. My parents posed me backstage on a variety of musical instruments—on top of a timpani, in the curve of a double bass. Then I was perched on a table by the stage door to watch my father sign autographs. I appear to be completely fascinated by all this.

In fact, I spent a large portion of my childhood on top of various musical instruments. I was photographed at two on a piano while Papa played Christmas carols for the children in a Boston orphanage. I graduated to the piano's keyboard when, at five, I was awarded a medal in a local piano competition, but a year or so later it was back up on top. For the celebration of Papa's twenty-fifth

anniversary as conductor of the Pops, Debbie and I were led onto
the stage of Symphony Hall and placed on the grand piano near
the podium.

Papa himself made stabs at portraying himself as a devoted husband and father. The Boston Pops Tour Orchestra press book
stated confidently:

Married since 1942 to former Boston debutante Ellen Bottomley, the
maestro takes pride in supervising the musical activities of daughters
Johanna and Deborah and son Peter. The Fiedler menage in suburban
Brookline bursts with the vitality of a happy, secure family, sparked by
Father Fiedler himself . . . In Boston, "the land of the bean and the
cod, where Lowells speak only to Cabots and Cabots speak only to God,"
everybody speaks to Arthur Fiedler.

Meanwhile, inside the house on Hyslop Road, no one was speaking much to anyone else. If our family burst with anything, it was
anger and resentment. Mummy was angry with Papa because of
his preoccupation with music and his long absences, and he was
angry with her because she interrupted his concentration with her
complaints and demands. Both of them were angry with the three
of us—Mummy because we could not take care of ourselves, were
not perfectly behaved, and prevented her from being with Papa.
Papa, who hadn't wanted us in the first place, was angry with the
load of responsibilities we had created, the financial drain we rep-
resented, and the amount of Mummy's time and attention we demanded.

The three of us were also angry. Sensing that no one was enthusiastic about us, we fought with one another bitterly. We knew
there wasn't much parental love to be spread among us, so we
resented the affection or attention shown to the others. Any love
lavished on a brother or sister meant that much less left for us.
Instead of being supportive of one another, we competed. Instead
of helping each other through the many difficult and painful episodes we shared, we, like our parents, retreated to our separate
rooms to lick our own wounds.

Because Debbie and I were the closest in age, our competition
was the most savage. If I did well in school, she would kill herself

to do better. If she was more popular with her schoolmates, I would flaunt my appeal to grown-ups. We fought over who was prettier, who was thinner, who got higher grades in school, who played the piano better. When we made up elaborate games to play, usually centered on a fantasized family far different from our own, the games would deteriorate into more fights. I would flee to my room, slam the door against any intrusions, lose myself in a book or a record, or make up my own stories.

We all lived in a state of constant tension. Almost everything we ever did was preceded, accompanied, or followed by anger or regret. I remember trying to do my best with each project I tackled —digging up dandelions or practicing the piano or finishing my schoolwork. When I did well, no one ever said "Good job" or "You must be proud of yourself." And if ever I failed, there would be endless and indignant recriminations. I crept around the house, trying not to disturb anyone, hoping to find a quiet corner where I could settle down with my latest book.

I cannot remember either of my parents playing with us. "I've never been an extraordinary family man," my father was the first to admit. "I don't understand children or their world, and do not speak their language. I am strictly an old-fashioned father. I don't believe in being a pal to my [children]. The children should look up to their father as the head of the family. A pal, indeed! A father should be the head of the house." There was also the age difference. When we went out with Papa, people who stopped him on the street would ask whether we were his grandchildren. "I just let them grow like Topsy," he said of us. "At my age, I didn't romp on the floor with them or play basketball. I don't think they suffered for it."

He was openly contemptuous of his friends who wanted to spend time with their families. "What are you going to do now?" I remember him saying scornfully to a Boston Symphony musician trying to extricate himself from a lengthy postrehearsal conversation. "Go home and play with your kids?"

None of this was an act. He had no interest in playing with us, although he was always ready for a conversation about a book or something we had read in the newspaper. We would no more have asked him to play a game than we would have run up and given him a spontaneous hug.

Our musical education didn't inspire much more involvement on Papa's part. I loved music and listened to records and the classical music radio stations as much as I could, perhaps because it was a way to get close to him. But he confined his interest to finding us a good piano teacher, placing the pianos we practiced on in distant parts of the house, and giving us strict orders never to touch the keyboard when he was home. One day he came back from Symphony Hall unexpectedly to find all three of us working away on our respective instruments, and he roared at my mother, "This house sounds like a goddamned conservatory!"

On a rare occasion, however, usually a cozy winter Saturday afternoon, he would decide to "help" me practice. "Practicing with Papa" was the most dreaded ritual of my childhood; he couldn't have known how my knees were shaking, how notes on the page suddenly seemed to be there for the first time. Five minutes after we sat down together at the piano, the keys would be so wet with tears that my trembling fingers would slip all the more as I attempted to get through a few measures of "The Happy Farmer." These were the only times Papa would become so enraged with me that he would rap my knuckles with a pencil or his hand, just as his own father had done to him. He was driven beyond endurance by my clumsiness. His screams of "RHYTHM!" still echo in my ears.

Afterward, the tension evaporated by all the shouting and crying, my father and I would have a companionable chat about why I had so much trouble with my music, and I would experience an almost cathartic sense of relief. The next time I went back to the piece we had worked on, I would miraculously find that I knew it inside out. I think I could probably play "The Happy Farmer" today.

Despite these sessions, my father may once have harbored hopes that I could be molded into a musician. After all, there was my perfect pitch, all that singing and dancing, and my first encouraging years of piano lessons. He wrote to my piano teacher just after I had begun studying, at five years, "She is a very sensitive child. I think she has made great strides and, without wishing to be a doting father, I think she really has some talent and certainly a goodly amount of intelligence."

Two years later he was discouraged. He wrote, "It is too bad Johanna dislikes practicing so much, because I think you will agree with me that she has quite a good mind and physical aptitude for the piano. Unfortunately I haven't got the time or patience to work with her. I also feel she could advance more rapidly. However, I think one day she will wake up to the fact that playing the piano can be enjoyable."

I never did wake up to that fact. Other children of well-known musicians have gone on to careers in music and overcome the problem of having to compete with a famous parent. Papa was just as mystified as I about my inability to excel at an instrument, and he never pushed me to think of music as a career. "It's no life for a woman," he told me frequently. Certainly neither of my parents gave any of us the self-confidence essential for a life as a performer. I loved music, and it remains one of the great joys in my life, but I could never make myself work hard enough to be very good, either on the piano or, later, the viola. I go to concerts frequently and find myself watching the musicians with great regret. "If only I'd practiced," I think to myself, but now it is far too late. Was it all the shouting? The lack of encouragement? Until I read my father's letters to my first piano teacher, I never knew he thought I had an iota of musical ability. Whatever happened, none of the three of us became a professional musician. My brother and sister still practice and play; I can't conceive of playing a musical instrument for pleasure or relaxation. I have never owned a piano, and I haven't opened my viola case in years.

ADDING to the atmosphere of anxiety that hung over Hyslop Road was a sense of doom that was carefully nurtured by my mother. My father, she liked to remind us, had decided to have a family only after nearly dying of a heart attack. And that hadn't even been his first serious coronary episode; an earlier attack when he was about forty-five had been almost as severe.

My mother looked for any excuse to create drama, and Papa's

health provided endless material. One of my father's greatest battles over the years was against his own body. He deeply distrusted doctors, although he often claimed that if he hadn't been a musician, he would have been a physician. As a result of this distrust, he tended to ignore his physical ailments until he was really sick; minor illnesses had the chance to develop into serious conditions because of his procrastination.

When I was a little girl, too young to understand the implications of what was going on, Papa had one of his biggest health scares. He had been on his annual transcontinental tour with the Boston Pops Tour Orchestra and had lost his usually hearty appetite. This concerned everyone traveling with him because eating in local restaurants was one of his great delights when on the road. But he refused to see a doctor and went ahead with the ten-thousand-mile tour, conducting fifty-eight concerts in twenty-six states in fifty-three days. He was concerned enough, however, to see the doctor as soon as he got back to Boston in April. The examination revealed that he had cancer of the colon, and a biopsy showed that the tumor was malignant. Even my father couldn't argue that the necessary operation be postponed until after the Pops season, which was about to begin. He entered the hospital immediately.

FIEDLER HAS EMERGENCY SURGERY, read the headlines in the Boston papers, and there was much speculation about whether he would be well enough to open the seventieth anniversary season. Since the operation was on April 20 and the Pops opened on May 3, even Papa couldn't get better in time for the season opening, but he channeled all his will power into his recovery. He refused radiation therapy, having been told it would weaken him further, and clung to his belief that he could will himself to recover. "You just have to grin and bear it," he wrote to his sister Elsa. "Take the pleasant things with the unpleasant things. Occupy your mind, keep your thoughts off yourself, cheer up, and try to find food you would enjoy eating."

On June 5, Papa walked onstage at Symphony Hall "as suntanned and lively as ever," the *Boston Herald* reported. "My surgeon is amazed that I was able to start as soon as this," he crowed in a letter to a friend.

But his return and the standing ovation were not enough reassurance for him. Each season at the Pops the biggest audience success was always an orchestral arrangement of the most popular hit tune from the past year. That year, it was "The Ballad of Davy Crockett." His first night back, Papa came out to conduct "Davy Crockett" wearing a coonskin cap and brandishing a toy rifle. The photograph ran in almost every newspaper in the United States. Now the whole country knew that Papa was "back in the saddle," as he liked to say.

My mother, though, had trouble coping with the occasional breakdowns in Papa's health. "You don't know what it's like to live like this," she said often. "He is going to drop dead on the podium one night and there's nothing I can do to stop him." She talked so insistently about Papa's imminent demise that we were all convinced he would not be coming back every time he left on a trip. And, as always, the implication was that this worry was something Papa was inflicting on her, not something that she was exaggerating out of all proportion.

When I was about ten, Mummy took Debbie and me to the Pops one Saturday night. We were still young enough that going to the Pops was a special, grown-up treat, and we were carefully dressed in our best Easter outfits. I remember the dainty straw purse decorated with daisies I carried that night, and how I surreptitiously slipped one of my favorite stuffed animals into the bag to take to the concert. I thought I was a pretty sophisticated ten-year-old, but I needed to bring along a little reassurance.

I certainly needed it that night. Mummy went backstage during intermission and returned to our seats looking even more tense than usual. "Papa isn't feeling very well," she told us. "We'll be going home right after the concert."

When we went backstage at the end, I saw immediately that she wasn't exaggerating this time. Papa's color was a frightening shade of gray, and he was slumped on a chair in the Green Room. My mother went to get the car, and we all piled in without waiting for the usual autograph seekers and congratulatory fans Papa greeted after concerts. In the car on the way home, I reached out tentatively and took Debbie's hand, not sure whether I was trying to comfort her or myself.

Papa's cardiologist was waiting for us on Hyslop Road, and he and my mother helped Papa upstairs. Debbie and I huddled in our adjoining rooms, listening to serious-sounding murmurings first coming from Papa's room, then to the sharply raised voice. The doctor apparently wanted to admit Papa to the hospital right away, but my father, true to form, refused. Foremost in his mind was that he had a live telecast scheduled for Monday, less than forty-eight hours away. He was absolutely determined to do it, and, in the end, he did, although he was forced to cancel several recording sessions and concerts in the days that followed.

Mummy assembled all of us in front of the television set that Monday night so that we could watch what she promised us would be "Papa's last concert." We sat there, staring at the little black-and-white screen, convinced that Papa was going to keel over any minute and die. At the end of the concert, as Papa returned for several final bows, my mother seemed almost irritated that he was still ambulatory.

Afterward, Papa admitted that he had been a little apprehensive. "There are times when you don't know whether to go on," he said. But if a doctor told him to take any precautions, to rest in bed even for a few days, his immediate reaction was "The hell with that. The worst thing that could happen would be to drop dead."

MY FAMILY certainly didn't turn to religion to ease the pressures among us. My parents' different faiths caused constant friction between them and had almost prevented their marriage in the first place.

At the time my mother and father married, the Catholic Church insisted that a Jew marrying a Roman Catholic had to renounce his or her Judaism. This, quite naturally, enraged my father. He did not practice his religion, but he considered himself a Jew; as he said firmly to the priests whom my mother's family had provided to instruct him in Catholicism, "I may want to take it up again someday."

Fortunately, my mother's mother, that "pillar of the church," as

my father sarcastically called her, was well acquainted with the
Archbishop of Boston, who promptly procured a Vatican dispensa-
tion from this requirement. My father, in the meantime, readily
agreed to abide by the church's other stipulation, which was that
all of his and my mother's children be brought up as Catholics.
This presented no problem, because he had no intention of having
children.

Papa's religious upbringing had been rudimentary. "My father
never went to church, nor did my mother," he said, "but they set
an example that the Golden Rule was all you need. You know what
is right and what is wrong, and I think people who don't have the
umbrella of religion develop a stronger sense of conscience. Music
was the only 'religion' of my family."

My father's family was so nonobservant of religion that, even
though he grew up in a predominantly Irish Catholic part of Boston, the neighbors were unaware that the Fiedlers were Jewish.
"We weren't very Orthodox in our religious observance," he once
said, "and most of my friends thought of me as 'that Austrian kid
from up the street.' "

He developed into a combination of cynic and idealist and often
stated that he wanted to be remembered first and foremost as "a
decent human being." His code of behavior was firmly based on
two of his mother's adages: "Do unto others as you would do unto
yourself," and "You can never raise yourself by lowering someone
else." "What more do we need?" he would say. And he tried to
live by these simple axioms. Occasionally, he would slip with the
second, and I would hear him make a derogatory remark about
another conductor. But the remarks usually had to do with the
person's pretensions or what Papa perceived as dishonesty. He
despised, for example, Serge Koussevitzky's habit of going by the
title "Doctor," which derived from a series of honorary degrees
and which Papa therefore felt the Boston Symphony's long-time
music director was not entitled to use. He thought Leonard Bernstein had no business talking to the audience during concerts, thus
breaching the natural boundary between conductor and audience,
and often referred to Bernstein as "the talking conductor." But
despite Papa's characteristic sarcasm and belittling remarks to his

friends and family, he never derided Koussevitzky's or Bernstein's or any other major performer's musicianship or technique, even when he disagreed with certain things they did while conducting.

My mother, on the other hand, strove hard to keep up the appearance of her Catholicism, although she never seemed to me to possess authentic faith. She clung to the rites and superstitions of her childhood religious training without a moment of questioning. "Jesus, Mary, and Joseph" was her response to anything that astonished her, and she would frequently intone, "In the name of the Father and the Son and the Holy Ghost, amen," when she was trying to summon the patience to deal with my father.

My grandmother May Kenney Bottomley had taken her flock of five children every Sunday to the so-called French Church in Boston, where, although Mass was said in the traditional Latin, everything else was in French. This rather surprising affectation in Boston, one of the most un-Gallic cities imaginable, appealed immensely to the upwardly mobile Irish-Catholic nouveaux riches. Mummy loved that church; after spending a year at school in Switzerland, she dropped French phrases into her conversation at some of the strangest times. She never went away on a trip—she was *"en tournée."* She found many chances to talk about So-and-So's *"idée fixe"* or *"bête noire,"* and she was always apologizing to lunch guests for the simplicity of the meal. "It's really *à la en famille,"* she'd say.

*"À la en famille* in family style," my father would add, never one to let a mistake slip by unnoticed. He spoke fluent French himself.

Mummy took us to the French Church occasionally, but not often. It was not our parish church, and Mummy was a well-raised Catholic lady who knew her responsibility to her parish. Our parish was St. Lawrence's, a lovely little church on Route Nine in Brookline, where we became friendly with the two or three priests who celebrated Sunday Mass, although we never got to know any of the other parishioners and never saw anyone we knew on our visits. Debbie and I made many reluctant trips there on Saturdays for Confession, walking as slowly as possible from Hyslop Road, dreading the moment of entering the dark box where the mysterious priest was hidden behind an opaque scrim. Mummy sent us to Confession frequently, saying we would "feel much better after-

ward," though she rarely went herself. Since I was not a naughty
child, I often had trouble thinking up sins to confess. Having evil
thoughts about my sister and brother and having lost my temper
were my major fallbacks, and they were always applicable. The
priest would give me five Hail Marys or two Our Fathers as a
penance, which I would get out of the way by praying at the altar,
lighting a votive candle, and then flying back up the hill toward
home.

The other disadvantage that kept Mummy from joining her
mother at the French Church was that its last Mass came at eleven
A.M. Long before Vatican II, churches in Boston had timidly begun
having Masses later and later in the morning. Mummy's favorite
was the Franciscan Shrine, way downtown, near the New England
Medical Center. A little after noon on Sundays, she would shove
us all in the car and drive as fast as possible into Boston in order to
make the twelve-thirty Mass. Mummy had a theory, one I never
heard articulated by anybody else, that you could say you'd gone
to Mass if you got to church by the Consecration. Since the Consecration came two thirds of the way through the ceremony, we usually made it with seconds to spare. Of course, by going only to the
last part of the Mass, we missed the sermon and the Collection as
well as many of my favorite prayers like the Credo. But, officially,
we had been to Mass, and that was all that mattered.

I saw early that Mummy's theatrical religious observances did
not make her a nice woman. In fact, she could be outright vicious.
She told my father's favorite sister, Rosa, to her face how much she
disliked her; she told me my father's family was cheap and vulgar,
and I was just like them. She would snap at my father's secretaries
or other people in a way that made my skin crawl with embarrass-
ment. She kept telling me that she was a good woman because she
went to church regularly, but I stopped believing her when I was
very young. Papa continued to abide by his simple principles, and
they made much more sense to me.

My mother, her mother, and her sister had all gone to school at
the Convent of the Sacred Heart, a socially correct Catholic school
in Boston that Papa considered academically unchallenging. She
had every intention of sending Debbie and me to Sacred Heart,

but Papa, who watched all the Sunday comings and goings with a jaundiced eye, put his foot down. "It's time to stamp out illiteracy in this family," he said firmly to my mother, not even yelling. "The girls are going to a good school." There was no fight, because even my mother knew when she was defeated. Debbie and I were sent to the Winsor School.

Mummy did insist that Debbie and I take catechism classes. Every Thursday afternoon, we were driven to the Cenacle, a convent in the Boston suburbs, and were drilled in Catholic catechism by a forbidding series of nuns in preparation for our First Communions and, later, for our Confirmations.

"Let me look into your eyes," one of the nuns used to whisper as I tremulously entered the classroom. "I'll be able to see by your eyes if you've been bad this week or not." I was terrified by the nuns when I was small, frightened by their long, black habits and harsh-looking wimples, and convinced that they had extrasensory powers.

Going to church and to catechism class made me anxious and upset. Papa, who had agreed to have his children raised as Catholics, went around on Sundays looking furious and muttering, "Religion is a crutch," or "Religion is the opiate of the masses," or "If you're so goddamned religious, why can't you get to church on time?"—this as my mother was racing toward the car to make it to the last Mass of the day.

Debbie and I finally got sick of the mad dashes on Sundays, and we began walking to St. Lawrence's with Celie for ten o'clock Mass. Papa had a certain respect for our rebellion against Mummy's helter-skelter observances, so when Mass was over, we'd sometimes find the family Volkswagen parked on Route Nine, with him at the wheel reading the Sunday paper. We would thank him with enormous enthusiasm, and after a grunt in return, he would head up the hill toward Hyslop Road, gears shrieking and transmission groaning as he drove with his typical lack of attention and expertise.

When I left home for college, I stopped going to church for good. "Don't you feel guilty about leaving the church?" people asked me. "Don't you miss the comfort of it?" I didn't. My primary feeling was of relief. At last I could stop doing something Papa didn't want me to do. I no longer had to sneak off to Mass or to Confession or to catechism class. In a family where nobody confided in anyone, it was one less secret to keep.

THE ISSUE OF RELIGION made holidays difficult times, but Papa hated them for other reasons, as well: they involved family get-togethers and they required spending money. In time he began to see them as a means of creating some publicity, but that didn't take away the sting of family togetherness and gift-giving obligations. Christmas shopping was a particularly heavy burden, but Papa evolved a ritual that made the chore a little less repugnant. He incorporated Christmas shopping into his public persona until his eccentric habits became part of Boston lore.

Every Christmas Eve, at about five o'clock or just as the stores were closing, he would take Debbie, Peter, and me and rush off to the Chestnut Hill Shopping Center near our house. The four of us would sweep into Filene's or R. H. Stearns, which was, of course, by then completely empty. Anyone else coming to shop at that inconvenient time on Christmas Eve would have been greeted with clenched teeth by the salespeople, but everyone was enchanted to see Papa. The saleswomen would compete to wait on him, and since his last-minute shopping had become famous in Boston, they actually waited for him if we were late.

Papa would dash around the store buying his gifts for the family. He always got the same things for Mummy—a bottle of her favorite perfume, Arpège, and a pair of leather gloves. He would pick up some small item for each of the three of us, sign a few autographs, utter some witticisms about how much he hated Christmas, and hurry back out into the December cold. As he shouted, "Merry Christmas to all!"—and he always did—it must have been easy for those watching to believe that he really was the Santa Claus figure people thought he was. We knew better; we were on our way back home to another miserable, tense Christmas Eve dinner.

Papa had discovered the public relations use for holidays early in his life as a family man. In 1949, an article purportedly written by him (but actually composed, as were most of his published writings, by his devoted press agent, who worked in the Boston Symphony's press office) appeared in one of the Boston papers at Christmastime:

When you ask concerning my Christmas plans, I am not now really the free agent I was a few seasons ago. For now I am subject to the demands, not of my public, but of my two daughters, Johanna and Deborah. Subject to their approval, I intend to follow the pattern they have established in recent years by having a double Christmas. According to this plan, we shall celebrate at our house and again at Nana's [Mrs. Bottomley's] house with the participating forces augmented by the cousins. Aside from the two trees and two conglomerations of toys and games, I am happy to report that the musical side of the holiday really does appeal to the kids. They actually register delight sitting down at the piano with Papa and running through a set of good old carols. It makes a concert with what the critics call "a small but enthusiastic audience."

That is not the way I remember Christmas. Thanksgiving, Christmas, and Easter were among the few occasions when members of both my mother's and father's families would convene, and the atmosphere was so filled with dislike that it was almost unbearable. Mummy hated her Fiedler in-laws, whom she considered common, and the Fiedlers were deeply suspicious of the Bottomleys, whom they perceived as undisciplined alcoholics—somehow ignoring the fact that their beloved Arthur drank just as much as any of the Bottomleys. In turn, the Bottomleys were mystified by the Fiedlers, most of whom had returned to Boston just before World War II, communicated with each other in German, and maintained their Middle European dress and demeanor.

No one liked or got along with anyone else, so the only thing to do was to drink. When the family began arriving, Papa would come downstairs looking like a thunder cloud; Mummy wouldn't come down at all until the last possible minute before dinner. The three of us children would be put to work passing hors d'oeuvres to the glowering adults while Papa served drinks. As we got older, we learned that Papa's mood improved as he drank, so, to hasten the process, we would surreptitiously add more liquor to his already potent cocktails. This usually worked, and he became more expan-

sive. He was still sarcastic to the members of the family he disliked, which included almost everyone except for his sister Rosa
and a couple of my mother's brothers. But with Papa, that behavior
passed for good-humored holiday cheer.

Eventually Papa found a solution to Christmas by performing an
annual concert with the Denver Symphony that necessitated his
leaving Boston early on Christmas morning. That left only Christmas Eve for us to survive; at least the holiday was slashed to
merely one dreaded evening. He related this twist of fate to the
*Boston Herald* with deep regret in 1972 when the paper asked several prominent Bostonians to recall their most memorable Christ-
mases. "[It is] not memorable [to spend Christmas Day aboard a
plane to Denver]. But truly the Christmas spirit is there since my
wife and children are so understanding about my leaving on the
holiday. They realize that it is my life, my work, and we celebrate
on Christmas Eve together."

Papa also "wrote" a "Memorable Christmas" article for the *Boston Sunday Advertiser* in the 1960s, describing a flight on Christmas
Eve from Chicago to Boston in the midst of a blizzard. He related
dramatically how worried he had been when he saw the snow in
Chicago, where he had gone to tape a television show. "My spirits
rose as my chauffeur skillfully but slowly navigated the snow-
clogged streets to the Chicago airport. I would be home in a few
hours."

Meanwhile, back in reality, I was at home watching the gathering blizzard with my own set of anxieties. I was sixteen and had
had my driver's license for only a couple of months. I knew that
my mother, beset by her usual holiday depression, was not going to
be able to drive to the airport that night. "Yummy, you go and pick
up your father," she said to me, as I had been afraid she would.

I went out into the snow and tried without success to get the
Volkswagen out of the driveway. Then I forced my way through
thigh-high drifts to the street, only to find that the pavement was
thick with ice beneath the fresh snow. Back in the house, I told my
mother that the situation was impossible, but she was adamant.
Someone had to pick up Papa at the airport and I was the only
driver in the household. Our frugality was so instinctive that I'm

sure no one even thought of calling a taxi company, not that a cab would have been available in that weather on Christmas Eve.

Finally, in desperation, I called a friend of my father's to whom I was particularly close and asked for help. Because he is one of the nicest people in the world, he came right over even though it was Christmas Eve. He had driven Papa on several cross-country tours, so a blizzard was hardly a challenge for him. On the drive to the airport, I jumped out at every stoplight to scrape as much snow as I could from the windshield. Papa stormed off the plane exhausted and in an unspeakably ugly mood and the three of us slithered in the little car to Hyslop Road, where my mother and father immediately had a screaming fight.

Papa's version for the newspapers was a little different. He recounted how his flight to Boston had taken off despite the atrocious weather, and how the plane flew through the storm, plunging into high winds and turbulence:

We finally came over Boston. The city was obliterated by the storm. The plane dived downward and slid through the snow to a bumpy stop. As I forced my way through the howling night to the deserted terminal I heard a happy cry. It was my elder daughter—some claim she is the apple of my eye, but I really love each of my children one hundred percent— who had somehow, quite miraculously, forced her little car through all the drifts to meet me and take me home at this very late hour of Christmas Eve to my family and my fireplace.

This was my most unforgettable Christmas.

MUCH HAPPIER MEMORIES of my childhood came from the animals we lived with. Around animals, especially dogs, the loving side of my father came to the fore. His boyhood homes in both Boston and Berlin had teemed with animals, including canaries, parrots, cats, and turtles. But dogs were the Fiedlers' first love.

For as long as I can remember, I had heard stories from my father and my aunts about Nicky, a wire-haired fox terrier that my father's Uncle Gustav had given his nieces and nephews in the early 1900s. The little dog was so beloved that when Emanuel retired from the Boston Symphony and moved his family back to

Europe, they took Nicky with them. I'm sure there was never a question about Nicky's making the voyage; when I was a little girl fifty years later, we took any portable animals we owned with us on our annual treks to San Francisco for Papa's summer concerts. Papa would even have the dogs taken off the planes, which in those days had to stop in Chicago, so that we could give them water and take them for a walk.

Nicky had obviously been a full member of the Fiedler family a generation earlier. In the old pictures of the Fiedlers' life in pre–World War I Berlin, Nicky is prominently featured. His terrier energy explodes from the faded snapshots, so much so that he is often the central figure. Against a backdrop of Europeans in stiff, formal poses, Nicky is all-American, bursting with spirit, almost jumping from the picture into the present. Maybe I just imagine this because I heard so much about him for so many years. My father talked about him as though he were still alive, and my father's sisters all had Nicky stories. He was one of those dogs so loved that they stay alive forever.

As Papa became better known, his passion for dogs made good publicity copy in Boston. A July 1945 article about the Esplanade Concerts contained several anecdotes about the problem of dogs running loose at the performances. Papa was asked what he could do to reduce the dog population. " 'I am not,' the conductor replied with some spirit, 'a dog catcher. In fact,' he added, 'I like dogs very much.' "

One of his favorite memories about the Esplanade series was of the night a large, mixed-breed black dog clambered up onto the stage during the concert and settled down at my father's feet for the rest of the program. Papa was enchanted. "I have always had dogs and enjoyed them, and they don't bother me at all," the *Boston Globe* reported his saying after the incident. "Right now, I don't have one, however. I have tropical fish. And I don't bring them to concerts . . ."

He gave up his tropical fish soon after I was born, although I was told that, as a baby, I loved to gaze at the fish; in fact, watching them was one of the few things that could calm me down when I was upset. I missed them when they disappeared, but I was even more enthusiastic about the next pet that arrived.

Having settled down, more or less, to family life, Papa was finally ready to get the dog he had wanted for years. My mother emphatically did not want a dog; she thought animals were dirty creatures, essentially feral and uncontrollable, and she fought their intrusion into her household as long as she could. But she was fighting a losing battle with my father.

Sparky came into our lives when I was about two. We had just moved to Hyslop Road. Debbie had just been born, so the family was undergoing major adjustments: from one child to two; from the relatively minor responsibility of renting an apartment to the ceaseless demands of owning a large house, something my father never really learned to cope with; from a household that had consisted only of the family and the long-time housekeeper, Louise, to a staff that at one time comprised a housekeeper, a cook, a valet-butler-handyman, and a children's nurse. Into this chaos Papa brought Sparky.

He chose a particularly unfortunate day to bring the puppy home. Louise had the day off, and my mother was making one of her rare attempts at cooking. She was trying to create one of her own favorite dishes, creamed chicken—or chicken à la king, as she preferred to call it—which my father and the rest of the family happened to detest. Mummy liked rice with her creamed chicken, so she had it on the menu. She carefully filled a pot with rice, added water, and turned on the gas burner. By the time Papa arrived home with Sparky, the pot had boiled over, and rice was covering the kitchen. Mummy and Celie, who was then supposed to be only the children's nurse, tried to clean up the mess while Debbie and I roamed around, unsupervised. It was a typical scene, everyone tells me, from the early days in my parents' household, before Celie managed to take control and get everyone organized. Into the rice-filled kitchen walked Papa with his surprise puppy.

Sparky was a robust and active male Dalmatian. His favorite activity was rushing up to my baby sister as she was trying to propel herself around by clinging to furniture and giving her a

good shove with his front paws. I thought this an absolutely wonderful idea, since it saved me from having to push her over myself,
and I immediately saw Sparky as an ally against the interloper.
Fortunately, my sister inherited the Fiedler passion for dogs and
grew up to forgive Sparky and the rest of his species.

Mummy did not. Her vigilance was eternal. As each of us grew
up and added our own pets to the family, she became the more
determined to wipe out all animal life under her roof.

I blamed my mother completely for the arrival of Debbie. Since
she hated Sparky, Papa loved Sparky, and Sparky kept pushing
Debbie over, it was clearly Papa, Sparky, and me against Mummy
and Debbie. I began sneaking downstairs at night and climbing
into Sparky's bed, where I would cling to him and fall asleep
feeling somehow comforted. Of course, no one else thought it a
good idea for me to be spending my nights under the stairs on the
dog's cushion.

"Why do you want to sleep with Sparky?" my father asked.

"I'm going to marry Sparky when I grow up," I responded, and
was surprised when my father started to laugh.

"I think you might change your mind about that at some point,"
he said gently. I knew I wouldn't.

My mother had saved the bride and groom from the top of the
wedding cake of a brother and had given them to me to play with.
I disposed of the groom and substituted a china Dalmatian that
was one of my most cherished possessions and then proceeded to
create elaborate weddings for the happy couple. I'm sure my
mother and father thought they had given birth to a deviant child,
but I knew that I loved Sparky more than anything else in the
world, and, even more important, I knew that Sparky loved me.

Sparky loved Papa most of all, but that was okay, because I
loved Papa the most of all the humans I knew. When my mother
came home with my brother Peter, I was most worried about
Sparky's reaction. I can remember watching my father feed Sparky
under the table at lunch one day. "Do you love Peter more than
Sparky?" I asked anxiously.

"It's different" is what I remember him saying, with a laugh, but I was mystified that he could even conceive of loving another creature as much or more than his beloved Sparky.

Sparky went everywhere with Papa. He went to Symphony Hall more often than I did, but because I loved him so much, I forgave him. Papa drove a convertible with the top down, even in the middle of Boston's icy winter, and Sparky would sit beside him in the front seat, his ears flapping in the wind. Every Sunday that Papa was home, we took Sparky for long walks through Brookline. Papa and I—and Debbie and Peter when they became big enough —trotted along the sidewalks and the paths around the Chestnut Hill Reservoir, Papa carrying the walking stick that had belonged to his father, and Sparky galloping in circles around us.

Sparky's favorite hobby was collecting items from other people's property. He came home regularly with children's toys, assorted doormats, and, on his proudest day, a bra he had dragged off someone's clothesline. My mother fussed, but my father was unconcerned and actually quite proud, at least until Sparky started turning up with what was undeniably garbage.

Papa shot off a letter to the Board of Health in Brookline:

From time to time, my dog comes home with bones and food scraps of all sorts. I called your office a month or two ago in regard to this, as undoubtedly some garbage cans must be uncovered. I personally discovered one, while following the rounds of my dog, at 166 Fisher Avenue. The name of the owner of the house is P.

I think for all purposes such as rats, vermin, etc., that the container should be under ground level and with a cover. There is such a contraption at the above-mentioned address, but there is also a large container full of swill which is entirely uncovered . . . much to the joy of my Dalmatian . . . I would appreciate it if this communication remained confidential.

I wish I could report that Papa continued his vigilance on Sparky's behalf for the rest of the dog's life, but reality soon intruded. My father began to travel almost constantly, and Sparky was left at home with the rest of us.

ONE SUNDAY, when I was about ten years old, my father decided to teach me how to drive. Sundays were always difficult days for him; he had a horror of inactivity. If he was at home and had a concert at night, he could get through the day with a long walk in the morning, lunch, and a nap. But if there was no concert, the empty day loomed in front of all of us. He would have an extended cocktail hour before lunch to arm himself for the endless stretch of time he would have to be in the house. When he couldn't get away, drinking helped him escape or at least tolerate having to be at home.

At other times, he drank to calm himself for his work. Not only did he have a drink—usually gin on the rocks—the minute he walked into the house from Symphony Hall or a trip; he also drank before and after concerts and during intermissions. Because of his history of coronary disease, he had gone through periods of almost paralyzing anxiety about dropping dead while conducting. One of his doctors had mentioned in passing that alcohol was good for relieving anxiety, and suggested that he have a small drink before he went onstage each night. I doubt the doctor had meant the several ounces my father would consume. "Oh, I never drink on the job," he joked. "Only before, after, and during intermission." "We can smell him coming," a Pops cellist said to me once, to my annoyance. I explained the medicinal value of alcohol and was met with an incredulous stare, which I decided to ignore.

Papa had had several gins on the rocks the day he decided to introduce me to driving. I was a little dubious about the whole project, but since the lesson meant I'd receive his undivided attention, I couldn't refuse. Carrying his glass, he led me out to the front driveway and together we got into his Cadillac. Papa always had a small car—he owned one of the first Volkswagens in the United States, having bought it on a trip to Austria—but he liked to have a big expensive car as well. When I was little, the big car was a Cadillac; then it was a Lincoln Continental, which he thought had proved more reliable on his cross-country tours. In the last years, he allowed himself the luxury of a Mercedes-Benz— although by then he no longer drove.

I was overwhelmed by the size of the Cadillac, but I reminded myself that Papa was there. Seating me in his lap, he taught me how to put my feet on the pedals, though I could barely reach

them, and we set off. Our driveway was made of gravel because
Papa liked the sound of the pebbles under the tires as his car
swept in, and it curved around and down a fairly steep hill to the
garage behind the house. This hill was wonderful for sledding in
the winter but less wonderful for maneuvering an enormous car
whose steering wheel blocked my line of sight. Somehow I managed the first couple of turns, but then I felt the car beginning to
pick up speed as we started down the hill. "Slow down!" my
father was shouting, laughing at the same time. Panicking, I
slammed my foot down firmly on what I thought was the brake,
but in my terror I had stepped on the accelerator, and the car shot
away down the hill. We veered off the driveway, clipped a pine
tree, drove up a set of brick steps by the back door, and crashed
into the house. My father was still laughing, and he continued to
think the whole thing funny until he got the bills for the crushed
stairs and the dents in the car.

THOSE SUNDAYS may have been alcohol-drenched, but at least
Papa was home. As the family grew, and the responsibilities and
the tensions mounted, he spent more and more time away. Before
1950 or so, he had occasional guest-conducting assignments outside Boston; afterward things began to change, and his first extended engagement away from Boston inspired a brief attempt by
my parents at traveling as a family.

Papa was invited to conduct a series of summer concerts with
the San Francisco Symphony in the early 1950s, thanks to his long-
time mentor Pierre Monteux, who was then the music director in
San Francisco. The concerts grew in popularity each season, and
my father went back every summer to the city he eventually regarded as a second home.

Papa loved San Francisco. He relished the weather, which was
much cooler in the summer than Boston, and the excellent restaurants. He became one of the city's leading celebrities, and his fame
in San Francisco was untouched by the tinge of disdain and conde-
scension he often encountered among native Bostonians. In a city
founded by pioneers and adventurers, my father's European roots
and Jewish heritage were not regarded as fatal flaws, as they were

in Boston. Relieved of having to "behave" like a proper Bostonian, my father let his fun-loving side free in San Francisco; his sojourns there were almost a return to his bachelor days. This was especially the case when, after the first few years, we stopped going to San Francisco as a family.

In the beginning, though, before Peter was born, we all went to California in the summers. Some of my earliest memories are of the three-day train trips across the United States. Mummy and Papa shared a sleeping compartment, and Celie shared another with Debbie and me. I can remember peeking out the train window early in the morning and watching the exotic scenery streaming by. I can remember, too, the exhausting ritual of changing trains in Chicago, where we boarded the famous "City of San Francisco" after a twelve-hour layover.

Debbie and I were fussy eaters. Celie often reminisced about how I would never eat a bite if my mother tried to feed me but how I'd happily gobble down my food if Mummy was out. Papa was not normally exposed to children's meals at home, but on the train he was forced to confront the futile rituals my mother would go through to get us to eat.

I'm sure there was a nerve-wracking amount of whining and fussing from two exhausted little girls on these trips, but my father reached the very end of his patience on one occasion. The train had stopped in the Rockies to take on food supplies, including some fresh brook trout, one of his favorite dishes. The waiter swept into the dining car with a plate of trout and plunked it down in front of him, the fish intact, its eyes staring glassily up at us. Debbie took one look and became hysterical. She cried and screamed until Celie pulled her out of the dining car so that Papa could eat his dinner in peace. I suspect strong doubts began to creep into his mind at that moment about the wisdom of traveling with a wife, a nanny, and two small children.

In San Francisco we lived in a series of hotels. Debbie and I were healthy, active children, used to living in a house. We didn't understand the necessity of keeping quiet to accommodate the other guests, so the six weeks in California were an unending battle between our natural exuberance and the grown-ups' attempt to keep us subdued. One of the few times I can remember being spanked was in San Francisco, when my mother lost her patience on Celie's night out and paddled both Debbie and me with her weapon, the "big brown hairbrush," which under more benign circumstances was a clothes brush used on Papa's formal wear.

After Peter was born, my parents decided that going to California with a brand-new baby was impossible. "Hotel life is no good for children," my father explained to friends with great relief. We did accompany Papa on occasional long trips while I was growing up, but there was no more regular travel as a family. I was sorry, because I hated being left behind when Papa went away. I may, in fact, have been the only member of the family who felt that way.

The San Francisco trips were just the beginning. In 1953, at the age of fifty-nine, Papa formed the Boston Pops Tour Orchestra. "We'll cover thirteen thousand miles," he happily told a reporter days before the first tour started. "We'll play sixty-seven concerts in sixty-four days. We're going in two buses, with a trailer for our instruments and baggage. I'm traveling in my own car."

The previous spring, he had been forced to use a free-lance orchestra for the Boston Pops season because the Boston Symphony had gone on its first tour of Japan. The substitute orchestra had played so well, with such enthusiasm and zest, and with so noticeable an absence of the petulance that marked the regular Pops, that my father found himself enjoying the season more than he had in years. Why not, he thought, take an orchestra like that out on the road? He had long wanted to tour with the Pops but had been unable to arrange any trips because of the group's busy schedule.

With the sponsorship of Columbia Artists Management, he put together an orchestra made up of free-lance musicians from all over the country. "I auditioned hundreds of musicians," he said, adding, "I decided to use all men to have it look as much as possible like the regular Pops. But several women came to audition, thinking they were welcome, and four of them played so well I couldn't turn them down!"

The first tour was an enormous success, and the tour became an annual event. During the rest of my childhood, I noticed that

Papa's mood would take a vivid upswing right after New Year's. His battered tour trunks would come out of storage at Symphony Hall and be set up in his bedroom so that the packing ritual could begin. Papa, who had a fetish for gadgets, had designed the trunks himself. They were higher than the standard wardrobe trunk so that the four sets of tails he traveled with would not wrinkle. Often they had to compensate for the inadequate dressing rooms he encountered in many of the theaters where the orchestra played, so each was equipped with a built-in mirror, towel rack, bottle opener, shoe compartment, a screenlike door that ventilated his perspiration-soaked concert clothes, and a specially outfitted drawer for the bottles of Jack Daniel's and Tanqueray gin.

Papa soon had the tour down to an exact science, living on as strict a schedule as traveling would allow. The orchestra journeyed from city to city on the morning of each concert, because almost every one of their appearances was a one-night stand. Papa rode in his own car with his librarian and close friend Bill Shisler and the orchestra's concertmaster. They became a cheerful, rowdy trio, and the car was their home away from home. Since the daily drives were often long, there was a huge salami for sustenance, usually nestled in the glove compartment or occasionally swinging gaily from the rearview mirror. There was plenty of beer to drink with the salami; and to keep Papa occupied, the car was festooned with thermometers in every conceivable location, inside and out. "Why do you have a thermometer in the glove compartment?" I once asked in bewilderment.

"You never know when you might need to find out what the temperature is in there," he replied with dignity.

The weather was frequently horrible, since the tours were always in the winter, but my father and Bill regarded each trip as a great adventure. "I've developed a system for living under tour conditions," Papa reported to the *Boston Globe* in 1962. "I get a good night's rest, rise reasonably early in the morning, and we take off for the next stop. The daily distance might be eighty miles or a hundred and eighty or sometimes three hundred. When we get there, we check into the hotel and I have my main meal of the day, since I never eat before a concert, then a walk around town for exercise, then to bed for rest until the concert time . . . Of course there were some places where everything closed up early and you had trouble getting a bedtime snack after a concert. To compensate, however, there must have been fifty-two parties given after concerts." (There were fifty-nine concerts in all on that particular tour.)

The tours ranged from forty-seven concerts in 1954 to eighty-one in 1956, and the intrepid orchestra covered most of the United States and Canada. People heard the Pops in towns and villages where no symphony orchestra had ever ventured before. Years later, people in these remote places would remember that, before orchestral touring became common and when concerts and operas on television were rare, my father and his orchestra had been out exploring the country. These tours did not exactly hurt record sales; my father wrote countless letters to RCA imploring them to get their promotions organized and be sure that a Fiedler display was prominent in each town the orchestra visited.

By the early 1960s, Papa began to find it difficult to recruit special orchestras for these trips; many musicians were reluctant to leave their home bases and jeopardize their free-lance work. So he decided to conduct "readymade" orchestras rather than give up the trips, and started touring annually with such groups as the Baltimore Symphony, the Buffalo Philharmonic, the New Orleans Philharmonic, the Denver Symphony, the National Symphony, and even the Yomiuri Nippon Symphony Orchestra from Tokyo, which marked the first time a Japanese orchestra toured the United States. Each of these orchestras incorporated "Pops" into its name in some way or other, because the Boston Symphony received a generous fee just for the use of the Boston Pops imprint.

When Papa went off on tour, Mummy stayed in Boston, with three small children, a large house, at least one large dog, and a different kind of day-to-day monotony. My parents' lives grew apart as my father discovered life on the road. And as he became more well-known, the trips became more frequent.

Our lives began to be defined by Papa's increasing schedule of engagements. January, February, and most of March were con-

sumed by the Boston Pops Tour Orchestra. If, for some reason, the
tour was a little shorter one year, Papa might go to Europe, where
he conducted frequently in London and less often in countries on
the continent. He spent late March and part of April in Buenos
Aires, a city he loved for its cosmopolitan atmosphere and its fare.
"The food down there is very good," he told a reporter. "They
make good Argentine wines, both red and white, and excellent gin,
too."

Back from South America, my father launched into the Boston
Pops season, with its heavy schedule of recording sessions and
broadcasts. The Pops extended over nine weeks, with a rigorous
program of six evening performances a week as well as rehearsals
and recording sessions during the daytime. For most of his tenure
as music director of the Pops, my father conducted almost all of
the concerts; his associate conductor, Harry Ellis Dickson, did one
or at most two a week up until the very last years before Papa died.

As Papa's career progressed, his relaxing weeks in San Francisco
were interrupted by other appearances. By the 1970s, he had an
annual series of engagements that kept him flying back and forth
across the country all summer. He conducted at the Saratoga Performing Arts Center with the Philadelphia Orchestra, the Hollywood Bowl with the Los Angeles Philharmonic, the Ravinia Festival with the Chicago Symphony, and usually twice with the Pops
at Tanglewood. Somehow, he squeezed in concerts at Denver,
Vancouver, Toronto, Baltimore, Washington, Miami, and many
other cities, as well as keeping up a regular weekly series in San
Francisco. By the end of the summer, he was exhausted and more
than ready for the brief spell in early September when there was a
pause in concert activity all over the country. This was the period
when many orchestras took vacations or went off on tours, but
early September to us was the time when Papa was home with
nothing to do. It wasn't our favorite time of the year, because by
the time I was a teenager, my father was so used to travel and
activity that he could barely tolerate a couple of empty weeks at
home. He and my mother could have gone away together then, but
by these years they had little interest in spending uninterrupted
time together.

Since he wasn't interested in vacations—"I've tried cruises and all I wanted to do was to get in a taxicab and go somewhere"—he came home instead. He would race frantically and ineffectively back and forth between Hyslop Road and the silence of Symphony Hall, where everyone else had gone away after the end of the long B.S.O. season. The whole family was relieved when orchestral activity resumed in mid-September and Papa's trips began again.

His autumns and early winters were a tapestry of guest-conducting engagements. His calendar eventually became so full that he would conduct a concert in one city at night after having rehearsed another orchestra in another city during the day. When he was eighty, beginning to feel tired for the first time, Papa made a rule that he would conduct in only one city per day, and he thought of this as a drastic cut-back in activity.

In June 1975, Richard Mohr, one of my father's producers at RCA Records, approached Papa about making a record with Sherrill Milnes in London. Papa, who loved working with opera singers and loved London, was greatly tempted. But even he was forced to admit that the recording would be impossible. He wrote to Dick:

Dear Ricardo,

My calling you on the telephone yesterday really was a most difficult task for me. I had made up my mind that I wanted very much to make this record with Mr. Milnes, and also to have the pleasure of a few hours in London. We have been having hectic activity here [during the Pops]— I had not stopped to examine this London trip thoroughly. I finally got out my August dates and they are really mind-boggling:

Aug. 1–Baltimore, concert
Aug. 2–Boston
Aug. 4–Tanglewood
Aug. 5–rehearsal & concert, Tanglewood
Aug. 7–two rehearsals, Tanglewood
Aug. 8–Tanglewood, Boston Symphony concert
Aug. 9–Chicago, rehearsal
Aug. 10–Chicago, rehearsal & concert
Aug. 11–Santa Barbara
Aug. 15–Hollywood Bowl, concert
Aug. 16–Hollywood Bowl, concert
Aug. 17–San Francisco, concert

Aug. 18–Tanglewood
Aug. 19–Tanglewood, rehearsal & concert
Aug. 21–Saratoga, rehearsal & concert
Aug. 29–San Francisco, rehearsal & concert with Alae Fitzgerald

Normally, I love these challenges, but when it came to leaving Saratoga with the Philadelphia Orchestra on the 22nd, doing the week in London, and having a rehearsal in the morning of the 29th in San Francisco, I thought that was too much of a good thing.

I appreciate very much your understanding, and you know that if it were a matter of extraordinary importance, I would have seen this through. But you can't teach old dogs new tricks!

My father was eighty years old that summer.

All of this activity had an unsettling effect on the family left behind. Most children look forward to the end of the school year, but as Papa's summer seasons alone in San Francisco became a fixed part of our lives, Debbie and I began to dread early June. School was a scheduled, organized, reliable part of our lives. Then, in the spring, the Pops season would begin and we would undergo the shuddering adjustment to having Papa at home again, going from a fatherless collection of strays to a tightly organized group whose lives revolved around his relentless work schedule. The Pops and the brief Esplanade schedule ended in July, as did our sense of routine and focus; Papa would fly off to San Francisco, and the long summer vacation was upon us.

The rest of us could not escape as he did. We stayed on at the big house, each of us in his or her own bedroom. There was little conversation, except for fighting, and no confiding or sharing. My mother's behavior grew increasingly strange, and the three of us children were sad and confused. We had no one to talk to, not even each other.

# THREE

## Papa

MY FATHER left us alone in Boston when he went to San Francisco every summer, but his own father, Emanuel Fiedler, had taken his family with him every summer when he traveled to Europe. The Boston Symphony did not perform in the summer, and the Fiedlers spent that time in Sambor or with Johanna's family in Vienna. Occasionally Emanuel would return to the United States, leaving his wife and children in Europe, but most of the time they traveled back and forth across the Atlantic together. Then, in 1915, Emanuel decided to retire from the Boston Symphony.

Emanuel Fiedler's decision to uproot his family and return to Europe after twenty-five years mostly spent in Boston was a happy one for him and Johanna. But it created a difficult adjustment for my father, a fifteen-year-old boy who had managed to have an American childhood in spite of his parents' unyielding European discipline. Resenting his parents' decision, he rebelled by losing interest in his education, which would have been difficult to resume in Europe. "I had to relearn everything I had ever been taught—in German. That was not to my taste. I had had enough of studying Latin and Greek and algebra and all that sort of thing. I think I was really trying to ooze myself out of it." Of course there were duties he could never "ooze" himself out of. "You have to remember that I was still practicing my violin and piano daily. That was my duty, though I didn't enjoy it." But music had never been negotiable in the Fiedler family.

Papa was resentful of the break in his studies that resulted from the family's return to Europe, and later in life was embarrassed by his abbreviated education, although he compensated as much as possible by a voracious reading of histories and biographies. As a result, he was thrilled when, after conducting a concert in honor of the Massachusetts Institute of Technology, he was presented with an official dark red MIT jacket by the Class of 1917. "The Class of 1917 might have been my class if I had been intelligent enough," he wrote in his thank-you note. "I was proud as a peacock to wear the MIT emblem." And he wore that red jacket at many of his concerts for the rest of his life.

Papa was resentful and bored during the first months in Europe, but Emanuel and Johanna thrived. They had first gone to Vienna, but found it staid and tedious after the liveliness of the United States, so they moved to Berlin, then considered the most exciting city in Europe. Johanna had lived an isolated life with few friends in Boston; in Europe she blossomed. She held a kind of salon in Berlin, opening the Württembergische Strasse apartment every Friday night for a range of guests from diplomats to journalists to actors and musicians.

Emanuel was completely undaunted by the fact that he was in his fifties and was going to have to start a new career. He knew his tiny Boston Symphony pension wouldn't support his family; but there was music everywhere in Berlin—several opera companies and orchestras, innumerable chamber music groups, and a dizzying schedule of recitals by great artists from around the world. Soon Emanuel re-established himself, working as concertmaster of the Komische Oper, and he playing regularly with the Berlin Philharmonic, then under the direction of his good friend Artur Nikisch, a former music director of the Boston Symphony. They had been so close in Boston that Emanuel had named his only son after the conductor.

Emanuel never expected to return to Boston, but in 1936 the rise of Hitler in Germany forced him to do so. He was miserable, dragging himself in the mornings to the counter of a drugstore on Beacon Street, no substitute for his beloved coffee houses in Berlin. But once again he relied on his violin for survival. He practiced as hard as ever, although he was in his seventies by then, and it wasn't long before he was an active violin teacher. Occasionally he played as a substitute with his former B.S.O. colleagues in Papa's Esplanade Orchestra. No matter how bad things were at home or in the outside world, for Emanuel and my father there was always music. Emanuel turned to his violin; Papa went off to the next concert.

But Papa as a boy had a hard time adjusting to Berlin. Having announced that he was sick of school, he decided to try the business world, and he found a job as a copy boy at a German fashion magazine. He ran errands and did filing and, not unpredictably, loathed the work and left after three months.

Meanwhile, the invigorating musical world in Berlin, so different from Boston, quickly began to fascinate him. "When I got to Berlin, somehow or other, all of a sudden, there was an awakening. I mean that music began to interest me. I loved the sound of orchestras and bands and so forth. I thought maybe this would be something I'd like to do." He had, of course, continued to practice. And yet, "I was never trying to perfect my technique by practicing hours and hours to become a great technician on any instrument. Right away, I was really fascinated by the career of a conductor."

Arthur went to Emanuel, who by this time was concerned about what his son was planning to do with the rest of his life. Since the Fiedlers had been musicians as far back as anyone could remember, there had not been a great deal of career planning in earlier generations. "I told my father that I would like to have a musical career—I wanted to be a conductor." What Emanuel thought about the realistic possibilities of this career is not known, but he arranged for his son to audition at the Royal Academy of Music in Berlin, one of the most prestigious conservatories in Europe.

Papa was one of only thirteen students accepted in September 1911. "I was very fortunate to pass the examinations. I was about fifteen or sixteen. I had to play the violin and I played the piano and they interrogated me. And I was considered a foreigner, and of course they gave preference to their own.

"My idea was right away to enter a conducting class, which I did. But I also took violin lessons on the side, music theory and history and that sort of thing."

The schedule at the Royal Academy was strenuous. The regular weekly program was six days of study and practice from eight in the morning until the evening. Papa studied the violin with Willy Hess, a former concertmaster of the Boston Symphony. His conducting teacher was Arno Kleffel, a music director of the Cologne Opera, and he studied composition with the famous Hungarian composer Ernst von Dohnányi.

He also played second violin in the Berliner String Quartet, a group in which his father played first violin. In the summer of 1912, he toured Europe with an orchestra conducted by Johann Strauss III, nephew of Johann Strauss II, the Waltz King. Papa remembered Johann Strauss III as an ill-tempered man, but he acknowledged that, thanks to the tour, he absorbed the Viennese musical tradition of waltzes and polkas that was so soon to disappear in the rubble of two world wars. Years later, he would be recognized as one of the few conductors in the postwar world who still understood the Viennese tradition.

Also in 1912, he made his public debut as a conductor. A program from the Ochs-Eichelberg Konservatorium for March 25, 1912, notes that Herr Arthur Fiedler *aus Boston* would conduct "Drei Deutsche Tänze" by Mozart. "I got my first whack at conducting when I was quite young, when I was seventeen, in Berlin. It was no great orchestra, [being] made up of military band musicians."

It may not have been a great orchestra, but this concert decided Papa on a career. He had always been thrilled by the sound of a big orchestra, and now he had experienced the exultant power of lifting up a stick and having a large number of people do what he told them to do. "I became intrigued with the idea of hearing and manipulating a large group and enjoying the sound of many musicians. I began to feel more and more that I was doing what I really wanted to do."

The Royal Academy in Berlin was a mere two blocks from the city's legendary Kurfürstendamm, a boulevard lined with cafés and restaurants. Here he discovered another lifelong passion—the pursuit of beautiful women. "What makes them beautiful is not perfect features and couture clothes. It's the expression. And the voice. A woman sends out something of herself with the glance."

Photographs of Papa at the time show a slender, almost beautiful young man, with enormous dark eyes and thick black hair. His friends from the conservatory cheerfully acknowledged that, as the handsomest among them, my father easily stole their girlfriends. At the same time, he was such a good companion that they all loved him anyway. He soon perfected certain techniques for picking up women in the Berlin cafés, but he also enjoyed the company of his male friends, a form of relaxation he would always treasure.

This combination of studies, free-lance work, concertizing, and socializing was exhausting; he was overextending himself physically, another lifelong proclivity. Because he was still living at home with his family, there were battles over the schedule he kept. He tried living on his own for a while, but he returned to the Württembergische Strasse apartment when Emanuel and Johanna accepted that their son was a young man of eighteen living his own life. Although he was living under his parents' roof, he was earning his living and was responsible for his own finances and his own actions.

By 1914, he rarely thought about Boston; he knew that there were no career possibilities in the field of conducting in the United States. Puritan Boston and the Yankee ethic must have seemed a million miles away.

In music, there was no comparison between Boston and Europe. "I realized," he said, "that if I were to become a really famous conductor, eventually I would get back to the States, because most American orchestras featured conductors who had made a name for themselves abroad. But it seemed to me, even if I had had to confine my career to Europe, I would have been just as happy professionally."

By the time he turned nineteen, he had received a professional offer from a small opera company. Germany was full of such opera houses—every city had one—and they were used by young conductors then, as they are today, as places to learn the repertory, amass invaluable experience, and possibly conduct performances.

But World War I interfered with his plans to accept the offer. He was on vacation in Bohemia when Archduke Franz Ferdinand was assassinated in Sarajevo. Uneasy about the developing conflict and hearing that men of his age were being drafted into European armies, he returned to Berlin. The night he got back, August 4, 1914, England declared war on Germany.

Papa stayed on at the Royal Academy for another year because he did not see his own situation as immediately dangerous.

My family was still living in Berlin. I was, not yet being twenty-one, what you call a dual citizen. I was Austrian by Austrian law; you are what your father is until you become of age. Which meant I could have been drafted into the Austrian army, which I didn't look forward to. And according to American law, I was an American because I was born in this country and had an American passport.

On the night of May 7, 1915, he was playing chamber music at the home of Kurt Hirsch, the owner of a prominent German wire service, when he heard that the liner *Lusitania* had been sunk by a German U-boat. My father could probably have maintained his indifference to the international situation a little longer, but Herr Hirsch pointed out that since American passengers on the *Lusitania* had been killed, the entry into the war of the United States seemed inevitable; he warned that anti-American feeling in Germany could only intensify. And there was the Austrian army and the draft situation.

Papa went to see the American ambassador the next morning. "What should I do?" he asked. "I want to complete my studies at the academy. What can the embassy do if Austria tries to draft me into their army?"

The beleaguered ambassador replied, "Get out of Germany

right away, today. Don't lose any time. Because if Austria says you've got to go into the army, we don't want to be involved. We don't know how long the war is going to last. When it's over you can come back and resume your studies." Papa went to Holland that night. All the money he had with him was about three hundred dollars, lent to him by Kurt Hirsch; his parents were unable to contribute anything at all.

Papa's leaving Germany before completing his musical education was an accident of fate that had a lasting impact on his life as a musician. Under different circumstances, during the next few years—his last year at the Royal Academy and his tenure in the nurturing atmosphere of a provincial German opera house—he would have broadened his proficiency, polished his technical skills, and gained a measure of self-confidence.

Instead, there was always a detectable insecurity in my father's approach to music. By the time he died, he had probably conducted more concerts with more orchestras than any other conductor in the United States, but he worked as hard studying his scores in his eighties as he must have done in his twenties. When I look through his scores, I am amazed by the forest of markings he inked and penciled in the music. He used any kind of writing tool that was handy, so it is easy to see from the different colors of ink or pencil how many times he went over a piece.

Papa conducted pieces like Elgar's "Pomp and Circumstance March No. 1" or *On the Beautiful Blue Danube* waltz literally thousands of times. But I was never surprised when, before a concert, he would call one of the musicians into his dressing room to go over a few bars in these or any other familiar piece on the program. He never stopped learning, questioning, and working, and he never allowed anyone else to stop, either. I wonder whether he would have felt the need to be so punctilious had he not lost those last years of training. Papa was certainly among the first conductors not to have the advantage of full traditional European training. There were almost no American conductors at that time, in any case, and the generation of European conductors just a little older than my father had already had a chance to test their skills in a protected musical environment. Papa had no such chance, and as a result it was necessary for him to revise completely the way in which a conducting career customarily took shape.

Once he was safely in neutral Holland, he and another American musician from the Royal Academy took a small apartment in Amsterdam. The fate of his conducting career was pushed to the back of his mind while he concentrated on surviving. Amsterdam, overwhelmed by refugees from the German advances all over Europe, had no jobs for a musician. Returning to Berlin was clearly impossible, so he made the only remaining choice as his money dwindled away. With just about the last of his loan from Herr Hirsch, he booked passage to the United States on the *S.S. Rotterdam*, bound for Boston.

After a twenty-day trip across the Atlantic, delayed by U-boat warnings, British blockades, and searches of the ship, Papa returned to Boston five years after he had left. He was alone and, believing that he had left his chances for a conducting career behind him in Europe, he was miserable. He was a boy when he had moved away from Boston; now he had no idea how to get in touch with anyone he had known in his earlier life. He rented a furnished room, stuffy in the summer heat. "Everything was so strange. It all looked so gray and oddly unfamiliar, and I didn't meet anybody I knew; I felt dismal and lonesome and old; and I felt as though there wasn't a damned thing I could do about it."

But young and lonely as he was, he knew there was no point in sitting around in his dismal room feeling sorry for himself. Besides, he couldn't afford to sit around and be depressed; he had completely run out of money.

Both of my father's paternal uncles were in the Boston vicinity, and he soon located them at their summer jobs, playing in New England resort hotels. Uncle Gus was close, at the Atlantic House in Nantasket Beach, but he didn't know of any work available in the town. So he sent his nephew to Uncle Bennie, who was leading a small orchestra on the island of Nantucket. Bennie couldn't afford to pay Papa, but he did provide him with lodgings, and Papa ultimately passed a pleasant summer working in Uncle Bennie's orchestra, playing chamber music with wealthy vacationing Bostonians in his off hours, and discovering that there were attractive young women in New England as well as in Berlin. With the pittance he earned for his chamber music activities enlarged by his talent for playing cards, by summer's end he went back to Boston with a little money in his pocket.

Life once again became dreary, because the only winter work Papa could find was playing the violin at the Kimball Hotel in Springfield, Massachusetts. He was overcome by discouragement as he compared the provincial New England town with Berlin, its rich cultural life, the Royal Academy, and everything else he had left behind. He tried to compensate by educating himself, reading through shelves of books in the Springfield Public Library. Fortunately, the misery lasted for only three weeks.

I remember I was playing at one of the lunch sessions in the dining room and a bellhop came and said I had a long-distance call. It was the manager of the Boston Symphony, who told me that, on account of the war, there was a vacancy in the orchestra's violin section—one of the men couldn't get back. Dr. Muck had known me and met me. [Karl Muck, the music director of the Boston Symphony, had previously held the position when Emanuel was a member of the orchestra.] He said, would I accept it. I was delighted. So I got into the orchestra.

During the last week of September 1915, Papa walked into Symphony Hall and became a member of the Boston Symphony Orchestra's second violin section, through the same stage door from which he would be carried to an ambulance sixty-five seasons later. For those sixty-five years, Symphony Hall was the place he would think of as his true home.

IN 1915, KARL MUCK was in his sixth season as music director. A respected and renowned musician, the very model of a European music director, with two doctorates in philosophy in addition to his musical training, Muck had been the music director of the Royal Opera in Berlin and was a close friend of Kaiser Wilhelm. The Boston Symphony is generally regarded as reaching one of its greatest artistic peaks during the Muck regime, but his closeness to the Kaiser was well known and a cause for uneasiness in Boston as the United States drew nearer to war.

My father was an impressionable twenty when he first became exposed on a regular basis to the extraordinary personal magnetism that is essential for a famous conductor. He was also lonely and homesick. Emanuel was a strong, if remote, father, so Muck's authoritarian bearing, combined with the inherently dictatorial quality of his position, must have filled a familiar yet empty place in Papa's life. In later years, he would stress how much he had admired Muck:

He was a very educated man. He had a Ph.D., legally, not honorarily. He loved mathematics, as many musicians have. A very precise man. Never sentimental—something I hate in music—and very productive in his use of rehearsal time. Knew what he wanted. Highly industrious. Would take home instrumental parts that needed treatment, like the woodwinds, and put in markings—always in very good taste—in his own immaculate hand.

Many of Papa's own idiosyncracies and characteristics reflect Muck's professional influence. My father, too, was a perfectionist about markings, in his own scores and in the individual musicians' parts. The B.S.O. librarians dreaded his arrival in the orchestra library because he typically opened up the first piece of music he came upon and glowered at any messy markings, smudges, or torn pages. "Look!" he would shout. "Look at this! Shame!"

Like Muck, my father also prided himself on his precision. He was maniacal about timings and efficient in his use of rehearsal time. He arranged to have every piece he conducted timed at each performance; then he would compare the length of the latest version with earlier performances. He was happiest when there was no deviation.

Karl Muck even affected the way my father began to dress. Newspaper stories about Papa from back in the 1920s, when his career began to flourish, mention his clothing. He bought expensive clothes even when he could not afford them, and by the time I was a child he had all his suits made in London. His clothes were so well made and well maintained that they lasted for decades, a point of which he was vociferously proud. One of the saddest memories I have of his last years, when he became thin and shrunken, is his admission that he needed an entirely new wardrobe. He hated to give up his good old clothes, but he hated even more to be seen in suits and tuxedos and tails that no longer fitted perfectly.

Nothing he wore, however, was ever *obviously* expensive. Papa had totally embraced the Bostonian notion that the more money you have, the less it should show. Toward the end of his life, he bought himself one of the few material objects I ever remember him coveting—the elegant Mercedes-Benz. But I don't ever remember him driving it. "It's too good to drive," he once said, and I think he believed that.

This lack of pretentiousness had as its source another of Papa's B.S.O. father figures: Henry Lee Higginson, the Boston Brahmin who founded the orchestra and accurately reflected the values and attitudes of his peers. Major Higginson often gave the musicians lectures about fiscal responsibility. He would remind them that he was a banker by profession, and would offer to help them with any of their financial problems. He counseled them to save their money and not be extravagant. He would show them his own shoes, pointing out that they had been repaired many times and were still perfectly good. The major was also renowned for his habit of steaming uncanceled stamps off letters. Papa was as impressed by this thrift as by the major's generous underwriting of the orchestra's annual deficit.

A young man when he joined the orchestra's second violin section, Papa was wholly cut off from his family in Germany and was to have no communication with them until the war ended, three years later. For the first time in his life he was separated from a family whose members were intensely engaged with one another. Their involvement may have taken the form of anger or resentment rather than warmth and affection, but the emotional bonds were strong.

Under these circumstances, it was only natural that the Boston Symphony and the people attached to it provided Papa with a sense of "home" and "family" and gave structure to his days. Indeed, he already knew many of the older musicians—they had been colleagues of Emanuel's only a few years earlier—and, of course, there were his two uncles, who both lived in Boston.

This sense of home was especially important in the midst of the growing national xenophobia about Germans. Of the ninety musicians in the orchestra, he was one of only eight who were American-born. Many of the others were Germans, but he did not feel foreign or out of place. For the rest of his life, his orchestra colleagues would be among his closest companions, friends with whom he could relax and behave in any way he wanted. With them, there was never any need of a façade.

But in those early Boston days, Papa did feel the necessity of a façade, especially when he was with people outside the circle of Symphony musicians. His response to the suspicion directed toward Germans was to use his exoticism as a shield, something he did not need to do when he was among his colleagues. Being a member of the orchestra was a joy to him musically, a comfort in his loneliness and isolation, and an honor personally.

PAPA'S FIRST YEARS with the Symphony went smoothly, and he began to feel more at home in the city. He had an outgoing personality and quickly made friends with the older musicians, despite the age difference. He joined chamber ensembles and participated enthusiastically in the time-honored orchestra traditions of discreet horseplay during rehearsals and gentle conductor baiting—although never with the martinet Dr. Muck. Papa switched from violin to viola in his second season, saying he found his new instrument "more interesting."

As World War I intensified, the orchestra was haunted by the conflict, even before the United States entered the war. The German musicians who made Papa feel so comfortable were looked on less happily by the citizens of Boston. Some members of the audience, sympathetic with the Allied cause, began to feel uneasy at the concerts.

Major Higginson, who had studied music in Vienna, believed steadfastly in the Germanic orchestral tradition, but he was also a Civil War veteran and deeply patriotic. The ethnic make-up of his orchestra and the explosion of anti-German feeling called for him to perform a balancing act he found increasingly difficult to manage. Higginson, in the Boston Brahmin tradition, truly believed that he knew what was best for the orchestra artistically, unpopular as it might be politically, and this lordly perspective prevented him and the B.S.O. trustees from seeing objectively the public's growing anti-German sentiment. For the first three seasons after the war broke out, the dismay about the orchestra's Germanic influences was held at bay by the ensemble's brilliance. But when, in 1917, the United States entered the war, the anti-German sentiment became acute, and patriotic gestures gained new significance.

Early in the 1917–18 season, there was an explosive incident. A last-minute request for the orchestra to perform "The Star-Spangled Banner" at a concert in Providence was turned down by Higginson; the orchestra had not prepared the piece, and Higginson did not wish to embarrass Muck, a German in the land of his country's enemy. Muck was never even consulted about the decision, yet when outrage broke in the press over the orchestra's refusal to play the national anthem, he was the focus of all the blame.

A few days later Higginson was forced to announce that Muck would thereafter include the national anthem on his programs, and he attempted to assume responsibility for the incident. As a result, he too was regarded with suspicion. Muck did not help the situation when he bluntly told *The New York Times*, "Why will people be so silly? Art is a thing by itself and not related to any particular nation or group. It would be a gross mistake, a violation of artistic taste and principles for an organization such as ours to play patriotic airs."

Anti-German outrage spread beyond Boston and across the United States. Operas in German were banned at the Metropolitan Opera; Danish music was banned in San Francisco because it was rumored that the Danes had smuggled supplies to the Germans. The entire country was becoming obsessed.

My father, born and raised in the United States, still seemed very European in Yankee Boston, and he became an object of anti-Teutonic prejudice. People shouted, "German spy!" at him in the streets. Loaves of bread delivered to him arrived full of holes, because vigilant neighbors had poked them to make sure he wasn't receiving enemy messages baked inside. At a seaside bungalow he rented in the summer of 1918, neighbors reported him to the authorities because he had hung Japanese lanterns in his garden. He had indeed hung the lanterns in an attempt to make the dreary little house more festive, but the neighbors were convinced that he was using the lights to signal the German U-boats they were sure were lurking just offshore. The police and the FBI investigated and found no evidence of treachery, but he was made to feel uncomfortable until the war was over.

Karl Muck did not get off that lightly. Only a few weeks after the national anthem incident, sentiment ran so high against him that the police had to be stationed at the Boston Symphony's concerts in New York. Muck offered to resign, but Higginson refused to accept the gesture, pointing out that the remainder of the season would have to be canceled, denying employment to the American musicians as well as to the Germans.

In March 1918, Karl Muck was arrested in Boston during a rehearsal of Bach's *St. Matthew's Passion* and interned in a Georgia prison. In June 1919, he was deported.

The actual charges that led up to Muck's arrest involved his indiscreet liaison with a young Boston woman under the age of legal consent. Incriminating letters written by Muck to her had been sent, anonymously, to the immigration authorities. Although Muck denied anything more than a flirtation, and although his wife steadfastly supported him, for Boston this was the last straw. He returned to Germany a bitter man, emotionally devastated, and never again returned to the United States, though he received many lucrative offers.

These events had a profound effect on my father. He greatly admired Karl Muck and absorbed as many lessons from his downfall as from his years of prominence. Papa developed an almost compulsive discretion and secretiveness about his personal life, especially about any romantic involvements. He also became convinced that an artist should never be perceived to be political in any way. It was evident to him that only danger and disgrace could result from mixing art and politics, and this was a position he strictly maintained for the rest of his life.

IT IS IRONIC that just as Papa was being suspected of disloyalty because of his German ancestry, he was beginning to feel a firm sense of loyalty to the country of his birth. When the United States entered the war in 1917, Papa, twenty-two years old, attempted to enlist in the Navy. Aware that he was too short—he was five feet seven—and thin to meet U.S. Navy standards, Papa stuffed himself with bananas and drank gallons of water before going to the enlistment examination. However, he still weighed in at under 120 pounds and was not accepted, much to his disappointment.

Then in 1918, although he had not grown any larger, he was drafted by the Army. He was given time to finish out the 1917–18 B.S.O. season, but then he resigned from the orchestra, gave up his apartment, sold his furniture, and, in a move that broke his heart, gave away his dog, Muzzi.

Dispatched to Camp Devens in Massachusetts for basic training, he immediately discovered that he loathed Army life. The severe life in the barracks and horrible food, which he largely refused to eat, made his life a misery. Only the fact that several of the other American musicians in the B.S.O. had been drafted and stationed at the same camp made his life bearable.

Two weeks after his arrival at Devens, my father was sent for a postinduction physical. "Who the hell sent *you* here?" the Army doctor asked in horror. "You have flat feet. The Army can't use you. They should never have taken you in the first place." His medical discharge quickly followed.

For some reason, my father considered the question of service to his country unresolved by his World War I experience. When the United States entered World War II, he launched a series of free concerts for members of the armed services and, in 1943, enlisted for active duty in the U.S. Coast Guard Temporary Reserve. He was given the rank of apprentice seaman and assigned to patrol Boston Harbor one night a week, looking for submarines and searching incoming and outgoing vessels for contraband. The only submarine he ever spotted turned out to be a low-lying barge, but my father was so proud of his endeavor that he even wore his uniform to conduct the Pops on Navy Night in 1944.

The ludicrous episode during World War I, however, created yet another disruption in Papa's life. He returned to Boston homeless, jobless, and, because Muzzi had run away from her new owner, dogless. But the Boston Symphony came to the rescue once again. Because of the war, they had been unable to fill Papa's seat in the viola section, so after a brief summer vacation, he gratefully went back to work at Symphony Hall.

LIKE EVERYTHING ELSE in the world at the end of World War I, things changed rapidly around the Boston Symphony. Major Higginson, emotionally and financially devastated by the war years, retired. A board of directors took over and began looking for a conductor to replace Muck.

The orchestra's situation was dire. Major Higginson had been the financial underpinning. Some of the musicians had been dismissed as enemy aliens and others had gone home to Europe in disgust as soon as they could after the war ended. The trustees turned to France, an ally in the war, not only for the next two music directors, Henri Rabaud and Pierre Monteux, but also for musicians to fill the many vacancies, and the 1918–19 season opened with what was essentially a new Boston Symphony. Papa remained, as did Uncle Bernhard, and in 1918 Uncle Gustav joined the orchestra's violin section.

Pierre Monteux became music director of the Boston Symphony in 1919. Papa, always susceptible to the appeal of a convenient father figure, had just lost two such men, Karl Muck and Henry Lee Higginson; he turned with enthusiasm to Monteux, a more gentle person than Muck, yet a rigorous musician with a legendary ear. He was also an adventurous explorer of new repertory who included neglected works of the past as well as contemporary compositions on his programs. Papa learned a great deal about mining of the symphonic repertory from Monteux and from his successor, Serge Koussevitzky.

My father's admiration for Monteux, whom he often referred to as "Maître," much as Karl Muck was always "Dr. Muck," grew as he watched the Frenchman rebuild the Boston Orchestra twice. The first time was after the war; the next was after a wildcat strike in 1920 that decimated the membership for the second time in three years.

My father himself had participated in that strike, more through comradeship with the other musicians than because of any deeply held beliefs. The walk-out came just before a Saturday night concert, but once he got home, away from the exhilaration of rebellion, he had trouble sleeping. Certainly he felt a loyalty to his colleagues, yet he believed he had an obligation to the audience, who had been left waiting in the theater. The orchestra had, he said, "played a damned dirty trick on our subscribers" and should not have struck right before a concert. He knew that his family in Europe depended on him financially in those hard days after the war, and that he had a responsibility to them as well.

Early the following Monday morning, my father went to see the orchestra's manager. He confessed that he regretted his actions, and asked to be reinstated as a member of the Symphony. The manager, who had promised to rehire any repentant musicians, agreed, and he was taken back, along with only four of the other strikers.

From then on, he was determined to err on the side of caution in similar situations. In the coming years he was distressed and angered by Boston Symphony decisions and restrictions many times, but he never again made a statement that challenged the management. Often, he failed to exercise the power he had which could have changed conditions he didn't relish. He had tried to use some lesser leverage during the 1920 strike and was terrified at how close he had come to losing his secure position. In the future, taking chances seemed uninviting.

Then, too, he had signed a contract with the Boston Symphony —he had given his word. The Symphony subscribers had paid in advance for a certain number of concerts, so it was wrong for the orchestra not to play. My father was brought up in a family where people stayed together more through obligation than because of love. He owed his parents obedience—in his studies, in his financial support, in a strict schedule of visits. He went to Berlin every summer, whether he wanted to or not. When Emanuel came back to live in Boston, Papa visited him every day, whether he had time or not. These were not duties he would ever question. Family implied responsibility. It's not too surprising that he waited until he was fifty years old to create his own family, and did so then only with reluctance. Nor is it surprising that he saw his quasi-familial relationship with the Boston Symphony in the same terms: commitment and loyalty fused by obligation.

After the crisis of the strike, my father's professional admiration of Monteux warmed to a close personal relationship. By 1924, he was keeping in touch with the older conductor during his summer vacations in Europe, and the friendship continued even though Monteux was not re-engaged by the B.S.O. at the end of the 1923–24 season. The men became closer when Papa began going to San Francisco in the summers during the years when Monteux was music director there.

Monteux and his American wife, Doris, came to our house in Brookline on many occasions. Monteux's beaming face and kindly manner must have enticed me out of my usual shyness, because I remember going up to him one time when he was in our library and asking him who he was. The old conductor, with his white military mustache and portly figure, smiled gently and said, "I am Santa Claus." Of course I believed him.

One Halloween he was sitting in the library when Debbie and I were about to go out on our trick-or-treating rounds with Celie. Dressed as ghosts, with old white sheets draped over our heads and round holes cut out for eyeholes, we were trotted in to say hello to the Monteuxs. As we came into the room, Maestro Monteux shrank back in his chair. "Oh," he said, "I'm so scared!" Debbie and I were thrilled; neither of our parents had ever paid much attention to us on what we considered one of the most important events of our year.

By the time Monteux was an old man, the Boston Symphony belatedly realized the orchestra's debt to him, and honored him as the fine conductor he had always been. His eightieth birthday was celebrated with a gala concert on April 4, 1955. Papa thought for a long time about what special thing he could do to pay tribute to this benevolent man who had been so kind to him years before. He began practicing the viola again, after not having touched the instrument in twenty-five years, and played in the viola section during the birthday concert, the only time he ever did so after his retirement as an active player in the 1930s. He was determined to play for Monteux even though he was about to enter the hospital for his colon operation; he would never have reneged on his promise to play for Papa Pierre, as he sometimes called the older conductor.

In 1959 my mother and father gave a large dinner party after Monteux's eighty-fifth birthday concert with the Boston Symphony. It was one of the few big parties they ever gave. I can remember hiding at the top of the stairs and peeking down between the railings at the grown-ups. I listened to the toasts made to Monteux, entranced by the wit and polish of the guests. Many of them, powerful people from the music business, had come up from New York for the concert, and I was drawn by what seemed to be their very un-New-England sophistication. It was all far more interesting than what I saw as the drab atmosphere of the city where I was growing up, but what was really the claustrophobia of life in an unhappy family. The drabness and claustrophobia were relieved, of course, on the magical occasions when Papa took me with him to Symphony Hall.

IN THE FALL of 1924, when Serge Koussevitzky arrived in Boston to begin his tenure as music director of the Boston Symphony, articles in newspapers referred to Papa, beginning his tenth season with the orchestra, as its busiest member. In addition to his regular seat in the viola section, he was also the keyboard player, performing on the piano, organ, and celesta when these instruments were required. "I played percussion instruments. I did general housework," he told an interviewer self-deprecatingly in the 1970s. "Somebody began to call me the orchestra's 'floating kidney,' " he said, "because in a single concert I would play in two or three

sections of the orchestra." He also helped out as a backstage conductor, to cue choruses and instruments playing behind the scenes.

Yet with all this activity, my father was frustrated. He felt
trapped in his life as an orchestral musician, even though he was
also involved in chamber music and in coaching and accompanying
musicians outside the B.S.O. He considered moving to New York;
in 1921, during his summer vacation, he spent a short time as a
rehearsal pianist on Broadway. But he loathed the hack work and
the endless rehearsals—although he later said that had he been
conducting the musical, he might have been able to work up more
interest. After a week on Broadway, he resigned and returned to
Boston.

That turned out to be a major decision. New York may have
offered more professional opportunities, but he never again considered leaving Boston. Its smaller and less competitive artistic community must have seemed safe to him, and I suspect the real
motive was his reluctance to leave his familial life with the Boston
Symphony.

When Koussevitzky arrived, Papa had to deal with a brooding
and quixotic man. From the beginning, there was little sympathy
between them. The Russian conductor was an immediate success
in Boston, but even after being securely established in the city for
several years, he did not lose his innate suspiciousness and defen-
siveness.

Koussevitzky had come to conducting after an unusual career as
a soloist on the double bass and, later, as a music publisher when
he was forced to immigrate to Paris during the Russian Revolution.
He had married well, however, and his wealthy wife helped him
establish an orchestra in Paris and, with it, his reputation as a
conductor. But he retained a lack of confidence in his technical
abilities as a conductor because of the gaps in his early training,
and masked this insecurity with extraordinary cruelty toward the
musicians in his orchestra. The Boston Symphony musicians were
terrified of him throughout his twenty-five-year tenure as their
music director, and, although they frequently joked with one another about his conducting inadequacies, they never dared show

him any disrespect. Still, Koussevitzky seethed with doubt, and kept a sharp eye out for any competition or conspiracies that might weaken his musical power in Boston. My father was young, ambitious, and locally popular; Koussevitzky made sure to monitor his developing career.

Meanwhile my father, as he wrote, was asking himself, " 'Are you going to play the viola all your life?' And I said, 'What about this conducting business? Are you going to give that up completely?' And I said, 'No.' "

Papa's determination to become a conductor required a good deal of faith in the 1920s. There were few orchestras and no tradition of Americans conducting the ones that did exist. Because the war had prevented his serving the planned apprenticeship in Europe, he assumed it would be impossible for him to compete. Nobody would take an unknown young American without European experience and entrust him with an expensive orchestra. "I said, 'How am I going to get started here?' Well, I did something novel. I organized amongst my own colleagues a chamber orchestra which I called the Boston Sinfonietta. Everybody thought that name was ridiculous. 'Sinfonietta. What does that mean?' It means small symphony. Everybody thought that was a crazy name, but I took it. And in the meantime hundreds of them have sprung up all over the world."

He saw his Sinfonietta as his own little Boston Symphony. It was founded in 1924, Koussevitzky's first season in Boston, and its members were all B.S.O. musicians. It was back-breaking work for Papa. He had to recruit the musicians, find an agent to book concerts, dig up the repertoire for an ensemble that was unique at the time or arrange other works to make them suitable for the Sinfonietta's size, and do all the fund raising. The Fiedler Sinfonietta gave its first public concert in October 1925 and its first Symphony Hall concert in January 1927; it received excellent reviews for both.

I never heard any of its live performances, but that little orchestra played on continuously in the family consciousness. Papa cherished his achievements with the Sinfonietta above anything else in his career except for the founding of the Esplanade Concerts. He remembered his years with the Sinfonietta as a golden time, a period in his life when he was conducting music everyone admired and respected. The Sinfonietta was untainted by publicity campaigns and showmanship; its repertoire was purely classical and serious. Its records still exist—Mozart divertimenti and serenades, Handel concertos, works by Bach, Corelli, and Telemann, and the world première recording of Paul Hindemith's Viola Concerto, with Hindemith himself as soloist. In later years Papa never stopped trying to convince the record companies to make records with the Sinfonietta, but they had little interest. After my father became famous, the Sinfonietta never performed in public again.

KOUSSEVITZKY was initially supportive of my father's fledgling conducting efforts; he attended several of the Sinfonietta concerts and offered encouragement. He was probably less pleased by the references to himself that cropped up in some of the glowing reviews, such as the one on the Symphony Hall debut: "These twenty-two men are under as sensitive a control, as responsive to it, as though they were under Mr. Koussevitzky himself."

Papa now had outlets in addition to his position in the orchestra, but he couldn't ignore the fact that he was still *in* the orchestra. He was restless, like most orchestral musicians, and compensated for the monotonous grind of orchestra life by a certain amount of creative mischief, even though his behavior once backfired, with disastrous results.

The heat in un-air-conditioned Symphony Hall often became unbearable during the Pops season, making the musicians even more restless than usual. On May 18, 1926, their pranks went too far, enraging the Pops conductor Alfredo Jacchia, who decided that my father had been the instigator. Early the following morning, Papa received a letter from George Judd, then the B.S.O.'s assistant manager:

It has come to my attention in such a way that I cannot think that there are any sufficiently extenuating circumstances to make it possible to excuse your lack of dignity and deportment at the Pops concerts. It is my suggestion that since these concerts seem to you so trivial, you do not play for the balance of the present season. Although this has been going on for some time, Mr. Jacchia's patience was exhausted last night and I am entirely in sympathy with his disappointment in your behavior. Until further notice it will therefore be understood that you are not a member of the Pops orchestra for the present season.

Papa was horrified by the possibility of expulsion from the Boston Symphony. Just as he had after the strike, he quickly apologized, employing all of his considerable charm on both Judd and Jacchia, and he was reinstated. He didn't stop there. Within months he had become a close friend of Jacchia's and visited him several times during his summer sojourns in Europe.

The solidity of his reinstatement was proven a few weeks later. Jacchia, with his classically impetuous nature, became infuriated with the B.S.O. management over a trifling matter at the end of the 1926 season. He resigned on the spot and refused to conduct the final Pops concert on July 4. The management, left with no conductor at the last minute, turned to Papa, whose conducting with the Sinfonietta was well known in Boston.

The concert was a splendid success. "Arthur Fiedler received an uproarious reception from a capacity audience that was insistent on encores after each number," the *Boston Herald* said. Knowing that Jacchia had decided not to come back, and flushed with his first major popular triumph, he wrote to the orchestra's trustees, applying for the job as conductor of the Pops:

It will be no secret to you that I hope to be seriously considered as a candidate for the position of Pops conductor left vacant by the resignation of Mr. Jacchia. Presumably you have known of my ambition to be a conductor, and that my education and training were shaped with that in view. It would be ideal to describe in detail the musical advantages which I have enjoyed that I feel certain qualify me for this work; you are familiar with my record in the orchestra for the last eleven years and doubtless know something of my experience as accompanist for singers and instrumentalists. I mention these seemingly irrelevant phases of my work merely to indicate how comprehensive my musical experience has been.

More pertinent is the training as a conductor which I had in Germany and my experience as an orchestral leader abroad and throughout New England as conductor of my own symphonic ensemble. The success of my activities in this field is indicated by numerous press notices which I would be happy to show you on your request.

It was indeed fortunate for me to have had an opportunity, though at eleventh-hour notice, to prove my fitness at the final Pops concert of last season. I trust that you recall the generous reception tendered me both by the audience and the press. Particularly gratifying to me was the fine spirit of cooperation which my colleagues proved to me, and which I feel certain I could depend on in the future.

Two other phases [sic] that you might care to consider are, firstly, that I am not only an American citizen, but a native of Boston, and although far from being a chauvinist where art is concerned, I think that, everything else being equal, an American and Bostonian might be given the preference; secondly, I have reason to believe that the large following which I have built up in musical circles would conceivably prove an important business asset.

To sum up, I believe that I am qualified for this position by the education, training, and experience which I have had, by the familiarity with the repertoire which my work in the orchestra and as conductor have gained for me, and finally by my heartfelt desire and reasonable confidence in my ability to make a success of this position.

It goes without saying that I will be deeply grateful for any courtesy which you show this application.

I was astonished when I came across this letter several years after my father's death, because it violates many of the principles he had stressed. "Never blow your own horn," he would say over and over, and I never did hear him blow his. He was self-belittling almost to a fault—it was almost as if he believed some of the terrible reviews he received over the years. He would often open a score and shake his head. "This is awfully difficult," he would say to anyone who happened to be present, even members of the orchestra, in front of whom most conductors went to extensive lengths to appear omnipotent.

The length of the letter is also unusual for him, as his normal letter rarely exceeded one paragraph. My father, an articulate man, was a firm believer in succinctness in conversation. "Start in the middle!" he invariably roared at anyone embarking on a patently long, discursive story or joke. But his hunger for the job of Pops

conductor must have led him to abandon his characteristic terse-
ness.

It is the clarity with which he expressed his longing for the
position that surprises me the most. "Don't wear your heart on
your sleeve," he would admonish me. Letting someone know you
wanted something was tantamount to admitting that you were vulnerable. For most of my life I truly believed that to show vulnerability was the stupidest thing you could do. When someone once
asked me, quite simply, "What's so bad about being vulnerable?"
I discovered that I had no answer. Papa had never explained that
part.

The roots of much of his bitterness and bleakness of spirit, I
think, lay in the constant disappointments of his relationship with
the Boston Symphony. An orchestra was never meant to be the
substitute for a family; anyone from the management looking at
my self-possessed father probably could never have fathomed his
emotional investment in the Symphony. His application to become
Pops conductor was one of the only times that he showed how
badly he wanted and needed the acceptance and approval of that
august Bostonian institution.

The trustees, with typical caution, made no immediate decision,
and Papa was forced to wait. Then, in January 1927, the Boston
Symphony announced the appointment of a new Pops conductor,
Alfredo Casella, like Jacchia an Italian.

Papa was severely disappointed. In later years, he would cite the
episode as the only time in his life he had ever asked for a job; the
rejection was a blow to his pride he was careful never to risk again.
He turned his disappointment to action and immediately looked
around for a new project.

My father had noticed for some time that classical music was not
available to most Americans. When he was in Europe, he saw that
music was everywhere: beer garden concerts in Germany, concerts
in the outdoor wine cafés in Austria, concerts in the parks in
France and Italy. Many of these concerts were with good orchestras or symphonic bands. In the United States, however, a person
had to be rich to hear a symphony orchestra. Only the moderately
priced Pops concerts were available to people of average means,

and they were still beyond the reach of most Bostonians. Papa thought this strange. Why shouldn't music be for everyone? Why should only wealthy people be able to go to concerts?

I thought of organizing some free concerts in Boston. The idea was a very simple one. It occurred to me that if you sought the great things in literature, you had a free library to go to. If you wanted to see great works of art, you had a free museum to go to. If you wanted to hear great music, you had to dig in your jeans and buy a ticket. Why?

I am still under the impression that music is the most easily accepted of the arts. You don't have to be able to read or anything. There's a certain thing about music, whether it's the rhythm or the pictures that you portray in your own mind when you're listening to music or the association of ideas—I don't care what it is—music has the largest appeal.

And I knew it takes money to run a library and to run an art museum. Well, I thought I would see if I could find the money to run a few concerts.

There was more to Papa's thinking than populist cultural philosophy. Certainly he did have altruistic motives for starting a series of free outdoor concerts, but he never deceived himself about his primary reason. "I was ambitious to establish myself as a conductor, and it appeared to me that my best move was to create my own opportunity."

He chose the Charles River Esplanade at the foot of Beacon Hill as the perfect site for his free outdoor concerts, and he began fund raising. It took him almost two years to convince a group of about fifteen wealthy Bostonians to put up the money for the first season and almost as long to win the backing of the Metropolitan District Commission, which eventually erected a shaky wooden bandshell to house the orchestra. Then he hired members of the Boston Symphony, who were happy for the summer employment, to make up the new orchestra.

On July 4, 1929, my father conducted the first Esplanade Concert and opened the first series of free outdoor concerts ever given by a symphony orchestra. In defiance of all the pessimistic predictions, five thousand people came to the performance and all of them behaved with a decorum that would have been appropriate in Symphony Hall. The program consisted largely of the "light

Emanuel Fiedler, my father's father, around 1920. *(Author's collection)*

My grandmother, Johanna Bernfeld Fiedler, as she looked around 1900. *(Author's collection)*

My father at his tenth birthday party, in 1904. *(Author's collection)*

As a student in Berlin around 1913, my father (far right, hand on hip) played in the Berliner String Quartet with his own father, Emanuel (holding violin, far left). *(Author's collection)*

My father's favorite sister, Rosa, poses with Nicky, the family dog, in Berlin around 1915. *(Author's collection)*

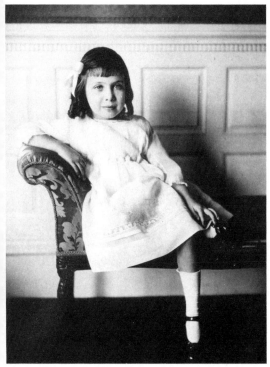

My mother, at seven, poses in her first communion dress in 1921, at her family's town house on Beacon Street in Boston. *(Author's collection)*

Jeanne Eagels, the actress who was my father's first love, in 1918, the year they met. She inscribed the picture "To my Ruffio," her name for my father. *(Author's collection)*

An early publicity shot of my father as a young conductor, probably taken in the mid-1920s. *(Author's collection)*

An Esplanade Concert during the 1930s. The orchestra is playing in one of the temporary band shells erected before the Hatch Memorial Shell, still in use today, was built in 1940. *(Author's collection)*

Papa discussing a score with his nemesis, the Boston Symphony Orchestra music director Serge Koussevitzky, in the late 1930s. *(Courtesy of the Boston Symphony Orchestra Archives)*

Papa in rehearsal . . .

. . . and in concert with the Pops, late 1940s. *(Author's collection)*

My mother's wedding picture, taken in the drawing room of her mother's home in 1942. She was married in a red velvet dress because she felt that marrying a non-Catholic made the traditional white inappropriate. *(Author's collection)*

At the age of nine months, I enjoy my father's conducting at my first concert, on the Esplanade, with (left to right) my father's sisters, Rosa and Fredericka, and my mother. *(Author's collection)*

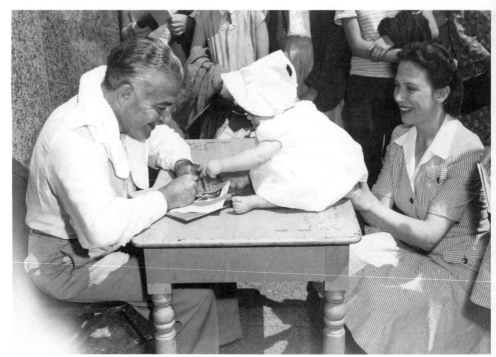

I help Papa sign autographs after an Esplanade Concert while my mother looks on. *(Author's collection)*

The Fiedler family in about 1950 on the terrace of the house in Brookline: (from left) my mother, Debbie, me, Papa. *(Author's collection)*

classics," but Papa also included "The Star-Spangled Banner" and never missed performing it for the next fifty years of Esplanade Concerts.

By the end of the first season, audiences had doubled, and Papa's national reputation was expanding. *The New York Times* and *Time* magazine did pieces on the concerts: "Last week, the experiment could no longer be considered experimental. The attendance amazed even optimistic conductor Arthur Fiedler. He is a new name to nationwide concertgoers but his musical lineage is a proud one. Now that the concerts are a reality, he finds himself—dark, stocky, energetic—something of a public idol. Boston ladies applaud himself as well as his music."

Even Koussevitzky, in Europe, heard about the success of the Esplanade's first season and made a point of congratulating my father on his return. Papa's success with his new concerts seemed complete; the Boston Symphony had noticed and approved.

Two months later, the stock market crashed. Papa's first concern was personal. He was completely wiped out. Once again, he had been reminded that the world was a precarious place where disaster was not only possible but almost inevitable. However, he rescued both himself and his newborn concerts. The second season opened on schedule in the summer of 1930, and the Esplanade Concerts survived the Depression, as they would World War II and its blackouts and the Boston Symphony's fluctuating commitment to the series. Papa never wavered about these concerts, long after he had achieved his goal of conducting the Boston Pops. "I think I've come to deserve a little credit," he said, "for making a thing like this possible."

The Esplanade Concerts also opened the Boston Pops to Papa, as he had hoped they would. An editorial in one of the Boston papers when the first Esplanade season ended stated, "Mr. Fiedler is closely in touch with popular taste [and] his concerts have built a new public for symphonic music." And the trustees noticed. The Pops conductor for the previous three seasons, Alfredo Casella, had alienated audiences by his overintellectual programming. Attendance dropped off, the orchestra was demoralized and disgruntled, and the Pops income, on which the B.S.O. depended, was diminishing rapidly.

In January 1930, my father was called to the manager's office at Symphony Hall and finally offered the contract he had wanted for so long.

I got the job, not under good circumstances because the management knew too well—and I think they were a little hard on me—that I wanted the job and I knew very well what Mr. Casella was getting and wanted to get somewhere near that, but I didn't. But I did get a three-year contract with an increase in pay each year, which at the third year was about half of what Mr. Casella got. And I started filling the halls and I'm glad to report that we did very well.

It was a mixed triumph: that question of his salary would haunt him for the rest of his life.

PAPA HAD BEEN READY with his plans for the Pops for a long time. In an interview with *The New York Times* a few days after the announcement of his appointment, he explained that he would go back to the venerable Pops tradition of programming popular music, stressing the distinction between the Symphony season and the Pops.

His debut as official conductor of the Pops was a great success. "The golden era of the Pops has arrived," the *Boston Herald* predicted. By the middle of the first season, the papers were reporting that the 1930 season had broken all previous attendance records, and my father was proclaimed "Boston's greatest stage-door sensation since the passing of the matinee idol."

Papa had finally achieved what he thought he wanted: he was the conductor of the Boston Pops. What he didn't foresee was the irreversible point he had reached as he forfeited any hope of being regarded as a serious musician. He gained broad exposure through his national radio broadcasts and highly publicized recordings, and his image became firmly fixed in the public's mind: he had become a Pops conductor, a conductor of light music. As he began to define what that kind of conductor was, he saw his original aspirations slip forever beyond his reach.

"The trouble is you get labeled," he said in 1972. "When I first started recording for RCA years ago I did an awful lot of large works, whole symphonies. But now when you go somewhere they always ask you, 'Will you play what you are known for?' 'Well, yes,' I say, 'but I'd like to do some other things, too.' They don't realize I can do other kinds of music. I wouldn't say Mahler or Bruckner, much as I admire those composers. But I conduct purely serious concerts when I can. I suppose every clown wants to play Hamlet."

PAPA SOON FOUND OUT that achieving the position he thought he wanted more than anything else in the world was a mixed blessing. For one thing, Koussevitzky began to view him as a dangerous rival.

In the beginning, the two men were able to maintain an outwardly friendly relationship, though there was discernible tension. In 1933, my father was invited by the owner of the Ritz-Carlton Hotel to start a series of chamber concerts in the dining room on Sunday evenings. The hotel was the most elegant in Boston, and the concerts were to be scheduled after dinner so that the musicians would play for an audience enjoying champagne or brandy. Since food and drinks were served at Boston Pops concerts in Symphony Hall, my father did not find this proposal objectionable. But he was careful to check with the B.S.O. management, because the musicians would be drawn from the orchestra. When he was told that the Ritz series sounded fine to the orchestra's administration, he went ahead and programmed a series—works for chamber orchestra by such composers as Haydn, Mozart, Rossini, Ravel, and Johann Strauss—and the first concert was given on December 10, 1933.

The concert was performed before an audience of Boston society, including my grandmother, one of my uncles, and my mother, who was singled out by the social column in the *Boston Traveler* the next day as "one of the most stunning girls in the room." The Symphony–Dinner Concert was proclaimed a delightful innovation and a great success.

Koussevitzky, who had apparently not been consulted by the

orchestra's management, did not agree. He arrived at the Symphony rehearsal the next morning in one of his legendary rages. "How can my men play in a restaurant?" he shouted. He forbade any of the musicians to play at the Ritz again, and no one ever did. "We were all scared of Koussevitzky," my father admitted. The series, of course, was canceled.

In 1936, a much more substantial and tantalizing project was proposed to Papa. A group of affluent music lovers from both Boston and New York approached him with the idea of starting a summer music festival in the Berkshires. There already existed a modest series of concerts in Stockbridge, Massachusetts, and the local summer residents had been impressed by the success of Papa's innovative Esplanade Concerts.

Nineteen thirty-six was the year that my father's own father and sisters left Berlin and moved to Boston. Papa, who had spent his summers in Europe up to this point, was delighted with the idea of a summer season in the Berkshires after the Esplanade Concerts ended. Since the orchestra in Stockbridge would be made up of Boston Symphony musicians, my father again went dutifully to the orchestra's management to clear the project in advance.

The management was quick to see the possibilities of this proposal, especially in extending the annual employment for the musicians. They told my father that their initial response was positive but asked that, as a matter of courtesy, the project first be presented to Koussevitzky. No one thought that the orchestra's music director would be the least bit interested in the Berkshire concerts. He always spent the summer in Europe and would seemingly have little interest in a rustic festival in western Massachusetts.

Koussevitzky was nothing if not unpredictable. Whether he knew that the proposal had first been made to my father and this fact influenced his decision is a matter of speculation, but he certainly saw signs that Europe was becoming unstable. Papa had already foreseen the Berkshire performances as much more traditionally classical concerts than the Pops or the Esplanade, but the Russian conductor considered this repertoire his bailiwick. Visions of an American Salzburg Festival seemed most appealing to Koussevitzky, and he decided to take over the Berkshire Festival himself, although even he could not have foretold the growth of what was to become Tanglewood. Of course Papa was disappointed at losing another opportunity to expand his repertoire, but he too didn't see the wider implications. He could not possibly have known that Tanglewood as it grew would not only be closed to him but would nearly destroy his beloved Esplanade Concerts.

Over the next few years, Papa found Koussevitzky increasingly difficult. "One year Koussevitzky would be very pleasant . . . and the next year he would walk right by you and you didn't know why; he was very subject to rumors. All you knew was that you were helpless; you didn't know what was in his mind."

In the spring of 1944, Koussevitzky had one of his abrupt changes in attitude. Papa had just come home from the hospital after his nearly fatal heart attack when he received a call from the music director inviting him to conduct the Boston Symphony on the winter subscription series. The concerts were scheduled for February 1945. Papa was thrilled but cautious. Koussevitzky was, after all, the man who had said, after being told that he had a known weakness for making promises, "Perhaps, but thank God I have the strength not to keep them."

Despite Papa's fears, however, the official announcement of his engagement was made in September 1944. Eager to prove that his musical abilities extended far beyond the light symphonic repertoire, he scheduled an ambitious program that included Dvorak's Symphony No. 4, a work that had not been played by the Boston Symphony in years. His happiness over the coming concerts helped him get through the sadness of his own father's death in October 1944, at the age of eighty-five.

Then, in November, Papa got a call from a Boston concert presenter asking whether he would like to conduct a special concert at Symphony Hall with Frank Sinatra as the featured soloist. The orchestra would be made up of Boston Symphony musicians, but it would be called Arthur Fiedler and his Orchestra to avoid any possible conflict with the Symphony or the Pops. Papa was intrigued, as he always was by a new idea that had potential; he liked popular music and was curious to work with Sinatra, the idol of the era. The concert was announced in mid-November and sold out overnight.

Koussevitzky was horrified; he saw Papa's participation as lending the Boston Symphony's prestige to a gross commercial venture. He went to the management and the board of trustees to vent his rage, and then called in the players' committee from the orchestra to berate the musicians for agreeing to play with Sinatra. His final explosion was directed over the telephone at my father. He said that he could not envision someone who was scheduled to guest-conduct the great Boston Symphony involved in such a disgusting concert, and he withdrew Papa's invitation to conduct the B.S.O. The phone call was followed by a letter.

My dear Fiedler:

I strongly feel that since your name was associated with a Frank Sinatra show in Boston, it can not remain on the list of guest conductors with the Boston Symphony Orchestra.

This is my firm, unwavering conviction. And my earnest advice to you is to find a way to cancel, of your own accord, your appearance with the Boston Symphony next February. If there is anything you wish to tell me, I could see you on Monday or upon returning from the Western trip.

My father was devastated, but he clung to his pride even in the face of such a tremendous disappointment. Unfair as Koussevitzky was in taking away the concerts, the idea that Papa himself was expected to come up with a reason for the cancellation was totally unacceptable. He wrote back two days later.

My dear Dr. Koussevitzky:

Thank you for your letter of November 30, 1944, which I have just received. Since you personally invited me, last spring, to appear as guest conductor with the Boston Symphony Orchestra, which invitation I accepted with great pride, there seems nothing else for me to do but accept your latest invitation to cancel my appearance with the Boston Symphony Orchestra next February, which I hereby do.

I can find no way or reason of my own to cancel my appearance with the orchestra because, of course, it is impossible for me to foresee the state of my health during the assigned week, nor can I possibly imagine a professional appearance which I would accept in preference to the honor of conducting the Boston Symphony Orchestra.

Therefore, the reason for this cancellation of my appearance is entirely in your hands.

Immediately after mailing the letter to Koussevitzky, my father went to Minneapolis to conduct the orchestra there. These concerts were his first major guest-conducting engagement outside Boston, with a serious program, and were a triumphant success. But any pleasure Papa might have drawn from the Minneapolis engagement vanished when he returned to Boston and found another letter from Koussevitzky.

My dear Fiedler:

The Brazilian Composer Hector Villa Lobos is now in this country, returning to Brazil late in February. The co-ordinator of Inter-American affairs in Washington, D.C., is anxious to have him invited as guest conductor with the Boston Symphony Orchestra. The only possible time for Villa Lobos' appearance in Boston is the week of February 19.

Would you be willing to postpone your appearance to some other time, as the invitation of Villa Lobos would be a "good neighbor" gesture towards his art and inter-American relations?

Papa replied:

Please excuse my delay in answering your letter of December 15 which I just found upon my return from Minneapolis.

I am perfectly willing to accept your suggestion of postponing my appearance to some other time as I believe the appearance of Villa Lobos is important for Boston, the orchestra, and the "good neighbor" policy of the Americas.

The change in guest conductors was not publicly announced until February, and it evoked no comment in the press.

"He was a very peculiar man," my father said in an interview almost thirty years later. "Mrs. Fiedler and I were at his last concert with the B.S.O. Though he had been very small and nasty to me, I said, 'I'm going up to congratulate him.' 'How can you do that for a man who was always stepping on you?' Mrs. Fiedler asked. 'I'm just being honest,' I told her. Twenty-five years is a landmark. I was at the threshold [of the Green Room] and all of a sudden he spied me. He had an overabundance of blood and he just got beet red and blue when he saw me. He made a beeline for me—guilty conscience, you know—and shook my hand and embraced me. He was very touched."

Just before he died, Koussevitzky did invite Papa to conduct a concert, although not with the Boston Symphony. He asked my father during the Pops season to substitute at a concert in New York that Koussevitzky had been scheduled to conduct. "I was in no great mood to do him any favors but I said, if I could. It was the Pops season, and I didn't want to make it too easy for him. 'Call the manager,' I said. 'If he'll release me, I'll do it.' He did; I did it; and the next thing I knew I was at his funeral."

My father's bitterness toward Koussevitzky never abated. On a visit to the Boston Public Library a few months before he died, Papa visited the Koussevitzky Room in the Rare Books section. He paused before a photograph that showed Koussevitzky standing next to both a portrait and a bust of himself. "He must have loved this picture," Papa remarked to Richard Dyer, music critic of the *Boston Globe*. Then one of the library staff pointed out an empty balcony that circled the entire Koussevitzky Room and suggested that it might be usable for my father's collection of memorabilia. "Well," Papa said, "it would be nice to be above Koussevitzky at last."

I don't know if the momentous events of 1944 had any bearing on the noticeable change that took place in my father's personality during his late forties. People who knew him earlier in his life constantly remark on his friendly, unpretentious, and open manner. He was sociable and outgoing; he loved people, parties, and new experiences. He played cards after concerts with his Boston Symphony colleagues and apparently made a great show of being "just one of the boys," even after he took over as Pops conductor.

The father I knew was very different. He was cold, forbidding, militantly unsentimental, and reluctant to show affection under any circumstances, especially to his family. He was bad-tempered, nasty to his former B.S.O. colleagues and sometimes to musicians in other orchestras he conducted. He kept people at arm's length: "You've got to keep people away from you. If you let them come to you, they'll devour you . . . The public will take your last drop of blood." And although he maintained that this attitude was not aloofness, he certainly was not the charming and accessible figure he had once been.

How much of this change had to do with his bitterness over what Koussevitzky had done and the lack of support he had received from the Boston Symphony management is hard to know. The change did become obvious after his loss of the Boston Symphony engagement. But it was around the same period that he had to deal with the death of his father, the stresses of becoming a husband and father for the first time, and the inescapable evidence that his health was fragile. His long-time image as a Wunderkind was behind him, and he never fully accepted this fact.

In any case, the intensity of his reactions in the Koussevitzky affair sharply influenced his relationship with the B.S.O. Any crisis with the orchestra—and there were several other explosions during his lifelong involvement with it—was extremely upsetting to him, much more upsetting than anything that happened with his own family.

# FOUR

---

# Mummy

---

WHEN I WAS GROWING UP, I used to wonder what had brought my parents together. They were so unhappy and unsuited for a life together that it was hard to imagine what had led them to think their marriage could work.

From the start, my mother and father seemed more incongruous than harmonious. They met for the first time in the winter of 1920, when my father was twenty-five and my mother was six. Papa, who had been back in Boston since 1915, was supplementing his Boston Symphony salary by free-lance operatic coaching.

"How I Met Your Father" was one of my mother's favorite stories. From the time we were little children, we heard the story over and over. Debbie, Peter, and I would roll our eyes heavenward when a certain look came over Mummy's face and we could tell she was about to launch into another recounting. Mummy never noticed; she was gazing into the distance, happily reliving the events of thirty-five years before.

"You know I was only six years old when I met him. My best friend when I was a little girl was Lydia Fuller, the governor's daughter [Alvin T. Fuller was governor of Massachusetts in 1920];

she later married my brother. Her mother was an opera singer *manquée,* and Mr. Fiedler used to come and coach her. One day I was playing with Lydia and suddenly there was this wailing you could hear all over the house. It was like a fire siren—but it was her mother vocalizing. I was taken in to be introduced to Mr. Fiedler. I was very properly brought up in a convent, so I curtsied very deeply and when I looked up into those eyes, I fell in love, then and there."

There were so many versions of this first meeting that I doubted any were true until I checked with my aunt, Lydia Fuller Bottomley. I had never believed this myth, but Aunt Lydia assured me that after she and my mother left the Fullers' drawing room on Beacon Street that day in 1920, my mother turned to her and said, "I'm going to marry that man someday."

"Mrs. Fiedler is an exceptional woman, who was exceptionally persistent," my father said many years later. "She decided one day she would marry me—and you know that what a woman wants, a woman gets. It is said that a bachelor lives like a king and dies like a dog. I didn't want to die like a dog."

The wedding of my mother and father twenty-two years after their first meeting was either a triumph of persistence or an imprudent passion between two people from completely different backgrounds who had completely different problems and expectations. Given the gap in their ages and upbringing, the unhappiness that characterized their relationship through its long history was almost inevitable.

My mother's antecedents were part of the great Irish immigration to the United States during the mid-nineteenth century. Her grandfather, known in family mythology as Grandpa Kenney, came to Boston in the 1840s when he was eighteen and began working in a grocery store. Soon he went into business for himself as a wholesale dealer and importer. By 1881, he was heading two of the largest breweries in the country. His business interests continued to expand into the fields of real estate, finance, and construction. He organized several financial institutions, including the Federal Trust Company and the Federal National Bank, and his real estate dealings, in which he was astutely guided by Joseph P. Kennedy, were particularly lucrative.

Grandpa Kenney married Nellie O'Rourke, a woman of his own background who later changed her name to Ellen because she thought it more refined. The couple had only one child, Mary Agnes, who became my mother's mother. The Kenneys were so prosperous that when Mary Agnes, known as May, married a prominent Boston surgeon, her parents gave her a town house on Beacon Street as a wedding present. Meanwhile, Nellie-Ellen had acquired the nickname of the Duchess, which everyone in the family called her for the rest of her life.

May's husband, John Taylor Bottomley, the son of English immigrants, was born in western Massachusetts. He graduated from the Harvard Medical School in 1894 (the year my own father was born) and went on to a distinguished medical career, which included a position as lecturer on surgery at Harvard. A man of cultivated tastes, he counted among his best friends the Irish tenor John McCormack. After Dr. Bottomley's premature death in 1925, McCormack wrote in his eulogy, "One of the dearest friends I ever had was a surgeon. The famous John T. Bottomley of Boston . . . I practically lived at his house, and his children to this day call me Uncle John . . . He was an excellent musician and played the piano with a marvelously delicate touch. His passion was to help the poor patients who could not pay for their operations. He gave his life for them."

Dr. Bottomley apparently died of a blood infection after pricking his finger on a hypodermic needle while treating one of his charity patients. My mother was eleven.

My mother seemed to grieve for her father for the rest of her life. In much the same way as Papa would later take me with him to rehearsals at Symphony Hall, Dr. Bottomley had taken her with him on house calls to patients. She was so happy to be with him that she didn't mind waiting outside when he went in to make his visits. "He always called me his 'good egg,' " she would say wistfully.

My grandmother May Bottomley was in her early forties when she was widowed and left with five children to bring up alone. My mother, the fourth, had three older brothers and a sister nine years younger. The boisterous boys and the baby girl claimed most of my grandmother's attention, and Mummy was left pretty much on her own. In addition, Mrs. Bottomley protected herself with a reserve and an almost chilly manner, despite her acid Irish wit, and was an aloof parent.

Immediately after Dr. Bottomley's death, the family moved to Switzerland to escape painful memories. When the Bottomleys got back to Boston, two or so years later, my grandmother pulled herself together, consulted with her husband's old friend Joseph Kennedy about solidifying her fairly substantial financial situation, and enrolled Mummy in her own alma mater, the Convent of the Sacred Heart. My mother proved the perfect pupil—captain of the hockey team, perennial winner of the prized blue sash as best-behaved girl, highly popular member of her class. She wasn't much of a student, but that was less important to her and her mother than her other achievements. After graduating, she considered her education behind her and turned her attention to making her debut into society, along with the other girls in her class.

Irish-Catholic girls had only recently been considered acceptable material for the debutante roster, but my mother continued to shine in her new activities and became a role model for the other convent-educated women who would follow her into Boston society. Or at least partway into Boston society. There was—and still is —a limit on how far a Catholic could penetrate the circle of WASP families who had founded the city.

Undeterred, my mother made her debut in December 1932, at a tea dance given by her grandmother. She wore "a simple Parisian model of dotted white tulle with a slightly raised waistline girdled in rhinestones" and carried a bouquet of roses and gardenias. The article in the *Boston Advertiser* about her coming-out party was accompanied by a large picture.

My mother had huge blue eyes and a brilliant smile. Tall and slim, she was outgoing and equally popular with men and women. She kept an extensive record of her social life in what was then called a "conceit book," a scrapbook jammed with newspaper clippings about parties and weddings she had attended and charitable

activities in which she had participated. She was a member of the
Junior League and performed enthusiastically with amateur theater groups. Since she seemed so sunny of disposition and happy
with her crowded social calendar, no one much noticed that she
kept herself fueled with alcohol. Her sister, my Aunt May, who
shared a bedroom with her on Beacon Street, remembers Mummy
gulping down glasses of brandy before going to Mass on Sunday.
No one in the family knew; her mother was distant and self-ab-
sorbed, her brothers busy with their own lives.

Boston was such a small city that my mother actually knew another member of my father's family quite well. In the 1920s, the
John T. Bottomleys summered at Nantasket Beach, at that time an
elegant resort close to Boston. They rented a cottage on the
grounds of the Atlantic House Hotel, where my father's Uncle
Gustav was the orchestra conductor. In the evenings, the Bottomleys would go over to the hotel to listen to the music, and the
Bottomley children became very attached to Uncle Gus.

In 1932, my mother and father met again. Mummy was part of a
charity benefit for disabled veterans of World War I, and Lydia
Fuller, who at the time was dreaming of a theatrical career, was the
soloist in "A Spanish Dance." My father's best friend, the pianist
Jesús María Sanromá, played the part of a Spanish guitarist, and
my father conducted the assembled forces. My mother was a Spanish lady; her role was to wave her fan in time to the Latin music
the orchestra was playing. Since she was not gifted as a musician,
she waved her fan in a rhythm that had nothing to do with what
was going on. My father, seeing one Spanish lady completely out
of synch with everyone else, roared at her in front of the entire
company. She was embarrassed—yet intrigued enough to ask Viola
Fuller, Lydia's mother and my father's former student, whether
the handsome conductor was married. "No, dear," Mrs. Fuller replied discreetly, "but I think he's engaged."

During the 1920s, my father's almost delicate beauty as a young
man had matured into robust handsomeness. He carefully cultivated a debonair image by dressing fastidiously, by driving a fash-
ionable new car, and by being with beautiful women. He had begun to become a part of Boston society—though not Boston

Brahmin society—partly through his close friendship with the Fullers.

He was especially famous, or infamous, for his enjoyment of female companionship. "I credit an exceptionally fine German housekeeper, who was an excellent cook, for my prolonged bachelorhood," he said. "Few bachelors have such a blessing. Also, I had no end of attractive friends of the opposite sex."

"If he's wearing a blue shirt, a bluer necktie, a blue double-breasted suit, blue socks and is engrossed in a polite tête-a-tête with any one of a hundred beautiful girls—it's Arthur Fiedler relaxing," reported the *Boston Post* in 1934.

While my father reveled in his reputation, and while there actually were many women in his life during the 1920s and 1930s, he also maintained two long-term relationships during this period.

Jeanne Eagels was a promising young actress in 1919 when Papa met her while she was appearing in a play in Boston. She was exactly his age and at a point in her career similar to his as a promising young conductor. She was also beautiful: small, blond, slender, and full of vitality, a type Papa would always find compelling. He was drawn to vivacious women, like my mother, who, being tall, dark, and statuesque, seemingly lacked the other attributes to which Papa was usually attracted.

But in Jeanne Eagels's case, the vitality in her nature was combined with a strong drive toward success. In an era when most women married, had children, and did not work, she must have stood out; she was single-minded in her dedication to the theater. I'm sure she loved my father—there are many pictures of them gazing adoringly at each other—but she was not about to sacrifice her career for another person any more than my father would have. He lived in Boston and she continued to live in New York, the center of the theatrical world. They were both young and on the way up, and for a while the relationship flourished as they built their careers.

Papa had a little difficulty accepting Jeanne's independence, however. He often talked about her to me as I grew older. "Why didn't you marry her?" I asked him once. He was sitting at his desk in Symphony Hall, and he gazed off over my shoulder. "It was funny," he said. "I remember once we were walking down Broadway after one of her big hits opened, and everyone kept stopping us and asking her for her autograph."

"Did you feel left out?" I said, a daring question for me.

He laughed, looking almost embarrassed, and took a sip from the glass he was clutching. "I guess I did," he replied with a chuckle.

But there was also a sinister side to their relationship. Over the six years or so that they remained involved, Papa became aware of the actress's reliance on drugs and alcohol. Though he certainly later developed a dependence on alcohol that was psychological if not physiological, he was never self-destructive. Jeanne was, and as her career blossomed, reaching its height with her acclaimed appearance on Broadway in Somerset Maugham's *Rain*, she began to drink and use drugs more heavily. Initially Papa explained away her mood swings as depression or lack of enough exercise and fresh air or the demands of a public life. Eventually, however, he could no longer fool himself about her problems and he began to extricate himself from the relationship. A clue to how difficult this must have been came a few years later when he singled out Maugham's *Of Human Bondage*, the study of an obsessive relationship, as his favorite book. In 1929, the year Papa's career began in earnest, Jeanne Eagels died of an overdose of barbiturates and alcohol. She was thirty-six.

Two years earlier, Papa had met another woman in Paris while on a summer trip. Pearl Delabeque was only nineteen, and she must have reminded him of the Jeanne Eagels he had met eight years earlier; like Jeanne, Pearl was small, blond, and full of life, and my father was quick to turn a chance flirtation at a sidewalk café into a full-fledged summer romance. Apparently he had no intention of anything more serious, but Pearl maintained a determination throughout their relationship that belied her youth. When it came time for my father to go back to Boston for the start of the 1927 Symphony season, Pearl announced that she too was going to the United States. Before he could panic at the news, she reassured him that she planned to settle in New York, and my father, ever vigilant about being trapped into a commitment, relaxed.

The next two years went smoothly. Papa and Pearl saw each other whenever possible and my father became attached enough to the young Frenchwoman to take her to meet his family in Berlin, the first time he had ever done anything so traditional. Pearl, encouraged by her success, made her next move in 1929. She disclosed to my father that the company she worked for was transferring her to Boston and that they would soon be living in the same city.

The move, although carefully calculated, had drawbacks that Pearl could not have foreseen. I doubt that even my father, who was conscious of his reluctance to enter a monogamous relationship under any circumstances, understood the complexity of this reluctance.

While the Boston Symphony had given him a home, my father, as he became more secure, began to look beyond the reaches of the orchestra for acceptance. He looked up to the Boston Brahmin trustees of the Symphony, those men who devoted their lives to civic duty, the patronage of the arts and educational institutions, and the practice of frugality and unpretentiousness. He wanted to become part of their world, the world he saw as the real Boston.

Pearl was not part of his plan. Papa was genuinely fond of Alvin and Viola Fuller and their children, and their patronage had been helpful to him in entering Boston society. But because the Fullers were Catholics and were considered nouveaux riches, my father's entrée was limited. Since part of Papa's social position was based on his eligibility as a dashing bachelor, a publicized alliance with any one woman, particularly a European outside the circumference of Boston society, would not be an asset. In addition, by 1929 his career as a conductor was poised on the edge of success, and he wanted to concentrate on his professional obligations without the distraction of personal obligations. To some extent, Pearl had miscalculated by deciding to move to Boston.

But my father, despite his objections to her move and his disinclination for an emotional commitment, was deeply attached to her. She moved to Boston and they continued to see each other.

Much as my father enjoyed the gossip about his reputation, he was punctilious about protecting the women with whom he was involved. William Berenberg, who became the family pediatrician years later, was working his way through Harvard College in the early 1930s by running a parking garage in Cambridge where Papa kept his car. My father had a standing arrangement with the student (whom he never recognized in his later guise as a doctor) that he would leave his battered car at the garage, and the student would drive him to a certain apartment building on Memorial Drive. From the years involved and the regularity with which Papa maintained this arrangement, the woman was probably Pearl, although Dr. Berenberg never knew her name. The student was instructed to return several hours later to the same building, pick up Papa, and drive him back to his parked car. Papa made it clear that he was visiting a lady whom he did not wish to compromise; parking his well-known car in front of her building would have placed her in a questionable position, according to my father's Victorian sense of morality.

I don't know when Papa's relationship with Pearl ended, but it was going on in the mid-1930s. Although she was rarely seen in public with him, people in Boston knew about her. There are a few yellowed newspaper clippings about my father and Pearl at parties and concerts, and her name is mentioned once or twice. Aunt Lydia remembers meeting her and being impressed by how attractive and charming she was. People assumed that she was a mysterious and wealthy Frenchwoman, because Papa was known to associate only with women from good families.

In time Pearl's independent streak asserted itself, and she became frustrated with her behind-the-scenes role. She began to see other men in Boston, men of excellent background, and started to push my father toward making a decision about marriage. He finally decided that, miserable as he was at the thought of losing her, he could not marry Pearl. She soon married someone else.

I heard about both Jeanne Eagels and Pearl directly from my parents. I think Papa was proud of Jeanne's fame, and once the misery caused by her emotional fragility was over, he thought back on their relationship with pleasure.

He never mentioned Pearl unless goaded by my mother; Mummy was the one who brought her up. She was never mentioned by name; for some reason, both of my parents referred to her as "Amie." In my mother's version of the story, Amie had been in love with Papa but realized that he would never marry her. Accepting her fate, she had subsequently married a dentist, according to Mummy. This was not true. In fact, Pearl had married a wealthy Bostonian. The moral of the story seemed to be that unless a woman was willing to wait eight years for the man she loved, as my mother was, her only alternative was to marry someone dreary and prosaic. This fable made a profound impression on me and led in part, I suspect, to my reluctance later to date anyone who wasn't a musician.

When I was grown, Papa told me about Pearl in his own way, still not speaking her name. He talked of his sadness at losing her and how endless his subsequent depression had seemed. I found out after he died that she had ended up living near Los Angeles; Papa saw her often when he was in California until nearly the end of his life.

After the Spanish dance fiasco, my father and mother met again under more auspicious circumstances, in March 1933. Once more, the Fullers were the catalysts. My mother and Lydia Fuller were serving as ushers in the Fuller home for a charity recital performed by Jesús María Sanromá. There was a Boston Symphony concert that night, and my father, accompanied by Koussevitzky, arrived late. He immediately caught sight of my mother, and ended up sitting on the stairs with her and Lydia Fuller. "She was a rather flirtatious, sweet young thing," he said later, "and I had always been welcome at her mother's home until I took up with Ellen. I was theoretically a confirmed bachelor, and I was considered to have designs on young ladies, which I most assuredly did."

My mother was just nineteen, my father thirty-eight. They began to see each other despite immediate opposition from my mother's family. The age difference and my father's reputation were drawbacks enough, and as things became more serious, the religious differences had to be confronted, too. Nevertheless, my mother was determined right from the start. She went to all his rehearsals with the cluster of local orchestras he conducted during those years, whether she had been invited or not. My father often ignored her when she appeared without warning and never hid the fact that he continued to see other women. Nothing discouraged my mother. "Mrs. Fiedler will tell you herself that she chased me for eight years until I gave up" was my father's description of the situation. "Most of my male chums had married by then and I didn't like finding myself alone. I married out of self-protection."

There were other considerations, of course. Papa had spent a great deal of energy hiding his relationship with Pearl from the proper and censorious Bostonians, and now he had to hide his relationship with my mother from her outraged family. He started to notice, however, that even rare glimpses of the couple together in public had a legitimating effect on his social standing. His name, which had appeared frequently in the music and gossip columns of Boston newspapers, now began appearing as well in the society columns. The Bottomleys may not have belonged to the upper echelons of WASP Boston, but they were wealthy and respected members of the community and had deep roots in the city.

"I had a very charming bachelorhood for about fifty years," my father liked to say, and it took him eight years to resolve his doubts about losing his freedom and his reputation as a man-about-town. Like all the women with whom he became involved, Ellen Bottomley was attractive, lively, and young. My mother was much more naïve than either Jeanne Eagels or Pearl: she lived at home with her mother until the day she married, she never held a job, she had never cooked or cleaned house. My father told me that one evening just before he and my mother married, she came to his apartment and they decided to have a late-night snack. He led her into the kitchen, took a loaf of bread from the cupboard, and suggested she make sandwiches while he boiled water for tea. She stared for a long time at the bread and at length admitted that she was totally mystified. She didn't know what the loaf was; she thought that bread came sliced, and she didn't recognize it intact. Papa said he almost canceled the wedding at that moment; certainly every doubt he already had was reinforced. But then he remembered that he had Louise, his devoted housekeeper, and he realized that Mummy would not have to get involved with mundane things like unsliced bread.

In fact, Louise became one of my parents' first problems. My mother developed a hatred of her that became almost pathological. Louise returned the feeling with much spirit; she was jealous of this beautiful but spoiled creature who had suddenly intruded on her cozy life with my father. The women fought bitterly for years, until Louise left at around the time Celie arrived.

I still wonder what led my father, a sophisticated, successful, and cosmopolitan man, to settle down with a woman who was a child, both emotionally and in terms of experience. My mother was a charming and beautiful child, and I think neither of them could foresee the unhappiness that lay ahead.

"In a weak moment, I popped the question to Ellen" is the romantic way my father described the official beginning of their life together. It was the summer of 1941; the two families, while not overjoyed, were reconciled to the inevitable after the eight-year courtship. Mummy and Papa set their wedding date for October.

But the wedding did not take place in October, and the postponement is mysterious. The family story is that my mother was so distraught over the delays caused by my father's reluctance to marry that she was struck down by an attack of strep throat and was sent by her doctor to recuperate in a warm climate. Over the years, there have been ominous murmurings in the family that my mother had become involved with another man, but I have never been able to confirm these rumors; however, my mother was a strong woman physically, and it is hard to imagine her so sick with anything that she would have postponed the wedding she had been plotting for eight years.

In December of 1941, the *Boston Evening American* scooped the wedding announcement:

FIEDLER AND BACK BAY SOCIALITE WILL WED
It was learned today that the engagement of Miss Ellen Bottomley, Back Bay socialite and a debutante of 1932, to Arthur Fiedler, popular Boston musical director, probably will be announced formally this weekend. Miss

Bottomley is the daughter of Mrs. John T. Bottomley of Beacon Street, and the late Dr. Bottomley, and is considerably younger than Mr. Fiedler.

On January 8, 1942, my mother and father were married at the Cathedral of the Holy Cross in Boston. Because it was a mixed marriage, the ceremony took place in the vestry. The wedding had almost been derailed one last time when my father discovered that he was expected to kneel in front of the officiating priest. He flatly refused, and a compromise was reached: my mother knelt throughout the ceremony while my father stubbornly stood by her side.

The Fiedler family, who had all moved to Boston to escape the persecution of Jews in Berlin, refused to come to the wedding because of my mother's religion. They did, however, agree to attend the wedding luncheon at Beacon Street. Only the immediate members of my mother's family were at the ceremony; even Lydia Fuller was not invited. After the brief lunch, with the two families eyeing each other suspiciously from opposite sides of my grandmother's drawing room, Ellen and Popie—as she called him—went to New York for a three-day honeymoon at the Hampshire House. By coincidence, their New York stay coincided with a Boston Symphony tour to New York, and they ended up giving a large party in their hotel suite for their New York friends and several members of the orchestra.

My parents moved into a large apartment on Marshall Street in Brookline, and, by all reports, had a good time together for the next four years or so. My mother went to all my father's concerts; they traveled together to his few guest-conducting engagements; and they took leisurely vacations in northern New England and Canada, since trips to Europe were out of the question during the war.

In letters my father wrote during those years, he describes himself as "very happily married." His career was also flourishing, a great relief, because he had worried that the added responsibility of a wife would somehow restrict his musical ambitions. In the spring of 1944, he received the summons that to him was the culmination of all he could expect from his conducting, the invitation—ill-fated, as it turned out—to conduct the Boston Symphony.

My father had dreamed of this moment ever since he began conducting thirty years earlier. Conducting the Symphony would validate his ability and fulfill the central ambition of his life.

Life seemed pleasant and gratifying during the first years he was married to my mother. Twenty years later the situation was so different that Papa would then do almost anything to avoid going home.

# FIVE

## Sinfonia Domestica

ONE SUMMER when my father was away and the rest of us were home, I woke up in the middle of the night because I heard noises on the lawn. Crouching at my bedroom window, I saw Mummy roaming across the grass, dragging the water sprinklers behind her; she had become obsessed about keeping the lawn green, even in the hottest part of July. For the first time, I became aware of her nighttime wanderings, the solitary pilgrimages she made through the house and garden that were some of the most haunting aspects of my growing up. I can remember those hot, dark nights, with the gentle spray of the sprinkler brushing against the gravel driveway since Mummy never got the flow aimed correctly. There would be the tinkle of Sparky's dogtags as he followed my mother around the lawn, and the flip-flop of my mother's sandals as she went back and forth across the grass. Those aren't sounds that normally generate terror, but my heart would pound in my chest as I watched and listened. I was only eight or nine, but somehow I knew that I was watching a person in the process of falling apart.

There was one summer I remember as being the most terrifying of all. Like many famous people, my father attracted the attention of crazed admirers, and once when he was away, a woman who had fantasized a romantic relationship with him began to harass us. First there were phone calls with heavy breathing; my mother had our phone number changed, but the campaign heightened. On a regular basis, the Brookline Fire Department would be summoned to false alarms on Hyslop Road. Then ambulances started arriving, responding to anonymous telephone calls for help for a supposedly ailing Mrs. Fiedler. The culmination came with several appearances of a fleet of hearses from the local funeral home to pick up various family bodies. Terrified as I was of fire, the fire engines scared me more than anything, but my superstitious mother was horrified by the hearses.

The police and fire departments quickly managed to trace the woman's phone calls, but the damage had been done. My mother's nerves were so strained, and she felt so vulnerable and unprotected with Papa away all the time, that she became even more fragile. Now I could hear her talking to herself as she watered the lawn at midnight.

Papa knew something was wrong, but his solution was to stay away even more. The cycle of absence and unhappiness began to feed on itself. By the time I was in high school, my father was home in the spring for the Pops, and that was pretty much the only time I saw him, except for a day or two here and there between trips.

My parents didn't talk about their difficulties. If the subject came up, their arguments were limited to "Why are you away so much?" from Mummy and "Why can't you understand about my work?" from Papa.

My mother didn't understand about my father's work, nor did she have interests of her own to pursue. She was known as my father's wife, and my father's official biographers referred to her only as a "former Boston debutante." For years, I thought being a debutante was some kind of profession, and my mother sincerely believed that my sister and I would be proud to follow her example.

Whatever skills had made my mother a good debutante were of

no help in maintaining a household. She was incapable of making or following a schedule, and we were never sure whether she would arrive to pick us up at school or take us to the dentist. She was never up when we left for school in the mornings, rarely sat down for meals, and was most accessible if any of us happened to be up late at night, when she did her wanderings. She spent most of the day shut in her tiny, windowless bathroom—she explained that it was the only place she felt she had any privacy. That was ridiculous, because none of us ever went into anyone else's room without first knocking; we weren't that kind of family.

When Papa was at home during the Pops season, my mother was the last to come down from her room for the daily ritual of lunch. It was something of a battle to get her to the table. "Ellen," Papa called day after day, ringing the brass dinner bell—from my grandmother's house on Beacon Street—that hung at the foot of the front stairs. When there was no response, the calls of "Ellen!" would become progressively more frantic. Papa finally taught Sparky to howl whenever he called "Ellen!" This was fine at lunchtime but became a little inconvenient after Sparky learned his lesson so well that he would howl soulfully every time he heard my father utter my mother's name, even when she was sitting in the room with them. In time, Mummy would appear, understandably reluctant to sit down for a family gathering at which tension was the primary fare. Usually these meals would end with my father exploding at my mother for some real or imagined infraction, and Mummy's rushing back upstairs to her room in tears.

Celie's day off was Wednesday, and that was the time of complete turmoil. Papa was careful never to be at home on Wednesday evenings if he happened to be in Boston. I found out years later that he would often go out with his B.S.O. friends then to hang out in local jazz clubs or chase fire department and police calls.

With Celie out, Mummy would be forced to go into the kitchen to try to put together some kind of meal for us. I have memories of her standing in front of the stove in tears while some revolting concoction bubbled over the sides of the pots. The kitchen would be strewn with other dirty, burned pots and dishes, the table unset, the whole scene as remote as possible from Celie's well-orchestrated, well-organized cooking procedure. Debbie and I would salvage what we could from the mystery dish on the stove. If, by rare chance, Papa was home, we quickly learned to get from the freezer the kosher hot dogs he loved. We would defrost and boil them, and serve them to him with a can of sauerkraut, and he would be almost pathetically grateful. On other occasions, in desperation he would make himself scrambled eggs with matzos, but since he made even more of a mess than Mummy, we tried to discourage him from cooking. Cleaning up the kitchen would be our responsibility.

When Mummy drifted upstairs, Debbie and I would try to avoid thoughts of our remaining load of homework and start working on the kitchen. Our goal was to get the room back to its usual pristine condition by the time Celie got home at eleven. We most often succeeded, at least to some extent. Then we would go back to our French or algebra or Latin assignment, wearily grateful that Wednesday was over for another whole week.

My mother began to drink too much. For years, my father had admired her ability to match him drink for drink; he had more fun when he was drinking, so it made sense to him that the same was true for her. But at some point drinking stopped being fun for my mother and became medication.

When I was very young, I thought my mother's volatility and unreliability, her sudden rages and irrational edicts, were just aspects of adults behavior. When I was in my early teens, something clicked into place, and I began to understand the connection between her moods and how much she drank. I was determined to keep this secret from everyone, firmly believing that no one else in the world knew what I did. My teachers at school by the ninth or tenth grade noticed something was wrong. "You look very tired some mornings," one said to me gently. I was called to the principal's office when my grades began to drop. "You have one of the highest IQs in the school," she said. "What seems to be the problem?" But I couldn't tell her or anyone else.

As it turned out, Peter and Debbie knew everything I did. Dealing with the problem was one of the few areas in which the three of us joined forces during my teens. We got the kitchen cleaned up every Wednesday night; if we found Mummy asleep on the library couch late in the evening, the three of us would wake her and coax her upstairs before Papa came home from his concert; we answered the phone for her and made excuses when she missed family gatherings; and most of all, we never said anything to anyone.

But apparently everyone knew. After her mother died, in the early 1960s shortly before I went to college, Mummy's drinking worsened to the point where her brothers and sister confronted her and she admitted that she had lost control.

The problem was out in the open, but instead of things improving, everything got worse. I went off to college, feeling lucky to escape the proliferating confrontations between Mummy and the rest of the family. My father now felt perfectly justified in hounding her about alcohol, but he knew nothing about alcoholism and refused to accept that she had a disease. He was sure that control of drinking was a matter of will power, so he was quite willing for Mummy to have a drink or two as long as she promised to stop there. Of course she couldn't have stopped after a drink or two, but he never seemed to understand that.

There were the requisite scenes of Papa pouring liquor down the sinks, his infuriated charges through the house looking for hidden bottles, my mother's hysterical denials of drinking followed by her pathetic pleas for forgiveness and her promises that she'd "never do it again." Although Debbie, Peter, and I, when I was home on college vacations, were almost grown, we cowered in our rooms during these frenetic scenes.

The saddest episode was when my mother's eldest brother convinced her to check into a hospital to get help. Mummy went off by herself, without informing my father, who was out of town. When Papa came home and found out where she was, he exploded. "There's no need for her to be in a hospital!" he yelled, probably worried that someone outside the family might find out what was going on. "It's all a matter of will power!" He immediately called Mummy in the hospital and demanded that she come home. She did.

My mother never stopped drinking for the rest of her life, despite several hospitalizations. Her doctors told her that she had to stop because her liver was in terrible condition, but to make their orders a little more palatable, they suggested that she could have a glass of champagne on festive occasions. That's all Mummy, or any other alcoholic, needed to hear. The festive occasions began to multiply until even a family lunch became, for the first time in anyone's memory, a festive occasion.

My mother's family kept trying to focus Papa's attention on the situation. From their point of view, he was an appalling husband and father, deserting his troubled wife and refusing to see the effect all this was having on his children.

Papa dismissed the warnings as "Bottomley hysteria"—"the Bottomleys are fatally addicted to exaggeration," he often said— and went right on pretending that there was no problem. He wrote to me after Mummy's first alcohol-induced stroke in 1972, "I think your mother is better, but she is taking some kind of pills, and I think, with her usual intensity, she might be taking too many of them. I have suggested that she call her doctor to find out if she should let up on them and reduce the number per day. Of course, she will never do this."

I was thrilled to escape from watching my mother's disintegration when I went to college, but I felt that I was deserting my brother and sister. Peter was enough younger that he was almost a stranger, but Debbie and I were so close in age that we were companions and comrades despite our rivalries. When I was at college, Debbie wrote letters to me expressing her sense of desertion and loneliness; I also missed having someone close to me who understood what life at home was like. But such feelings were not easily expressed in our family, and Debbie and I were Fiedlers. We couldn't comfort each other.

Left alone to deal with Mummy's problems—Papa was away, and Peter was too young—Debbie withdrew more and more. By her sixteenth birthday, she rarely left her bedroom except to go to school. No one was alarmed, because we were not a sociable group. On Debbie's birthday, she didn't come out of her room at all. My mother's response was pitiful. After knocking at the door and getting no response, she collected my sister's birthday presents, went back to the closed bedroom, and knocked one last time. Getting no answer, Mummy piled the gifts in front of the door and went back down the hall to her own room.

"Why didn't you go in?" I asked my mother later when she told me this story.

"The door was shut," Mummy replied, and I nodded.

Peter withdrew in other ways. He had made attempts to play with Debbie and me, but neither of us was receptive. We had our favorite escape, reading, and when we weren't reading, we played our private games together. There was no time or room for Peter, and his family label became "Peter the Pest."

Peter never shared our interest in books. In the years that separated him from Debbie and me, television had become an accepted part of life, even in our family. My mother, as she was left alone more and more during Peter's early years, also began watching television for escape.

When Papa was home, he would roar about Peter's being allowed to watch too much TV. After these tantrums, my brother would be monitored carefully to make sure he wasn't in front of the set. But Papa wasn't home very much, and Peter soon discovered that no one noticed if he went into the library and surreptitiously turned it on.

I can remember my brother seating himself in front of the television day after day when he came home from school, the volume turned down so that no one else could hear it. First he'd go into the deserted kitchen to help himself to a bowl of cookies; then he'd tiptoe across the house to the library. He would pull up a chair to the TV screen until his nose was only inches from the set, and would sit there for hours mesmerized, munching cookies and watching whatever came on.

Inevitably Papa came home from a tour and discovered what was going on and would shout and storm. Peter would cut back on his television watching, but soon Papa would go away again, and Peter would be back in the library.

MY MOTHER always said cheerfully that she never lost a moment's sleep over the question of my father's sexual fidelity. Since she was an insecure and suspicious person, I decided as a child that if she didn't see a need to worry, there probably was nothing to concern me about my father's life when he was away. When I grew up and began working for the New York Philharmonic and the Metropolitan Opera, I saw for the first time the way artists behaved when they were away from their families for long periods of time. Even musicians who tried to stay faithful to their wives, husbands, or lovers had a hard struggle. There was temptation everywhere, and the more famous the artist, the more tantalizing the possibilities that existed. I began to wonder about my father, who had traveled continuously nine months a year. Then I reminded myself that he had started traveling in his late fifties and probably had no interest in the "fooling around" that was omnipresent in the music world.

I was wrong. People would drop hints to me about Papa's avid interest in women while he was still alive, and, at first, I would get upset. Remembering my mother's words on the subject, though, I would console myself that Papa loved to flirt and that this was probably misinterpreted by people who didn't know him well. Again, I was wrong.

My father had an active love life until the very end. He met women at parties after concerts and invited them back to his hotel room. He sustained at least one long-term relationship with a woman in California, considerably younger than himself, and there probably were more. If a woman came to his hotel, often uninvited, and phoned his room from the lobby, he would usually invite her to come up and, if she was attractive, stay the afternoon.

It was years after he died before I accepted the fact that Papa had had another life, completely separate from us. I'm glad I didn't know earlier because, much as I missed him with things as I thought they were, I would have been even more devastated every time he left if I'd known the truth.

DURING MY LAST YEARS in grammar school and early high school, with my father's powerful presence missing for long periods of time, my mother did manage to assert herself in some limited areas. When Papa was away, the rest of us began eating things we liked instead of the meals he insisted on. An occasional feast of pizza substituted for boiled kosher hot dogs, and my mother's beloved creamed chicken replaced the chicken paprikash Celie had learned from Louise. The strict rules governing television watching were relaxed a little because my lonely mother became attached to some of the weekly series; she even installed a television set in the kitchen, although it was never turned on when Papa was home. These deviations inspired a small spurt of independence in me, and I would sometimes leave the house without being completely honest about where I was going. It wasn't that I was doing anything forbidden or going anywhere off limits; I just liked the idea of being free and not having to account to anyone for what I did. I also decided that I wanted my own dog.

Mummy had finally managed to get Sparky's bed moved from under the front stairs to a rear area we called the Back Room. The room was painted chocolate brown and had small windows facing onto the back porch, where our garbage receptacles were kept. One of our five pianos had been stuck in this dreary space, so Sparky at least had some company, since someone was almost always practicing there. I would go down to the Back Room regularly and sit with Sparky—I never forgot that he had been the loyal companion of some of my loneliest childhood hours—but I was growing up and had a widening set of responsibilities and interests.

I also had become fascinated by a breed of dog I often saw around Symphony Hall. The second harpist in the Boston Symphony raised chihuahuas as a hobby. Many of her Symphony colleagues had purchased dogs from her, and she farmed dogs out to other families when she ran out of space in her own house. I was enchanted by her home; the living room was furnished with two harps and about two dozen barking chihuahuas, and the first time I went there I thought I had found paradise. I was enchanted by the little dogs, so bright and spirited.

I began saving my money to get my own chihuahua. I saved literally for years to get together the seventy-five dollars I knew the harpist charged for one of her non-show-quality dogs. The appearance of the dog didn't matter to me; I just wanted something all my own to love and care for.

When I was fifteen, I had the money, and after innumerable confrontations with my mother, who, needless to say, opposed the idea, I went to the harpist's to choose a dog—and found Bambi. Bambi was large for a chihuahua, and her proportions were all wrong, but she was sweet and loving, and I picked her out immediately and took her home.

My father was in Buenos Aires when this happened, on his annual trip there. When he got home, I could hardly wait to show him Bambi and immediately took him up to my room, where Bambi was happily nestled on my bed. "What *is* that?" he asked.

As I look back, I can understand that he was exhausted from the long trip and probably anxious over the upcoming Pops season, but I was devastated. "That's Bambi," I said to him. "She's my chihuahua."

"That's a pretty funny-looking chihuahua," he replied, and went off to call the woman from whom I'd bought Bambi. In addition to being second harp in the Symphony, she was principal harpist of the Pops.

I was helpless. Within hours, Bambi had gone back to the harpist's house and in her place appeared Benedict. "We'll call him Bennie," my father said firmly. Bennie was a beautiful dog; I couldn't deny that. His father had been an American Kennel Club certified champion, and Bennie had all the classic features of his breed. He was also a little puppy and scared to death; he was so frightened and tiny that he couldn't even clamber over the threshold from one room to another.

Although I was heartbroken about losing Bambi, and desperately searching for a way not to blame my father for this treachery, I was touched by the new little dog's terror, and, understanding only too well what he was feeling, began to help him get from room to room. As part of the original deal with my mother, I was responsible for all his meals, so I fed him his three puppy meals a day.

As his personality emerged, Bennie turned out to be a delightful dog. He was a typical chihuahua: intelligent, vigilant, almost humorous; "these merry little dogs," in the words of one of the dog books Papa gave me. One was called *How to Raise and Train Your*

*Chihuahua*, and I undertook the frustrating task of attempting to educate an independent and strong-minded dog. I have almost always had a chihuahua ever since.

My father loved Bennie, too, and I think regarded him as partially his own dog since he had picked him out of the harpist's pack. One night after a Pops concert, when I came home a little later than my father, I walked into the house and found my father excitedly waiting for me. "Look!" he said, pointing up the stairs. "He's been waiting for you to come home. I tried to get him to come into my room, but he wanted to wait for you." On the top step I saw the silhouette of a little dog, ears pricked, sitting at attention. When Bennie saw me, he came flying down the stairs, and my father and I smiled at each other like the proud parents of a brilliant child.

I tried, as I fell in love with Bennie, not to exclude Sparky. Sparky was about as unhappy with Bennie's arrival as I had been with Debbie's, and I was determined not to make him as unhappy as my mother had made me. I tried to spend as much time with the old and failing Dalmatian as I could, but as he got older, sicker, and less responsive, I disappointed him more and more often. It still hurts to think of him, banished to the Back Room, sick and in pain from the cancer he suffered in his last years, and abandoned by my father, who had gone off to conduct all over the world.

Papa was in San Francisco when my mother decided that she had had enough; having seen Sparky's misery, I couldn't argue with her. She called the family veterinarian, who agreed that Sparky needed to find peace. He was fourteen by that time—he had come to live with us when I was about two, and I was now old enough to drive. I drove the poor sick dog to the Angell Memorial Animal Hospital one last time and handed his leash to the vet.

That night, my mother sent me to the airport to pick up my father, who knew nothing about Sparky's death. He and my mother had planned to go to Hawaii for a brief vacation—she had been scheduled to go to San Francisco to meet him but had missed the plane—so he was already furious when he arrived back in Boston, his only vacation for the next twelve months ruined by my mother's unreliability.

Then I told him about Sparky. We were driving on our secret short cut through the back roads of Brookline, and he started to cry. He hadn't paid much attention to Sparky in the last years, but I knew what he was remembering. He was thinking about the rambunctious puppy who had come to live with us all those years before, about the fires they had gone to together, about the walks around the reservoir on Sunday mornings and the rides in the convertible. Neither of us wanted to think about the sick old dog we had banished to the Back Room.

A few days later, Papa received a letter of sympathy from the veterinarian. "Don't be too sad about Sparky," the veterinarian wrote. "I'm sure he's up in Heaven somewhere, and he's probably chasing fire engines."

I LOVED THE DOGS, but music became my chosen escape as I got older—not, of course, as a performer, but as a listener. I loved to go to Symphony Hall with my father, and I could never get enough of the spirited atmosphere there, so different from our lugubrious house. Reading and making up stories remained favorite activities, and gradually I wove my love of music into them. I gathered all the information I could about what went on at Symphony Hall and what Papa did there, and I couldn't understand why my mother seemed so uninterested in orchestra life. Symphony Hall became my fairy land, and I was determined to go there every day when I grew up.

I watched my father go off to concerts and rehearsals looking happy and enthusiastic, and then I saw him come home with his shoulders stooped and a frown on his face. When I went to Symphony Hall with him, I saw a new Papa emerge. I feared and avoided the Hyslop Road father, the silent, glowering, explosive man who preferred to be by himself, with no one daring to disturb him. I was enchanted by the Symphony Hall Papa, outgoing, amusing, gossipy, acerbically witty, funny even when he was being cruel.

A so-called Boston Symphony brat, I spent as many hours as I could at Symphony Hall, just like all the other children of orchestra members. My father had been a Boston Symphony brat, too, fifty years earlier, when his father had been a member of the orchestra. But Emanuel Fiedler rarely took his children to work with him.

Papa remembered going to occasional concerts. "What I enjoyed particularly was when he [Emanuel] used to sneak me in to watch the rehearsals. I loved to spend time hiding behind the bass drum or something and watching the percussion players." I liked the idea that both my father and I as small children, half a century apart, stood wide-eyed backstage while the big orchestra rehearsed. I wonder whether he too looked in amazement around the darkened hall, the white Grecian-style statues in the second balcony hovering in the dimness, the huge rehearsal curtain separating the brightly lit musicians from the blackness of the auditorium.

I know people in the performing arts who refuse to bring their children to the theater; "the theater gets in your blood," a singer once said to me, explaining why she never had her young daughter at rehearsals. That's exactly what happened to me. Symphony Hall was a magical place, full of music and people making music, brimming with activity and excitement.

People at Symphony Hall seemed nicer than the people at home. The musicians gave me hugs and occasionally doughnuts from the orchestra lounge. They told me I looked pretty and asked me how school was going. The first harpist, who was Parisian, helped me with my stumbling French pronunciation and my grammar; the librarian showed me pictures of his new puppies; Papa's secretary painted my fingernails with her nail polish. None of these things or anything even remotely similar happened at Hyslop Road.

Going to a Pops concert was the most grown-up treat of my childhood, but I didn't get taken very often. The nightly ritual for us three children during the Pops season was to stand at the tall windows on the landing of the front stairs and wave goodbye to Mummy and Papa as they drove away for the concert.

On opening night each year, we weren't left behind on the stairs. Instead, we were in the car with our parents, trying to hide our delight at being allowed to go to the concert and staying up late. We had to hide our feelings because Papa was nervous and cranky and would yell at us if we made any noise.

At Symphony Hall, the management and the players would greet my sister and brother and me with great formality, making us feel very important; and Nana, our grandmother, would present Debbie and me with gardenia corsages. I would struggle to pin mine on the fragile material of my dress, and watched my mother in admiration as she secured what seemed like a whole bush of orchids to her shoulder with no effort at all. For most of my life, the scent of gardenias has invoked a thrill of excitement and anticipation.

Papa would be at his large mahogany desk in the Green Room, studying his scores and paying no attention to us until the time came to pose for the traditional opening-night pictures, which would run on the front page of the *Globe* the next day and accompany the social column in the *Herald* later in the week. My father, in white tie and tails for opening night, would look nervous; my mother, taller and exuding a tweedy Bostonian glamour, stood beside him. My grandmother, short and regal, with her hair massed on top of her head in the Edwardian style she kept all her life, stood beside my mother, and clinging to the fringes of the family group would be my father's sisters, frumpy and Middle European in the midst of all that New England self-confidence.

Then we would kiss Papa good luck and progress out from backstage to be seated at our usual tables in the auditorium, halfway back on the orchestra level. Once seated, we couldn't see Papa very well because the auditorium was not raked and there were tall people all around us. Debbie and I mostly concentrated on the pitchers of pink Pops punch that arrived instantly and the plates of Cheez-it crackers, a brand I still buy at the supermarket in New York City when I feel particularly in need of comfort.

Papa would come onstage, his shoulders erect, his left arm tucked elegantly against his torso. He made a quick bow to the audience, then turned to the orchestra. Diverting the audience's attention from their little green tables laden with drinks and food, especially in the festive and slightly intoxicated air of opening night, was a challenge, so Papa always began with a rousing march.

His conducting had a seductive verve that worked superbly on shorter pieces, such as marches, overtures, and waltzes. I would pat the fluffy skirt of my dress, take a long sip of Pops punch, and settle back to listen to the concert, timed to last exactly two hours: eighty-five minutes of music precisely, broken by two intermissions.

Mummy and the other grown-ups mostly ignored us. Our Fiedler aunts were usually seated with Debbie and me, since Mummy considered them tiresome and unsophisticated. There were five seats at each table, so Debbie and I sat with Aunts Fredericka, Elsa, and Rosa. My mother was with her mother—"Mother dear," as Mummy called her—and several of her brothers and their wives. There was no Pops punch at those tables. As our big pink pitchers arrived (the Fiedler sisters rarely drank alcohol), bottles and bottles of beer would be delivered to my mother's family. "I always gain so much weight during the Pops," my mother would say with a sigh. "It must be all the beer."

We would be rushed home the minute the concert was over, because we had to get up for school the next morning. But I never worried about not falling asleep; during the Pops season when Papa was home, I slept through the night. The only time I did wake up was when Mummy and Papa fought after coming home from a concert. I would hear them screaming at each other downstairs and would peek my head out my door to listen. I'd hear Debbie's door creak open as well. Sometimes she and I would exchange worried glances across the dark hall, but when we compared notes the next day, neither of us could figure out what the fighting had been about. The battles would end with the thundering sounds of one parent or the other dashing up the stairs, and we would quickly pull our heads back. One door would slam, soon followed by the slam of a second door at the opposite end of the corridor.

Once I was old enough to drive, I often took my father to Symphony Hall. I could watch close up as he changed from the Hyslop Road father to his Symphony Hall persona. The beginning of the drive was filled with elaborate directions on how to get to Symphony Hall, as if this were the first time I had ever gone there from

Hyslop Road. Gradually, he would relax and start telling me about any unusual piece on the program that night, sometimes suggesting that I borrow his score to follow along during the concert. Occasionally we listened to the radio, but he would snap it off if one of his own recordings came on; unlike most other conductors I know, he could never stand listening to his own work. Imperfections made him uncomfortable.

On the way to Symphony Hall, it was as if Papa's demons had fled and his dark side vanished. He returned with enthusiasm to the world of human discourse. His work was his life, and he never talked about his work at home. At some point, while I was still going to Papa's concerts religiously, my sister and brother stopped, which was probably healthy. But I couldn't extricate myself from the fascination of Symphony Hall and the new father who emerged there. I went to his concerts night after night to reassure myself that this good Papa was still inside the terrifying Papa from home.

I sat in his dressing room, listening to his preconcert consultations with the orchestra's librarians and musicians and his quick discussion of the evening's concerto with the soloist. I soaked up the adrenaline-permeated atmosphere that fills every theater just before a performance.

Papa went onstage at eight on the dot; he was constantly worried about the expense of a concert going overtime. It didn't matter that it wasn't his money at risk; he couldn't bear waste. I went out into the hall and experienced the almost jolting transition from the intimacy of backstage to the impersonal demeanor that my father and the orchestra assumed in front of the audience. Moments earlier, Papa had been trading dirty jokes with a percussionist or having his preconcert swig of bourbon. The orchestra members would have been complaining about the temperature onstage or the nuisance of wearing their jackets instead of playing in shirt sleeves, as they did on hot evenings. (They loved the informality, but my father didn't. "You look like a bunch of waiters!" he would roar on hearing that the musicians had voted that it was too warm to play in jackets.) But once everyone was onstage, the performance masks would drop into place, at least for the relatively serious first part of the concert.

Papa evolved a program format during his first years as conductor of the Pops which stayed pretty much the same during the next fifty years. When, in the early 1950s, he began his extensive guest-conducting activities, he followed that format as much as possible, although its three-part design with two intermissions was not practical with most orchestras outside Boston. No one had ever programmed concerts exactly like these before, and no one has since. His formula was unique, and grew out of his own personality. "It is all bound up with Arthur and the Boston Symphony and that hall," the composer Morton Gould, who worked frequently with my father, has said. "What happens now is not the kind of program I would do, and whether someone else could survive with Arthur's programs is something I don't know. An audience has a gut reaction to what is true, and the Pops are Arthur, who is authentic."

"It's quite a chore," my father once said about making programs. "But what *really* makes it complicated is that I like to please people." He made honest attempts to accommodate audience requests, but in general he hated the process of making programs. The only element of his personality that made any of this a little easier was his meticulousness. Every piece lasted almost exactly the same time it did every other time he had conducted it; intermissions ended on the dot; he had no qualms about interrupting applause if he was afraid the concert was going to run over the stipulated two hours; and he was even known to drop encores if things were running late, although he hated doing that. To my father, the adopted frugal Yankee, having a concert go overtime was unthinkable. Also, he sincerely believed in a motto he repeated over and over again, sometimes right as he came offstage, the audience still applauding happily back in the hall. "Leave 'em wanting more," he would say gleefully, and return for another bow.

"I mixed a little of the best of the old with a little of the best of the present and came up with a palatable concoction" was the way Papa would describe a program, and that is the most concise description I have come across.

He also threw into every program a generous sprinkling of encores, each announced from the rear of the stage by large cardboard signs that became noticeably dog-eared as the long season passed. Everything was paced so that only a few seconds' pause came between each piece, and the cumulative effect of this continual outpouring of music was amazing to see, night after night, as I did.

The first part of the program always began with the opening march. By the end of it, the audience had started to listen and enjoy themselves, and Papa could move on to the part of the program that I suspect he enjoyed the most: the light classics. He felt that much of this music was disappearing from symphony concerts —Sousa marches, Strauss waltzes, light, delectable things—and that someone ought to preserve it. He wanted to be the one, and he did his best. "The important thing," he said, "is that one doesn't let himself get into a rut."

And he knew what the audience wanted. "Each year we have an all-request concert. I can tell you right now what the requests will be next year and five years from now. *Bolero. The Blue Danube. The William Tell Overture.* Of course I'll play them; why not? *William Tell* is a fine overture. Toscanini performed it often, and if it was good enough for Toscanini, it's good enough for me."

The second section of the concert was the concerto. "A good Pops concert is a melting pot of music," Papa said. "The important thing is balance. It's nice to eat a good chunk of beef, but you want a light dessert, too." The concerto section was the chunk of beef, I suspect. The soloist almost always played a piece from the serious symphonic repertoire, another chance for Papa to conduct the music he really wanted to be doing all the time. He was, for example, proud that for many years he played more of the Mozart piano concertos than did the Boston Symphony Orchestra itself.

He was also proud of his soloists and was determined to present young artists at his concerts, remembering only too well how hard it had been for him to get a chance to perform during his early years. So he searched out young performers, always hoping to give a break to someone truly talented. In turn, young soloists were eager to appear with the Pops. It was a chance to play with a real

conductor and a real symphony orchestra in front of a real audience, a combination hard for a young artist to find. The fact that
the fees were nearly nonexistent didn't seem to be a problem.
When my father died, in 1979, a soloist's fee for a regular Pops
concert was the vast sum of seventy-five dollars.

When Papa said to me, as he quite often and quite unnecessarily
did, "You really should come to the concert tonight; we're doing
something very special," he was referring to the middle section of
the program. Over the years he presented a startling conglomera-
tion of concertos and serious works: rare performances of such
pieces as Beethoven's *Wellington's Victory*, Gershwin's *Second Rhapsody*, the world première of Piston's *The Incredible Flutist*, the American premières of Walton's *Façade* and the Khachaturian Violin
Concerto; the first Boston Symphony performances of Rimsky-
Korsakov's Symphony No. 2 and *Antar*, the Boston premières of
the Khachaturian Piano Concerto, the Shostakovich Piano Concerto, and the Poulenc Concerto for Two Pianos; the MacDowell
Piano Concerto and other compositions by composers rarely associated with the Pops, such as Telemann, Bach, Haydn, Handel, Prokofieff, Britten, and Ginastera. Papa would often go back to the
Green Room exhilarated after the second third of the concert. If
he was nervous about anything that night, the source of the tension was usually on that part of the program, and his mood would
improve once it was out of the way. Again he had proven to himself that he could conduct something on a higher level than "Her-
nando's Hideaway." The audience was respectfully silent for the
second section, but their relief when the third section began was
easy to sense.

"Nobody can make a perfect program," Papa often said after
about sixty years of trying. "I have no mission in these concerts,
except to do what I think people have come for, and that is to
enjoy an evening of music. Some people will come for the serious
part. Others say, 'The hell with all that. I want to hear the things
from Broadway and the movies and the Beatles.' "

Papa worked as hard on the third section as he did on the others,
if not harder. "I have always tried to stay in step," he once said
almost defensively, because staying in step had become harder as

he got older and more out of touch, as popular music moved far away from what he had known in his own younger years. Sometimes he programmed things that frankly frightened him. When the TV series "Evening at Pops" started, he worked with stars who played a kind of music he had probably never listened to. He gamely tried to keep up with Ella Fitzgerald, Pearl Bailey, Dizzy Gillespie, Roberta Flack, Tony Bennett, Chet Atkins, Boots Randolph, Bobby Short, Duke Ellington, and Eubie Blake, among many others. Some of these people performed in a tradition completely antithetical to Papa's classical training, and he would find himself lost; Ella Fitzgerald, Sarah Vaughan, and Dizzy Gillespie with their free-wheeling, improvisational styles were especially challenging. Papa tried everything from memorizing tapes of the rehearsals to restricting himself to beating time, to no avail.

One contemporary musical phenomenon that he had no trouble understanding was the Beatles. From the first time he heard them, Papa was convinced that Paul McCartney was a great melodist and that the Beatles should be taken seriously as musicians. "The Beatles had beautiful ideas and absolutely beautiful tunes. They were real innovators," he said. When he was in Liverpool in the early 1960s to conduct the Royal Liverpool Philharmonic, he went to the clubs late at night to see if he could add to his understanding of the roots of the Mersey sound. (He also squeezed in some dancing while doing his research.) For the 1964 Pops season, just after the Beatles' triumphant first tour of the United States, he commissioned an arrangement of "I Want to Hold Your Hand," thus becoming the first person to program the Beatles at a symphony concert. "I didn't know what the audience reaction would be, whether they'd like it or throw things at me," he said afterward. Characteristically, "The orchestra was very annoyed. They were *furious*," especially about having to sing the refrain, "Yeah, yeah, yeah."

"But the audience *loved* it." Papa felt vindicated; that was the important part. And incidentally, when the Pops musicians saw how much the audience loved the Beatles' pieces, they began to enjoy themselves just as thoroughly.

"Do we all have to face music with our hands in our hair and bowed down with eyes closed?" Papa would ask. "Thank God I have a taste for everything. I would hate myself for just liking one thing. 'How could he lower himself?' people ask, and I get tired of it. This damned snobbism is the thing I've been trying to fight all my life, every chance I get. You've got to give people a program that has something for everybody, a great variety of the best music played with love and kisses, but never over-gooed. You can't really enjoy something if there's no fun in it."

Papa called the last part of the concert "classical music for people who hate classical music," but these works were really not symphonic at all. He also occasionally referred to the pieces in the last section as "lollipops." They were usually medleys from musical comedies, arrangements of hit tunes, themes from popular television shows, and even the occasional TV commercial. What all this music had in common was that it had been arranged especially for the Boston Pops. The pieces were orchestrated as richly and as lavishly as the arrangers could manage. Pops arrangements were music for the people, performed by an ensemble originally created for the aristocracy. One colleague had a theory that Papa, with his strong New England work ethic, was offended by seeing any musician sitting idle at any moment during the concert, which was why the arrangements featured a full symphony orchestra, complete with double winds and percussion section, every instrument playing all the time and usually very loudly. (The list of percussion instruments Papa's arrangements required on a normal basis was mind-boggling: ratchet, chimes, vibraphone, bass drum and cymbals, two snare drums and brushes, tambourine, xylophone, glockenspiel, triangle, klaxon, train whistle, prizefight gong, police whistle, electric siren, slide whistle, maracas, tin shaker, castanets, temple blocks, and sleigh bells. "It's a bit fussy for the percussion section, and it might be a good idea for them to practice it," he regularly warned orchestras about to perform the new arrangements.)

"I enjoy the luxury of having a great orchestra play less than great music, perhaps," Papa admitted once. Hearing this large ensemble performing a piece like "Send in the Clowns" or selections from *Hair* would send the audience into a cheerful frenzy. I don't think I ever saw the last section of a Pops concert flop or fizzle. One stuffy B.S.O. trustee is reputed to have said, after attending a Pops concert, "This is really music for middle America." He added, "What's amazing to find out is that we are *all* middle America!"

The Boston Pops introduced many people to classical music. When Papa died, Leonard Bernstein recalled in a memorial radio program that the first time he had heard a symphony orchestra was at the Pops. "To me the Pops was Heaven itself. It was the first live orchestra I'd ever heard and I felt it was quite simply the supreme achievement of the human race. Of course the idea of conducting the Pops myself never occurred to me as a practical possibility. I merely identified with the glorious man named Fiedler and indulged a fantasy or two."

Then would come the last encore, which was almost invariably the piece my father probably conducted more than any other, "The Stars and Stripes Forever." When asked why, he would first shrug with irritation, and then patiently explain once again. "Because it's the sort of thing everybody expects of me by now, and because I think it's a damned good march and adds a little drop of patriotism without flag waving. Besides, it's so rousing that you can't play anything after it, and so it tells people it's time to go home."

Despite all his success, Papa himself never wholly appreciated how much the Pops meant to people. Another composer, Virgil Thomson, summed it all up: "The Boston Pops are really a lovely success story," he wrote in the *New York Herald Tribune*. "They have no budget troubles. They have no audience troubles. They have no program troubles. They just play everything and play it beautifully, and everybody loves them and comes every night to hear them."

AFTER THE CONCERT, my father would unwind with his friends in the Green Room. Joseph Spotts would bring in trays of sandwiches, and beer would be dispensed from a machine bought for my father by the orchestra to commemorate one of his Pops anniversaries. (Musicians used to sneak into the Green Room when they weren't playing to steal beer, until my father figured out what was going on and, to the orchestra's distress, put a lock on the dispenser and cut off the supply.) After about ten or fifteen minutes and a couple of beers, the tension of the performance would fall away from my father, and he would become more approachable and expansive.

Papa's coterie of friends in the orchestra—Pasquale Cardillo, the principal clarinetist; the librarian Bill Shisler; Harry Dickson; Bill Cosel, the producer of "Evening at Pops"—would often be joined by Papa's jovial politician friend John Cahill as they gathered for a beer, a sandwich, and the quick verbal disembowelment by my father.

Papa had an acid wit and few compunctions about displaying it in conversation. His friends were resigned to his barbs, and every night he attacked someone different. Harry Dickson would be derogated because he didn't drink: "Come on, Harry, be a man!" my father would roar, gesturing at the beer machine. John Cahill loved to bring his political cronies back to the Green Room to meet his distinguished friend. Papa was devoted to John, but that didn't stop him from snarling, "Don't solicit business for me, John!" as the genial Cahill encouraged autograph seekers to crowd into the Green Room. Patsy Cardillo was constantly teased about his love life, or what Papa imagined his love life to be. Since Papa was well aware that Patsy's marriage went through troubled periods, the joking had a bitter edge.

There were people Papa left alone. Bill Cosel seemed inviolable. I don't know whether it was because his contribution to Papa's career was invaluable, or because Papa had trouble finding a crack of vulnerability. That wasn't a problem in regard to me, but Papa rarely turned on me in front of the Green Room crowd. There was plenty of time for that in the car on the way home.

Once in a while, Papa would get morose after a concert, especially after such a momentous evening as the Bicentennial Concert. He would be quiet and pensive, and there would be an unguarded sadness in his eyes. The postconcert get-togethers would be abbreviated on those nights, and Papa would go home to Brookline to sit on the cool terrace of the house. He would stare into the darkness, perhaps trying to reconstruct the audience's bravos, perhaps enjoying the silence.

When Papa was conducting in other cities, he couldn't host his gatherings after concerts. If there was no party, he would go out for a drink and a snack with friends, but he seldom had to worry. There was almost always a party.

Papa loved parties all his life. Although at home or in the office he generally stopped drinking before he became inebriated, he invariably drank too much at social events. He wrote to a friend in 1975 after a party in his honor in New York, "What a helluva party! I never had so much fun with my clothes on. And then, to top it off, the wonderful supper at '21.' I can't remember how I got on the plane, but when I woke up I was home in bed and should have stayed there!"

When Papa was on the road, he did many one-night stands. His schedule was so exhausting that it is a wonder that he had the energy to socialize late in the evening before catching a plane early the next morning. But to Papa, parties after concerts were an essential part of his routine. "I like this. It suits me—gives me a chance to unwind. Some of the parties are great, some aren't so great, but they're all a tonic to me."

Because he was fascinated by people, he rarely found a party dull. When I began working in the music business and met other well-known musicians in social situations, I saw immediately that Papa was different. Other conductors would assume that anyone they were talking to would be eager to hear all about their last concert, their next concert, and their plans for the next several seasons. Papa never talked about himself. Instead, he pumped the people he was talking to about *their* lives; he was interested in regional differences, accents, any hobbies or eccentricities. And late at night, in the car or taxi going back to the hotel, he would turn to me, his eyes bright, and say, "Did you hear what So-and-So was saying about breeding spotted owls?" And if I had missed the tidbit, he would repeat it with great relish and infinite detail, no matter how much he had had to drink.

In Boston, the postconcert baiting sessions went on past midnight, and the energy Papa had left over from the concert would drain away. He'd be so exhausted that even he would be ready for the short drive home. His several beers, added to the bourbon he drank during the concerts, and the physical exertion would leave him quiet and sleepy on the way back. Just the same, every night as we started home from the concert, I would see the good Papa disappear once again.

As the car turned into the curving driveway on Hyslop Road, I had a sense of unease. It was twelve or twelve-thirty, and we had been gone for only five hours, but the gloom I always experienced was as deep as if we'd returned from a trip to a different planet. Our house would loom up in the moonlight, and I would quickly scan the windows to see who was still awake. Debbie's light would rarely be on; she went to bed early if she was home. Peter stayed up much later, but he was usually careful to be untraceable when Papa was expected home.

My mother's room faced on the back of the house, so we could never see if her light was on as we drove in. Her door at the head of the staircase was always closed when we went up to bed, and Papa rarely knocked to see if she was awake. We knew that once the rest of the family was in bed, she would come out of her room and go downstairs to wander.

Papa, bent over with fatigue, dragged himself up the stairs and down the long hall to his suite. "Good night," I called after him, and he would flap a hand in response. He could never look forward to a good night's sleep because he was haunted by insomnia. "I don't fight nonsleeping. Your body knows what it needs," he said defiantly. "I only sleep three or four hours a night." My room was next to his, and I knew that this was true. I could hear the short-wave radio by his bed murmuring all night long as he switched stations from continent to continent until the sun rose again over Brookline.

The dogs had waited for us to come home and put them out for their last walk of the evening. One of them often trailed up the stairs, following Papa to his door, on which a sign, stolen from some long-ago dressing room, said MR. FIEDLER. But even Papa's beloved dogs wouldn't cross that threshold unless invited; they would watch as the door swung shut and my father went into his rooms alone.

I would get into bed, lie in the darkness of my room, not afraid since Papa was home, too exhilarated by the hours at Symphony Hall to sleep, and I would think about the next day. Certainly, there were unpleasant meals and grim scenes with my mother to be endured, but the evening would come, and we would be off to another night at Symphony Hall, where Papa was entertaining and loving and the world full of color and light.

# S I X

## Backstage at Symphony Hall

AS I GREW UP, Symphony Hall became one of the things in life I thought my father and I shared. Of course we didn't; Symphony Hall and the Boston Symphony were his life's work, and for me they were the magic kingdom. But we were both happiest there, I thought. It took me many years to understand that my father's joy in Symphony Hall had a side that was tainted with bitterness.

When Papa became the conductor of the Pops in 1930, he and everyone else assumed that his biggest challenge would be to resuscitate the failing Pops season. That part of his new job turned out to be easy; Papa's personality and talents dovetailed perfectly with the taste and sensibility of the Pops audience, and his success was both immediate and abiding. But his difficulty in dealing with his former colleagues in his new position as their conductor was far more taxing; that problem did not go away in his fifty years with the orchestra.

My father was well liked by the other B.S.O. musicians before he took over the Pops, even though he was ambitious about his conducting, a characteristic that is traditionally unpopular with most symphony musicians. To orchestra members, the conductor is the enemy. No matter how much they may like him personally, or, far more important, how much they may respect him as a musician, every orchestra player regards the man on the podium with resentment and a kind of fear. The conductor has total control. He tells a hundred other people how to play, how to behave, even how to think during every minute he is in front of them. They, in turn, stare at him with an almost palpable contempt. Distrust and disdain flow between the conductor and the orchestra at every rehearsal, recording session, and concert.

Because he had once been one of them, Papa seemed a traitor to most members of the orchestra. They were lenient toward him when he conducted the Esplanade Concerts; they were grateful for the extra income and knew that he had started the concerts himself. Things changed when he was appointed by the Boston Symphony management to the Pops position. They regarded the move as his defection to the enemy.

Papa knew exactly what the musicians were thinking, since he had had the same thoughts for the fifteen years he was in the orchestra. He knew that the musicians didn't like him, and he didn't expect them to. "I don't give a damn if they like me," I heard him say a million times. I never believed him.

My father had a deep respect for the Boston Symphony musicians, despite their persistent hostility. I think he never stopped feeling hurt by their attitude. I used to watch him at rehearsals when he would stop the orchestra because someone was talking or not paying attention or fooling around—which happened frequently. His eyes, always expressive, would briefly seem to ask, "Why are you doing this to me? I was one of you. I know what it means to be a member of the Boston Symphony even if some of you young ones don't." The moment of vulnerability would be brief. Then his expression would harden and he would regard the musicians with something close to hatred. They would stare back at him with the same intensity. Papa and the orchestra were antagonists, and each side approached a battle almost with relish. But Papa's instinctive love for a good fight with the musicians was always tinged with pain.

Even Papa's famously precise ear became a cause of battle. Musicians regard intonation as an intimate and sensitive element of their work. Papa was "a bear," as one musician described him, on the subject of playing in tune, and his unrelenting insistence on perfect intonation grated on the orchestra. They particularly hated his conspicuous gesture to indicate when someone was playing sharp or flat. He would raise or lower his thumb in full view of both the orchestra and the audience until the correct pitch was reached. The orchestra would be furious, but Papa knew this was one area in which they couldn't fault him. Each time he tuned the orchestra in performance, he had a few seconds of gloating.

When I traveled with my father and saw him rehearse with other orchestras, I was amazed at the difference in the way he and they behaved toward each other. The musicians in other orchestras accorded my father a respect totally lacking in Boston. They tacitly acknowledged his reputation and his fame; some of them may have hated the music they were playing as much as the Pops musicians did, but they never expressed boredom or contempt. In return, my father showed a courtesy to them that he didn't bother with in Boston. Perhaps his comments were caustic, but the musicians away from Symphony Hall chose to laugh at them or even seem a little fearful when his remarks were too cutting. They never acted insulted or outraged, as the Pops orchestra did. So Papa made sure to leaven his criticism and sarcasm with enough encouragement to let the musicians feel challenged yet secure. In Boston, my father acted as though the orchestra neither wanted nor needed encouragement and praise.

And with the great orchestras—his favorite was the Chicago Symphony, although he never admitted that outside the family—I saw Papa almost obsequious for the only times in my life. Even in his last years, he felt so grateful to be conducting superior orchestras like Chicago, Philadelphia, New York, and Cleveland that he hardly made a correction, except of course in intonation.

Only once did I see him react to another orchestra as he did in Symphony Hall. In 1970, he was engaged to record the Paderewski Piano Concerto with Earl Wild and the London Symphony Orchestra. Papa had given the U.S. première of the piece with his pal

Jesús María Sanromá, and Paderewski himself had come to the rehearsals, so he had a long history with the work. Earl Wild was one of his favorite soloists; they played together many times, because Papa requested him as soloist whenever an orchestra he was conducting would agree. When he stepped in front of the London Symphony at the first recording session, my father was feeling happily secure, without the humility he would often exhibit at his first rehearsal with a world-class orchestra.

The London Symphony, however, is as famous for its feistiness as for its virtuosity. English musicians work schedules that would kill American musicians, and they regard the Americans as pampered and lazy. An English musician will often play a recording session in the morning, a rehearsal in the afternoon, and a concert at night, all three services in different locations, necessitating hours of driving through the murderous London traffic. They are too overworked and tired to put up with any nonsense from a conductor, except possibly from the one or two ancient maestri they may venerate at any given moment.

Papa was definitely not on the venerable list, even if he was old enough to qualify. The first recording session was on a Sunday morning, probably uncomfortably early after the musicians' usual Saturday night postconcert trip to the pub. Because of their tight schedules, the L.S.O. musicians were almost all exceptionally fast sight-readers, and they were accustomed to a quick rehearsal pace. Papa, on the other hand, was about to record a serious work with a top-rank orchestra other than Boston for one of the few times in his career, and he was not going to sight-read the piece. The clash was instantaneous. I knew a lot of the English musicians because one of my friends had married a London Symphony member, and I had been to many of their concerts and rehearsals. Most of the time, I admired their spunk and vitality, but when I saw how the rehearsal with my father began to deteriorate, I cringed in my seat. Eventually I moved to the back of the hall where the recording session was being made so that I couldn't hear the cutting remarks.

I wasn't the only one who couldn't hear what they were saying. Papa's hearing had deteriorated after years of standing in front of a blaring orchestra, an affliction suffered by many conductors. He also had a problem with the London slang many of the musicians used deliberately to heighten the tension with a conductor they didn't like. When the orchestra realized that he couldn't understand them, they were delighted and began to pretend they couldn't understand him either.

At the break, a few of them came over to me. Some seemed to forget that the conductor of the morning was my father, some didn't care, and some were deliberately nasty. "Who does he think he is?" expressed the prevalent attitude. I tried to defend my father with as light a tone as I could manage, but I knew the orchestra had made up its collective mind. They had decided that Papa was not up to their lofty standards, and although their professionalism ensured a beautiful performance for the recording, they gave Papa an extraordinarily hard time. Papa, as soon as he figured out that they were determined to be antagonistic, dropped any pretense at Bostonian politeness. He acted as rude and critical as they did.

Papa loved London and admired the city's five orchestras. I'm sure he was hurt by the London Symphony's contempt, but he never said a word about his feelings. Part of his restraint may have been caused by his knowing that I was friendly with some of the musicians, and he was too proud to admit any regret to me; but he also focused on what was important to him about his L.S.O. experience—the indisputable fact that he had recorded a serious work with one of the world's great orchestras. The record was, in fact, widely reviewed as an excellent performance of a rarely performed piece. He felt that, in the end, he had come out ahead.

The Boston Symphony musicians, who were almost as openly contemptuous of Papa as their London counterparts, occasionally acknowledged a grudging respect for my father. They admired his infallible ear and sense of pitch. They also reluctantly admitted his capacity for hard work, his professionalism, and his attitude that performing music was a job to be done as well as possible. His most frequent plea to them was "You are all professionals! Where's your pride in what you are doing? Shame!" Because most orchestra musicians are proud of their ability to be proficient under all circumstances, the B.S.O. reacted to my father's badgering by playing beautifully at the concerts no matter how unruly they had been at rehearsals.

By the time I began going to Pops rehearsals and recording sessions, baiting Papa had become a favorite sport of the musicians. In fact, the bickering became so rancorous—sometimes even obscene—that I was rarely allowed to go to a rehearsal. Papa did take me to recording sessions, because the musicians were a little better behaved in the presence of the microphones.

One of Papa's most venomous and unrelenting opponents in the orchestra was a woman who played at the back of the second violin section. She had acquired a reputation for sexual experimentation among her male colleagues, and since Papa always stayed on gossiping terms with his close friends in the orchestra, he knew all about her supposed activities. She expressed her disdain by talking constantly during rehearsals and by slouching in her seat with her legs crossed, something that drove Papa wild, because he felt it was disrespectful to the music as well as to the audience. "They're paying for this, you know," he would remind the orchestra. He saved some of his most seething looks for this woman, and she was delighted to return them just as fiercely.

One day she went too far. "Sit up in your seats!" Papa said to the second violins, since he rarely singled out one member of the orchestra. "Can't you be professionals?"

The woman slumped even further. "Fuck you!" she called out to Papa in the special voice musicians use, which seems to be inaudible but which they know perfectly well carries right to the podium.

Papa turned to her with his most courtly manner. "Is that an insult," he asked politely, "or an invitation?"

Some of the more innocent pranks became Pops traditions. One of the orchestra's most distinguished instrumentalists would bring his bowling ball to a Pops rehearsal once a season. No one ever knew which rehearsal he would choose, but everyone in the orchestra, including my father, knew that the bowling ball would inevitably appear. The musician would wait until what he considered the appropriate moment and then gently drop the ball from his seat in the middle of the orchestra. Bowling balls make a lot of noise when they are dropped, and this one would bounce leisurely down from one level to the next as it rolled toward the front of the stage and my father. And every year the orchestra would dissolve into hysterical laughter, right on cue.

The bowling-ball dropper was in fact one of my father's favorites, so Papa would laugh along with everyone else although perhaps not as deliriously year after year. He understood that these harmless incidents released a certain amount of tension, so he allowed them to continue, up to a point. One of the woodwind players also had an annual tradition; without any fanfare or obvious movements, he would put on a face mask while Papa was preoccupied with another section of the orchestra. When Papa looked back at the woodwind section, there would be Josef Stalin or Santa Claus or Groucho Marx waiting expectantly for his downbeat. He always laughed, because he liked that player, too.

He did not, however, like the cello section at all. He considered those musicians his most ferocious enemies, and they did their best to fulfill his expectations. The battle seems to have had its origins in a feud he had with one member of the section, his cousin Pepi Zimbler. After Papa had successfully launched the Boston Sinfonietta in the 1920s, he renamed the ensemble the Fiedler Sinfonietta. As he became more successful, he was forced to abandon the Sinfonietta, but he was indignant when Pepi resurrected the little orchestra and called it the Zimbler Sinfonietta. Papa regarded this as outright theft and broke off relations with Pepi; he even brought a lawsuit against him, to no avail. Several of the older musicians told me that Pepi's bitterness toward my father was so manifest that it may have been what infected his cellist colleagues. For whatever reason, any new young cellist who joined the orchestra seemed to behave obstreperously, in a boisterous manner rarely seen in a new young percussionist or trombonist.

One day not long before he died, Papa stormed home for lunch during the Pops in a towering outrage. The normal gin on the rocks was followed by a second, and then the facts emerged. That morning's rehearsal had been interrupted at several points by the quiet but unmistakable sound of a cow mooing. Papa first noticed the sound while he was correcting the woodwinds, but sharp as his ear was, he couldn't figure out where in the orchestra the sound was coming from. He went on with the rehearsal. A few moments later, the soft *"moooo"* floated out again from the rear of the stage.

Some of the musicians began looking around. Many, of course, were laughing, but others were annoyed by the intrusion. "Stop it, whoever you are," my father said irritably and, by reflex, glared at the cello section.

The mooing didn't stop. By the end of the rehearsal, Papa was in a fury. He was particularly angry that the mischief maker was operating in secret; in his own day as a troublemaker, half the fun was misbehaving out in the open, under the conductor's nose. "Coward!" he roared at the orchestra, looking fiercely in the direction of the lower strings. "Why don't you own up?"

Of course Papa knew exactly who the mooer was. After sixty-odd years around the B.S.O., nothing escaped him. Many years after Papa's death, I ran into the alleged cow at a party in Boston and asked him outright if Papa had been right to suspect him. Looking rather sheepish, if not bovine, he nodded; he had had a small device in his pocket that made the sound. The ironic part is that this musician now frequently conducts the Pops himself and, I imagine, runs into many of Papa's problems in dealing with the other orchestra members.

Sneakiness of any kind filled my father with disgust. As children we quickly learned to admit our misbehavior and suffer the ensuing tantrum rather than lie and face his extended moral outrage. In fact, the easiest way to quiet Papa, who was much given to shouting at us, was to admit our crime. There would be some further sputtering, but that would usually be the end of the incident.

Papa never held a grudge. Even in the case of the spiteful second violinist, Papa admired her playing enough to allow her to play a concerto at the Pops. Her attitude had nothing to do with her ability, he thought, and he always told the orchestra, "You don't have to like me to play with me." Most of the mischievous cellists played solo at the Pops if they wanted to. Any member of the orchestra who came to Papa's dressing room to ask a question or make a suggestion was treated courteously. His favorites might be offered a drink as well, but the others probably didn't know that.

Musician after musician I talked to in the B.S.O. commented on Papa's lack of vengefulness. Since most of them had at one time done their share of hell raising, they were grateful for the forgiving side of Papa's nature. He never fired anyone in his fifty years of battling with the Pops musicians. Actually, he did not have the contractual right to dismiss anyone, but he could certainly have suggested disciplinary action to the management. He never did. Maybe it was his sense of history. He himself was the only musician ever fired from the Boston Pops, a fact that still holds true.

Occasionally, the orchestra could get tired of his abruptness and belligerence. Several musicians gleefully recounted to me, many years afterward, the story of one Pops rehearsal when they won the battle with my father. He had been in a noticeably vile mood that morning and had bellowed at several of the musicians. At the break, they got together and decided on their revenge. When Papa walked onstage to begin the second half, there was absolute silence. Looking mollified, he began working. No one said anything when he stopped to make a correction; no matter how caustic he was, the only response was a complete hush. Finally Papa couldn't stand it a minute longer. "What's the matter?" he shouted. "Don't you like me anymore?"

At other times, Papa himself contributed to the ruckus onstage, although he was more likely to act up at concerts than in rehearsals, where he hated to waste time. He would beat a march in waltz time or conduct a familiar work using the baton upside down. When the orchestra spent an entire season playing the theme from *Jaws*, which everyone onstage—my father and musicians unified for once—loathed, the brass players one night showed up with a large rubber shark that they inflated and floated above the orchestra during the performance. The creature ascended into the air and moved gently in my father's direction. Without missing a beat, Papa reached up with his baton and pushed the shark right back at the brass. The trombone players shoved it back, and things deteriorated from there. But Papa and the orchestra had outsmarted themselves. The shark and its perambulations eventually became so popular that audiences began to request the *Jaws* theme as an encore every night.

Another evening, Papa irritably motioned to the first violins, who had moved back during the concerto to make room for the soloist, to return to their original position, closer to him. They began inching their chairs and stands forward as he requested— and so did the rest of the orchestra. Papa was almost squeezed off the stage, and he began to laugh, which of course only encouraged the next prank.

From time to time, the orchestra would toss their music up in the air at the end of a selection they hated. (Every musician I talked to mentioned his own least favorite piece from the Pops repertoire; "The Stars and Stripes Forever" ranked high on the list.) Papa would toss his score up slightly in response, the musicians would throw theirs a little higher, and soon pieces of music would be flying all around the stage.

The double bass players were probably the most creative section. They would choose appropriate places in certain overly familiar pieces and, at an unseen signal, would as one gracefully twirl their unwieldy instruments. Like the rest of the orchestra, the basses detested Christmas Pops, a sold-out series that involved endless playing of overorchestrated Christmas carols, a costumed Santa Claus scampering through the orchestra, and an overdecorated stage set complete with snow drifting across during the performance of "I'm Dreaming of a White Christmas." One night the bass section, driven to distraction, showed up with concealed umbrellas; as the fake snow began floating down from the ceiling, they all pulled out their umbrellas and raised them with a flourish. Papa thought this was so funny that the prank became another Christmas Pops tradition.

His most vicious tormentors were the members of his own family. Pepi Zimbler was relentless in his sullen antagonism toward Papa, and so was a cousin by marriage who played principal bassoon. Both would speak derisively to other members of the orchestra about Papa and his programs, sneering at the popular music he played and remarking that they certainly hadn't gone to Europe's finest conservatories to play that kind of trash. Their accomplice was a member of the viola section who had once been a member of the renowned Kolisch Quartet and had never got over it. He steadfastly refused to join in any extracurricular activities called on in a Pops score: barking in the suite from *The Incredible Flutist* by Walter Piston, whistling in the "Colonel Bogey March," or, worst of all, singing "Yeah, yeah, yeah" in "I Want to Hold Your Hand."

The other musicians alternated between agreeing with these self-styled "artistes" and disparaging their arrogance. "I'd hate to think what would have happened if one of them had got up to play a concerto," one of my father's supporters told me. "But of course they never did. It's very easy to sit in the middle of the orchestra and criticize."

My father himself had as little tolerance for snobbery among the musicians as he did with pretentiousness from concertgoers. He often told of stopping the orchestra when he was the brand-new Pops conductor. "Most of the musicians were foreigners. They looked down their noses at American music. Their hearts weren't in it . . . I said, 'Gentlemen, you are in America, you are making American money, you are playing to American audiences, you have an American conductor. We are going to play American music and we are going to play it well.' "

Most of the principal players, responsible for the solo passages and thus under more pressure than section musicians, were great fans of Papa's. They were gratified by the deference he unfailingly showed them, and they returned the courtesy by showing respect and, most important to my father, by playing beautifully for him.

Papa was always afraid that if he decided to concentrate on serious music, he would have to give up his beloved Pops, with no assurance that he would ever again work with as fine an orchestra. "There was a period in my life, when I first started, that I thought of going into the very serious side of conducting. Then I felt that, well, there are trials and tribulations. You go to a town and you have a second- or third-rate orchestra, or there's a faction that likes you and a faction that hates you. In Boston, I had the advantage of a marvelous orchestra at the tips of my fingers. I don't know; I just chose."

A music critic once told Papa that had he concentrated his energies more, his career could have gone anywhere. Papa laughed. "Well, yes, had I concentrated. People approached me to take over this and that orchestra in smaller communities in the United States. Well, that would have gotten me involved in local politics, which I don't like, and I wouldn't have had the kind of orchestra I have in Boston—it was a great temptation to hang on to *that.*"

His relationship with the orchestra's management was as complicated and touched with pain as his relationship with the musicians. He was hurt by the B.S.O.'s administrative indifference to him after what he regarded as years of loyalty, loyalty not just from him but from generations of Fiedlers. Over the years, one episode after another convinced him that the Symphony management was not just dismissive of him but downright contemptuous. He blamed himself because he was never able to confront the administration directly about what he saw as his mistreatment.

My father's feelings about the Boston Symphony Orchestra as an institution may have been tortured, but the orchestra's feelings about him were quite straightforward: they saw him, in the words of Michael Steinberg, a former artistic administrator and program annotator with the B.S.O., as "a sort of lowlife who has to be taken seriously because the Pops season provides the money to keep the B.S.O. going."

In 1976, the *Wall Street Journal* discussed the financial relationship of the Boston Symphony and the Boston Pops:

Increasingly the B.S.O. has come to rely on the Boston Pops [to bolster its income]. The Boston Pops has few of the financial problems facing the Symphony. Most of its tickets . . . are sold out in advance as early as the preceding fall, often in large blocks to companies and organizations. It can keep labor costs to a minimum by holding only one three-hour rehearsal a week, because the material, besides being simple and familiar, is repeated throughout the week. And sales of the Boston Pops recordings have reached some 50 million copies.

But the patrician Boston Symphony trustees and management— during my father's lifetime, members of the administration were almost as well born as those of the governing board—looked down their noses at their golden goose. One former B.S.O. administrator told me the reaction of his boss, the orchestra's manager at one period in Papa's tenure, when it was suggested that the Pops play

in Carnegie Hall while the Symphony was on one of its New York
trips. "It would not be appropriate," the manager declared. "It
would be like playing basketball in a cathedral." When Thomas
Morris became manager in the early 1970s, this attitude changed
dramatically; Tom Morris was the first B.S.O. manager to see the
enormous economic potential of the Pops outside Boston.

Perhaps this was because Tom didn't come from Boston. Bostonians seem to have a tendency to be provincial, regarding their city
as a Utopia and cultivating an indifference to what goes on outside
its environs. After my father began conducting most of his engagements outside Boston, the Symphony didn't notice the extent of
his activities. What they noticed was the healthy record royalties
and the plump receipts from the Boston Pops Tour Orchestra, but
they never grasped the extent of Papa's career. Most of it didn't
take place in Boston, after all.

Papa didn't help his situation. Just as the B.S.O. never understood the bigger picture of my father, he never saw the true picture
of himself in relation to the organization. His perceptions were too
hobbled by hurt feelings. And as he got angrier and felt less appreciated, he became more difficult to deal with.

"He never stood up for himself," a former B.S.O. administrator
told me. "He had a chip on his shoulder and just grumped around
and didn't do himself any good." The people who served as public
relations directors for the orchestra had keen recollections about
Papa, publicity being one area in which my father evinced no false
modesty. Somewhere he had got the idea that it was all right for a
conductor to care about his publicity. "I hated to go by his office,"
one said to me. "He always had something for me to do." Another
remembered the sign hanging in his office: "What have you done
for Arthur Fiedler lately?" A third reminisced about the time a
picture of Papa conducting the opening concert of the Esplanade
season ran on the front page of two of the three Boston daily
papers. Since the annual Esplanade opening attracted mostly dutiful press coverage, she was proud of her achievement and brought
the papers to my father's office. As she placed them on his desk,
she expected to receive warm thanks for her efforts. Papa spread
out the papers, glanced at the front pages of the *Herald* and the

*Record American,* then looked coldly at her. "What the hell happened to the *Globe?"*

"They treat us like second-class citizens," my father remarked in 1972, referring to himself and his orchestra, about the time that the B.S.O. management, under Tom Morris, began to capitalize on the popularity of the Boston Pops. "They have finally learned, however, that there's money in them thar hills, and money talks, you know." For years he had viewed himself as the victim of exploitation, so his cynicism was understandable. Subsequently, he was almost humble in his gratitude to Tom Morris when he realized that at last someone seemed to appreciate him and what he had given the orchestra.

There are many examples of the Boston Symphony's institutional indifference to my father and its manipulation of him. The administration must have understood early on that he was unwilling to challenge it, and, ornery as he became as the years went by, he never did confront the orchestra directly.

His salary was probably the major area in which he and the administration repeatedly clashed; the encounters were profitable for the orchestra and unprofitable, not to mention humiliating, for my father. He actively assisted, however, in maintaining the status quo that was so disadvantageous to him, so the Boston Symphony can't be perceived as being the only party at fault.

I never realized how shockingly low my father's salary was until the 1970s. I was going through a bleak period and decided that I needed some kind of therapeutic help. But I was working for an orchestra myself by then, and I couldn't afford treatment on my salary. Summoning all my courage, I approached my father for help.

I spoke to him on the terrace in Brookline just before lunch one Sunday. He listened carefully and asked me a few questions about why I was feeling so awful. I told him how empty life seemed to me just then.

"I think it's all a question of self-respect," he said surprisingly. "I have the same problem."

I was stunned. Papa rarely talked about his emotional problems; in fact, I had long ago decided that he had denied their existence so long that he didn't know anything was wrong. But very occasionally, he would make a remark indicating that under his proud façade lay a great depth of self-awareness.

"You know," he said, "I've never even felt that I could ask the Boston Symphony for a raise. They're still paying me the same thing they paid me when I started in 1930."

"How much is that?" I asked in continued amazement.

He looked at me ruefully. "Twelve thousand dollars a year," he said.

Papa at this point was conducting nine weeks of nightly concerts during the Pops, as well as Christmas Pops, New Year's Pops, Esplanade Concerts, and Tanglewood Pops. He and the Pops had sold over fifty million record albums, a gold mine of royalties for the Boston Symphony. When Papa died, his successor would be paid around twenty times as much for many fewer concerts. Yet he was still receiving a sum that even by the standards of 1930, when he became the Pops conductor, was minimal.

"Why?" I finally managed to ask.

"It's a question of self-respect," he repeated. "I had offers from other orchestras. But I loved the Boston Symphony—I didn't want to leave."

In the early years of his tenure, my father tried hard. From the beginning, he understood that he had been wrong to take over the Pops at a small salary; he knew, after all, what his predecessor's fee had been. It was almost as if he was so embarrassed by his desire for the position that, in restitution for this unseemly longing, he agreed to be paid far less than he knew was right. Besides, he must have thought, if he was a success, the B.S.O. would surely raise his salary. His judgment in this was as mistaken as it was in most financial matters.

At the end of his third season with the Pops, Papa wrote to William Brennan, the orchestra's manager:

When the contract for the Pops was offered to me three years ago at a very much smaller salary than my predecessor's, you advised me to accept this, as you were speculating on whether or not I could make a success of these concerts.

At the end of this first season you seemed very satisfied with the result and you promised me that you would try, should the second season be equally successful, to increase my salary in the form of an extra bonus, as my annual increase in salary was minimal.

You agreed with me that the second season was equally, if not more, successful and you told me you would speak to Judge Cabot [president of the trustees] about it, particularly since some of the concerts were broadcast and the Orchestra derived a substantial income from that.

Also, there was no mention in my contract of radio broadcasting, and, as you know, this entails considerable extra work, such as timing the particular choice of programme, and decided extra nervous strain, as it is not an easy task to try to interest two audiences at one time.

Meeting you at various times throughout the winter, I asked you whether you had spoken to Judge Cabot about this, and you said that the opportunity had not arisen. The next thing I was aware of was the regrettable death of Judge Cabot.

Therefore, I am asking you, if you agree with me, which I hope you do, that in spite of bad conditions throughout the country, the concerts have gone surprisingly well, even beyond my own expectations; and in as much as the Orchestra has again received an additional income through the sources of broadcasting, I would deeply appreciate anything that you can do for me in the way of receiving an extra fee.

I think you know me well enough to know that I am not of a grasping nature, but when a man works conscientiously and very hard to try to achieve success for his organization, his only definite proof of the mutual understanding of this is compensation in one form or another.

The letter displays my father's characteristic behavior when dealing with a professional organization he considered more powerful and influential than he. His tone was almost apologetic when he wrote to the Boston Symphony management or the executives in charge of one of his record companies, men to whom he saw himself as somehow being in thrall, because they controlled areas of his career that were of supreme importance to him. This is in sharp contrast, of course, to his manner toward smaller orchestras or companies, when he regarded himself as having the upper hand.

Unfortunately, his tone in his initial salary negotiations with the Boston Symphony set a pattern that was to persist for fifty years. I don't know how much of the pattern was hardened by Papa putting himself in an entreating attitude, and how much was the arrogance of the Boston Symphony's traditional paternalism.

George Judd was the B.S.O. manager at the end of the 1944 season, when the Esplanade Concerts received great press acclaim for keeping up the public spirit in the war years and throughout the blackouts. He wrote to my father in typical Boston Symphony language.

Both the Trustees and the Management want to express the admiration they hold for your part in this great civic enterprise. It has been a memorable season and your part in it is especially significant in view of the number of concerts which you were willing and able to conduct. If there were a way to do it, I'd like to see you awarded a badge of merit for what you do through these concerts to make it possible for all people of goodwill to come together as a Greater Boston family, all elements in our metropolitan area having equal opportunities to enjoy themselves in each other's company . . .

I look forward very much to seeing you here in September when we will, as you put it, try to work out our future plans free from any of the cobwebs that might surround our thinking in the midst of producing 100 concerts for 100 capacity audiences.

I'm sure the "future plans" Mr. Judd referred to were, in my father's mind, questions about his salary. In 1944, he had earned $7200 for the nine-week, nightly Pops season, and $1000 for the Esplanade Concerts. Whatever discussions ensued apparently produced no results; in fact, my father's fees from the Boston Symphony diminished over the next three seasons. His annual compensation was computed from payment for recordings, Pops, Esplanade, broadcasts, and a miscellaneous category entitled "winter." In 1944, he received a total of $16,200 for all of these. This was reduced to $14,362 in 1945, to $13,608 in 1946, and to $13,827 in 1947. At the same time, he was receiving a couple of thousand dollars annually for teaching at Boston University and a pittance from his few guest-conducting engagements. He may have received additional royalties from RCA that were not channeled through the Symphony, but I sometimes wonder whether Papa joined the Coast Guard Temporary Reserve because he needed the money.

In the late 1940s and early 1950s, Papa's income increased somewhat as he added regular concerts in San Francisco and the

Boston Pops Tour Orchestra. Things improved a little in Boston. By 1955, his Pops salary had increased to $12,500 for a ten-week season of concerts every night.

As Papa's career outside Symphony Hall expanded, he complained again about his compensation for the Pops. The orchestra's administration puzzled over how to reconcile my father's complaints with the obdurate refusal of the trustees to consider any increase in his salary.

For some inexplicable reason, Papa chose the controller of the Boston Symphony, James J. Brosnahan, to act as his intermediary with the trustees and management. In an equally bizarre decision, he entrusted his personal financial planning to Mr. Brosnahan, an employee of Papa's chief economic adversary, the Boston Symphony. For years Mr. Brosnahan would convey Papa's grievances about his pay to the B.S.O. manager and then report back to Papa. I suppose my father saw this as a way to avoid having to complain directly himself, but it was not an effective bargaining tactic. In 1960, the manager wrote to Mr. Brosnahan:

I raised the subject of Mr. Fiedler's pay with Mr. Cabot [president of the orchestra's board of trustees]. Naturally he finds that any increase in money to Mr. Fiedler results in the enrichment of Uncle Sam, the impoverishment of the B.S.O. and about nothing to Mr. Fiedler. I spoke of your thought of a company automobile for him, and Mr. Cabot thinks it would be hard to argue that it could be exempt from his income tax.

Do you have any other bright ideas that might improve things for A.F. without taking too much hide off the corp[oration]? If I sense Mr. Cabot's sentiments correctly, they are that A.F. has a jolly good thing out of his connection with the B.S.O. and the Pops already, and he is not deeply moved by suggestions that his rewards are insufficient.

"Your father was the smartest person about making a career in the music business that I ever met," Tom Morris said to me years after my father died. I stared at him in disbelief, having recently read the preceding memo and many like it in the B.S.O. archives at Symphony Hall. I was beginning to see my father as the querulous victim of the B.S.O. administration, miserable in his servitude but unwilling to participate in a confrontation. Tom, seeing that I didn't understand, explained several things to me. "He had the use of the Boston Symphony," he said, and we both understood he meant that, for fifty years, my father worked with one of the best orchestras in the world. This was not likely to have happened under any other set of circumstances, Tom felt, and Papa, realizing that, forfeited much of his bargaining power with the management and board in order to safeguard the relationship.

Papa also made brilliant use of the Boston Symphony's incomparable music library. He had the year-round use of the scores and parts, as long as they weren't being used by the B.S.O. itself; he had the fairly constant attention of the librarians and, once Bill Shisler joined the Symphony's staff, the service of a full-time librarian for all his concerts, both with the Pops and as a guest conductor. In addition, the Boston Symphony commissioned the Pops arrangements that were an essential part of the Boston Pops formula. Arrangements are expensive to commission, and the B.S.O. paid for them and allowed Papa to use them whenever he wanted.

His special stroke of genius was in his adamant refusal to let anyone else use the arrangements under any circumstances. This made the arrangements unique, something that no other orchestra and no other conductor could ever replicate. Conceivably, renting out the arrangements would have been a lucrative side business for the Boston Symphony, but that would have devalued a quintessential Pops asset. A short-term financial reward would have debased the long-term power of the orchestra's uniqueness.

For Papa, there was also the specter of Koussevitzky's eventual fate. Much as he had hated the older man, my father respected him as the music director of the Boston Symphony, and was shocked when, in 1949, the trustees made the seemingly casual decision to let the Russian conductor resign. The dispute that caused Koussevitzky to threaten resignation was a trifling disagreement that could easily have been resolved if the board had made the attempt. But no one, not even a music director of a quarter-century's standing, was allowed to threaten the trustees; they let him go. Papa looked on first with trepidation and then with horror as Koussevitzky became ill and died within two years. The lesson was all too clear: if he were to have the hubris to confront the trustees, he would be gone just as fast as Koussevitzky, and probably faster. Was he afraid that then he too would die? Maybe that seemed to him the inevitable result of exile from Symphony Hall —the ultimate price for defying the "family's" authority. So Papa stayed on in Boston, not quite quietly, but with a bitter, grating sense of his fate.

In 1962, Mr. Brosnahan approached the Symphony management with a new tactic from Papa:

Mr. Fiedler has again spoken about an adjustment in his Pops salary. The last time this was mentioned, Mr. Fiedler's tax status was such that any increase in payments to Mr. F. resulted in a like payment to the Federal government, leaving little or nothing for Mr. F. It is now my understanding . . . that since R.C.A. royalties on recordings by Mr. F. are part of Mr. F.'s earnings from the B.S.O., it is possible . . . to purchase further annuities for Mr. F. This could be an answer if it is desirous to adjust Mr. Fiedler's Pops compensation.

This suggestion apparently arose because much of Papa's compensation from the Boston Pops Tour Orchestra went directly into annuities that would be payable when he was earning less taxable income. The trustees kicked around this suggestion but decided nothing. Six months later, Papa quite rightly got angry about the continual delays and procrastinations. It was thirty years since his first letter to Mr. Brennan requesting a review of his salary, and little had changed. During the 1961–62 season, my father was paid $12,500 (exactly what he had earned in 1941–42) for the Pops season and $500 for the Esplanade. His record royalties and Boston Pops Tour Orchestra fees were several times his basic salary, but that money was not calculated into his salary from the B.S.O., which also, incidentally, benefited from these outside activities of my father's. He felt that the arrangement was fundamentally unfair.

Mr. Brosnahan tried again. "Mr. Fiedler paid me a visit yesterday . . . He spoke about the fact that his Pops salary has remained the same for the past eighteen years and, as he put it: 'What can be done about it? Can we buy annuities or set money aside on a deferred income basis?' "

The Symphony's manager dashed off a memo to Henry Cabot. "While you and I were talking about Mr. Fiedler, by some miraculous thought transfer, evidently Arthur was addressing Mr. Brosnahan on the same topic—with some force, I gather from Jim. Anyway, I think we will have to face up to this soon—Jim [says] Arthur's working up a good deal of steam—and I think we should offer Arthur an analgesic annuity of some sort."

Included for Mr. Cabot's edification was an accounting of Papa's total earnings during the 1961–62 season, $49,617.98, including record royalties that were now funneled to him through the Symphony offices. Mr. Cabot's reply was immediate: "I still think that $50,000 for a little over two months' work is enough. Bring this up at a Trustees' meeting."

Papa was not told of Mr. Cabot's response, so he had James Brosnahan approach the chief executive again in November. The only reaction this time was an offer by the B.S.O. to purchase annuities on my father's behalf with money due to him from record royalties instead of just passing on the royalties directly.

In March 1963 Mr. Brosnahan went directly to Mr. Cabot: "Mr. Fiedler has again called my attention to the fact that his salary as Conductor of the Pops is, in his opinion, inadequate. I did not mention the decision of the Board, reached at the meeting held on Dec. 19, 1962, that you were contemplating commissioning a portrait to be hung in Symphony Hall with suitable unveiling ceremonies to be held on his 70th birthday, two years hence."

Papa's Pops salary remained at $12,500. The portrait was never commissioned; in fact, neither my father's name nor his picture is to be found on permanent display in the public areas of Symphony Hall.

Not that the Boston Symphony couldn't express its gratitude. In February 1969 the manager wrote to my father, agreeing that Papa's dues to the B.S.O. pension fund be waived after fifty-three years, "with a very warm feeling of gratitude for the great support you have offered the Pension Institution over these many years."

Papa did not help himself financially when he conducted other orchestras. He flatly refused to engage a manager, someone who could have negotiated appropriate fees for him. "They didn't want to have anything to do with me when I needed them [as a young conductor]. Now they need *me*, and I don't want to have anything to do with them." Most people in the music industry interpret this statement to mean that Papa wasn't interested in paying commissions on his fees.

He was unable to stop the Boston Symphony from contracting Columbia Artists Management to book the outside engagements for the Pops, and these are the few appearances for which my father did earn fees commensurate with his experience and fame. Despite himself, he liked the Columbia manager who worked on the Pops, and always greeted him warmly when he arrived in Papa's dressing room at one of these concerts. "Here's the flesh peddler!" he would snarl, but then he would pull out his Jack Daniels bottle and give the agent a drink, a rare gesture of friendship and trust.

But Papa distrusted Ronald Wilford, the powerful president of Columbia Artists. "He's not a nice man," he warned me once at a party given by Seiji Ozawa. The remark was made in a dramatic stage whisper that Ronald could not have helped overhearing, since he was only five feet away. After Papa died, I talked over the incident with Wilford, whom I admired and who pointed out to me that he had constantly tried to convince my father that he was badly underselling himself. He also believed that Papa went to the wrong orchestras; he should have been limiting himself to the best few. "If someone walked up to him on the street and offered him a concert, he'd do it," Ronald said in complete frustration.

This was absolutely true, but my father believed he had an obligation to go to the small orchestras. Other famous conductors wouldn't consider them. He knew his audiences very well—they lived in small towns all across the United States and were a little frightened of "classical music." Papa had built his career in the 1950s with his backbreaking cross-continental trips with the Boston Pops Tour Orchestra, playing one-night stands in places no other symphony orchestra had ever been. He knew the importance of direct contact between the musician and his audience, and when he became famous, he wasn't satisfied to rest on his enormous record sales and massive fees from the "Big Five" orchestras. He remembered the people who had given him his success, and he kept conducting for them. Papa may have been a miser with money, but he was generous with his musical spirit.

The question of record royalties was more straightforward, since a large, profit-making corporation was involved, and Papa was successful over the years in increasing his share from a seventh of the gross royalties from RCA to a third. The Boston Symphony retained two-thirds. But in 1969 the Boston Symphony was faced with a dilemma when RCA decided not to renew its recording contract with the orchestra but wished to retain their relationship with the Boston Pops. The B.S.O. management approached several other record companies and entered into serious negotiations with Deutsche Grammophon. The German company, however, was interested only if the Boston Symphony deal included the Pops.

The B.S.O. realized that this was one situation in which they could not take their usual cavalier attitude toward my father's feelings. His recordings had become a major bargaining issue. Recognizing that loyalty was one of my father's strongest characteristics, and knowing that he felt an allegiance to RCA despite his fights with them over repertoire, the B.S.O. administration approached him with great caution.

Papa's instant reaction to changing record companies was negative, as everyone expected. I remember him moping around the house in the spring of 1969 over the prospect of being forced to leave RCA, the label he had been with since 1935. Just as he had been averse to leaving Boston and the Boston Symphony, he was not eager to sever the profitable and enjoyable relationship with RCA. He was personally close to many of the people at the company, especially his record producer at the time, Peter Dellheim, who had joined Bill Shisler and Bill Cosel as nearly adopted sons.

But the Boston Symphony had to move on, and, as always, Papa's ultimate loyalty was to the orchestra. There were solid reasons for him to join the move to Deutsche Grammophon. The RCA proposal for continuing with the Pops alone was for only four records a year, at least initially; in addition, Deutsche Grammophon was interested in exploring music my father had not conducted for years, including works by such little-known composers as Goldmark, Auber, and David, giving him the chance to record more serious pieces; and there was also the possibility of a more favorable royalty agreement.

But his reluctance was not all on a rational level, and he was genuinely sad about leaving RCA. Internal memos flew between B.S.O. administrators concerning Papa's state of mind about the recording issue, and there were constant efforts to reassure him about the beneficial aspects of the move in terms of recognition for him and the Pops. In June 1969 Papa grudgingly said he "would go along with" the B.S.O.

RCA in the meantime was busily appealing to Papa's sentimental side, a part of his nature he rarely exposed but which was a potent force. It enabled my father, for once, to keep the B.S.O. management on tenterhooks, something that his own self-esteem had never managed to do, but in the end Papa did what the Boston Symphony asked.

In December of 1969, RCA gave a luncheon at the Four Seasons in New York to celebrate my father's seventy-fifth birthday and to thank him for the thirty-five-year association they had shared. The *New York Times* article about the event commented: "The B.S.O., of which Mr. Fiedler has been an integral part of the past 55 years, has signed new recording contracts with Deutsche Grammophon and Mr. Fiedler has no choice but to go along with the orchestra in its new association." This was not precisely true, but my father did derive some pleasure from having the Symphony shown as the public villain in at least this situation. Although he loathed public speaking and what he referred to as "talking conductors," he made an exception at the luncheon; he gave a touching farewell to his record company, comparing his involuntary departure from the ranks of Red Seal artists to "a divorce from a wife you still love."

The exclusive B.S.O. contract with Deutsche Grammophon lasted only a couple of years, and by 1972 Papa was back recording with RCA, although he never again was an exclusive artist with any record company.

I HAVE OFTEN ASKED MYSELF exactly why Papa stayed on in Boston when he was clearly so unhappy and frustrated. He felt unappreciated—the orchestra didn't seem to value him enough even to exploit him—and, much as he admired the Boston Brahmins, I suspect he felt that his being Jewish meant he was viewed as "foreign," an outsider. The memories I have of my father dressed so correctly as a Bostonian in his tweed jackets with leather elbow patches or his made-to-order suits from London, all the while sprinkling his conversations with Yiddish expressions in a perfectly cadenced New England accent, were confusing. I also knew that my father had grown up with German as his primary language and, to all reports, spoke a *"hoch Deutsche"* roughly analogous to his accent in English. Yet he was only a generation removed from his family home town in Eastern Europe. My head would spin.

Papa's being Jewish certainly affected his relationship with the Boston Symphony management and trustees, but the major reason he instinctively hesitated to insist on his rights after a long and honorable career was that he conducted popular music. It didn't matter how many records he sold; it didn't matter how many honorary degrees he collected; it didn't matter how often he reminded everyone of the triumphs he collected outside Boston. He felt that the trustees condescended to him, and he accepted their behavior as appropriate.

My father often defended his decision to stay in Boston by acknowledging the excellence of the orchestra he had at his disposal. "It's always fun to drive a Cadillac, if you know what I mean," he said in interview after interview. He also developed a convoluted theory that the management in Boston was more liberal than any other in the artistic license it granted to its conductors. "I was born lucky, I think. I have a great variety of musical taste and I would be bored to do the same kind of thing all the time. This is one reason I've been tempted to stay so long in Boston. It is a tradition that Boston Symphony conductors can do exactly what they please. If you want to go out on a limb and hang yourself, hang yourself, that's all."

The Symphony management let Papa go out on a limb and earn

a fortune for the orchestra, but they scorned him for the way he earned that money, and he understood how they felt. In the final analysis, he forced himself to accept this; I'm not sure I will ever be able to do the same.

Life at the Boston Symphony improved for my father during the last five years of his life. When Seiji Ozawa became music director, the orchestra for the first time had a conductor who respected my father and his achievements. In sharp contrast to the outright hostility displayed by Koussevitzky and the indifference shown by his three successors, Ozawa seemed to revere my father. My father had already been conducting the Pops for several years at the time of Ozawa's birth, and Ozawa, the last B.S.O. music director that my father would know, honored the Japanese tradition of respecting older people. Papa responded warmly, soaking up Ozawa's affection and returning it with his own. He even overcame his traditional distaste for his colleagues' children when Ozawa's daughter was born. I can remember a party at the Ozawas' Tanglewood house where Papa spent most of his time with the two-year-old. Mrs. Ozawa intervened rapidly in this burgeoning friendship when she discovered that Papa was feeding her baby straight gin, probably one of the few ways he was able to show his liking for the little girl.

Papa's affection for Tom Morris's children reflected his delight at Tom's becoming the orchestra's manager. Tom sent the orchestra on tours and instituted Christmas Pops and New Year's Pops, both of which sold out immediately and then became traditions. He tried to guide Papa's choice of outside engagements and gently to advise him on cutting down his schedule, two endeavors inevitably doomed, despite Papa's liking for Tom. It is ironic that in those last years, when Papa's abilities were quickly declining, he at last enjoyed a camaraderie and sense of collegiality with both the orchestra's music director and manager. I think it helped him make a little bit of peace with the inevitable decline in his old age.

# SEVEN

## Papa and the Other Men in My Life

A S I GOT OLDER, my father seemed to find me more interesting. Maybe he appreciated my interest in everything that went on at Symphony Hall; maybe it was just that I was the first of his children to reach the age when intelligent conversation was possible. When I was around twelve, he began to pay more attention to me, and we spent more time together when he was in Boston.

He observed that I loved music and listened to it at every opportunity, and he responded. My mother certainly wasn't interested in the musical part of his existence, even though it was the most important to him. She actively resented his career because she felt it supplanted her in his life. So Papa encouraged me. He gave me one of his old record players and a handful of LPs he didn't want. Soon I was shut in my room listening to my new record collection whenever I could.

Papa would invite me into his private sanctuary to listen to new records he had bought or been sent, and he taught me how to follow along with the score. When I had learned to read an orchestral score, he lent me miniature scores from his precious collection to take along when I went to concerts. In the course of all this, Papa taught me an enormous amount about music history and theory. I started to feel closer to him and more comfortable when we spent time together.

My mother was incensed. She felt that Papa didn't spend enough time with her in the first place, and now he had turned to a gawky adolescent for companionship in the brief periods he was home. She complained bitterly about how loudly I played my records when Papa was away and even seemed irritated that my schoolwork wasn't suffering from my new fascination with music. I was just entering puberty, but Mummy ignored all the obvious signs of what was happening to me physically, leaving me swamped by the new symptoms and feelings. These were things I couldn't talk to my father about.

When I was in my mid-teens, Papa started taking me with him on brief trips. We went to Tanglewood when my mother didn't want to go, and he took me to New York a couple of times. We discovered, to our mutual surprise, that by this time I was more than able to hold my own in adult gatherings and could contribute intelligently to the conversations.

I was particularly surprised by my newfound ability since I was a disaster socially with my schoolmates. I was tongue-tied and awkward; my interests in music and literature were foreign to the hearty, hockey-playing girls I went to school with; and I'm sure I was obnoxious about the superiority of my own pastimes. Grownups, on the other hand, seemed to understand what intrigued me and encouraged me to learn more.

"You made a big hit," Papa would say to me after one of these adventures, and nothing could have been more satisfying. I had finally discovered at least one way to please him. I worked as hard as I could at overcoming my natural shyness around Papa's adult friends so that I could keep going places with him. Of course there was a fair amount of drinking on these occasions, and I used to cause some amusement when I asked for the only drink I then knew how to order—what Papa drank, gin on the rocks. I would end up with sherry or Dubonnet, but that was all right. The warmth of the alcohol made me even less shy, and it was easier to speak up.

As I grew, my father seemed to realize that he had a home-grown companion who would go with him anywhere on a moment's notice and be able to hold her own, even to his exacting standards. From the age of fifteen, I was a regular member of Papa's entourage when he went on "runouts." Runouts were concert engagements the Pops did around New England that did not require it to stay overnight. Papa loved these expeditions, and for the first time I was seeing my father relaxed and happy on a regular basis.

He was usually driven to these concerts by John Cahill, whom my mother disliked and often snubbed. Uncle John, as Peter, Debbie, and I called him, was the archetypal Boston politician. He was an elected sheriff in Somerville, Massachusetts, where he lived and owned a liquor store, although he never touched a drop of alcohol himself.

Papa had met him while serving with the Coast Guard during World War II. His first night on duty, he was greeted with incredulous stares and more than slight resentment from the other reservists. Uncle John later admitted that he immediately suspected a public relations stunt on the part of both the Coast Guard and Papa. "Grab a mop" were his first words to my father; they endeared him to Papa immediately.

Uncle John, whose rough style and enormous heart were accompanied by an unfailing nose for pretentiousness, admitted that he quickly discovered Papa to be one of the most down-to-earth people he had ever met. This side of my father was not my mother's favorite, but when he was with Uncle John he felt comfortable letting it show.

Papa and Uncle John always stopped at diners when they were traveling to or from runouts; they would sit at the counter or in a booth, arguing loudly about almost anything that came up in conversation. While Uncle John was driving, Papa would perch in the front seat beside him, sipping from a bottle of Jack Daniels. Unlike my mother, Uncle John would not have cared if Papa came to a meal without his shirt; as far as he was concerned, Papa could have eaten while completely nude.

Uncle John not only did not require elegant behavior, but would not have put up with it if Papa had tried it on. He had known my father too well and for too long, and he was confident that he had the friendship of the real Arthur, the one almost no one else ever saw. This new Papa was a revelation to me, and I begged to be taken along on runouts. But I was careful not to tell anyone at home about them. This other Papa belonged to me, and I guarded him jealously. I didn't want anyone else knowing about my secret father.

AS MY FATHER started noticing me more, I took a greater interest in what I looked like. Strangely enough, in a family obsessed with the necessity of presenting a perfect public front, none of us children was aware of the need to pay more attention to how we looked than just being neat and clean. Possibly this was because my mother couldn't imagine any other female in the family drawing attention away from her any more than my father could ever consider Peter handsome.

Mummy was an attractive woman in a Bostonian way and she was secure about her looks, if about nothing else. She was convinced that she was a great beauty, and, in fact, even well into her fifties, she looked years younger and had a natural vibrancy and radiance. How she managed to look so good when she was so unhappy and was constantly abusing her body, I don't know. By the time she was in her sixties, the drinking had caught up with her. She looked puffy and bloated, and once I heard someone backstage say, "That old lady is Fiedler's wife? That's amazing." My mother's fantasy world protected her from more than just my father; she was certain of her beauty until she died.

Debbie and I never even entered into competition with our mother for attention in the area of looks. One of the many problems of my family's public profile was the pictures of all of us that appeared now and then in the newspapers. Any shred of self-confidence we managed to attain was usually destroyed by a typically unflattering candid family portrait in the *Herald* or the *Globe*. I

would stare at my hideous hairdos, hating my short hair, then timidly ask my mother whether it would be okay if I grew it. My
mother would sniff and say, "With that little face? Your face is too
small to be covered with a lot of hair," and I would give up. Only
when I was ready to go to college did I stand up for myself and let
my hair grow long.

As a child I was skinny or overweight, with an expression in
most of my pictures of sheer terror. By the time I turned into a
teenager, I had pretty much given up hope. One night, however, I
overheard a Pops musician say to another, "That older daughter is
going to be very pretty when she grows up." I stared in the mirror
for days afterward, trying to figure out what he had seen that I
couldn't see.

I got almost no such reassurance from my parents. Papa certainly
never thought I was attractive when I was younger. "Why don't
you have some color in your cheeks?" he constantly prodded me.
"Get outside into the fresh air. You look like a piece of cheese."

Until I blossomed a little socially as an adolescent, I was para-
lyzed with shyness. Papa often had to jerk my finger out of my
mouth when I stood before a stranger. My convent-bred mother
taught me to curtsey when I was introduced to someone new and
insisted I go on doing this until I was taller than some of the
people I was curtseying to. Gawky as I was, I was firmly packed off
to dancing school, and when I appeared one afternoon in the front
hall in my first pair of very low high heels, Papa choked on his gin.
"She looks like a French prostitute," he said to my mother, chortling.

But as I got older, he expressed admiration. "You have very
good legs," he told me when I was in my late teens. "Look at her
profile," he said once to a whole room full of people at Symphony
Hall. "She's just the type I used to go for." He flirted outrageously
with me and, after some initial surprise, I flirted right back. After
all, I saw that this infuriated my mother.

Once, for some reason, he compared me with Clementine Chur-
chill. "Oh, don't be ridiculous, Popie," my mother said. "*She* was a
great beauty."

An early music lesson with Papa (who's got Debbie in his lap). My expression of trepidation was usual on these occasions. *(Author's collection)*

I played in my first piano competition when I was five. *(Author's collection)*

My father outside the house on Hyslop Road in 1948. *(Author's collection)*

Debbie and I onstage at the opening of the twenty-fifth season of the Esplanade Concerts, in July 1953. Also shown are (left) Christian Herter, governor of Massachusetts; (center) Michael J. Kelleher, fire commissioner of the City of Boston and one of Papa's good friends; and Papa. *(Author's collection)*

Papa and Sparky parked at the stage door of Symphony Hall in the 1950s. Note the Boston Fire Department plates and police-radio antenna, standard equipment on my father's cars. *(Author's collection)*

In 1953, while on the road with his tour orchestra, Papa was made a chief in the Otoe tribe in Stillwater, Oklahoma. *(Courtesy of the Boston Symphony Orchestra)*

During a concert in the early 1960s, the musicians of the Boston Pops Orchestra presented Papa with a beer dispenser for his dressing room. Here he thanks them as he samples a product of his new gift. *(Photo by Photography Incorporated, courtesy of the Boston Symphony Orchestra)*

Papa loved posing for his record covers. This photograph, a take-off on a famous advertisement for Tabu perfume, was used on the album of "Great Music for Great Lovers." *(Courtesy of RCA)*

A major part of my adolescence was spent at Logan Airport in Boston, either dropping off or picking up my father. In this photo, he has just arrived and does not look happy to be home. *(James R. Holland)*

Papa and I rarely had a meal together in public without an interruption by a fan. Here we are having breakfast at a White Castle in Washington, D.C., because Papa hated paying hotel prices. *(James R. Holland)*

A rare photograph of the whole family together, taken at Papa's seventy-fifth birthday party, in 1969, following a concert he conducted with the Boston Symphony: (left to right) Peter, Papa, Debbie, me, my mother. *(Photo by Photography Incorporated, courtesy of the Boston Symphony Orchestra)*

Papa driving his very own fire engine, a present given to him on his seventy-fifth birthday. *(Courtesy of the Boston Symphony Orchestra)*

Papa with Sparky II, the puppy given to him by the Boston Symphony Orchestra for his eightieth birthday, in 1974. *(Photograph by William Shisler, courtesy of the Boston Symphony Orchestra)*

Papa and I at a party in New York in 1977, two years before his death. *(Author's collection)*

How I'll remember Papa best: at work, studying his scores. *(Courtesy of the Boston Symphony Orchestra)*

"So's Yummy," Papa replied. He probably said it to irritate her, but I still felt a small glow.

He never stopped hounding me about matters of taste. "Never leave home without taking one thing off," he said as we went off to concerts; he thought I had a tendency to wear too much jewelry. "You look like a Gypsy."

Sometimes he'd say, "Those earrings are too big for your face." I'd often ask for his opinion of dresses I bought, because his taste was much more reliable than my mother's. He bought me the only hat I've ever worn, and he enjoyed picking out my shoes and handbags—especially when I paid for them myself. But his taste was conservative, and after he was gone, it took me years to try even cautious experimentation with clothes. I had not learned to trust my own instincts.

I certainly never tried to dress like other girls my own age, mostly because I had no friends. I hated the Winsor School because of the other students. Most of the girls were the daughters of the same Boston Brahmins who were Symphony trustees or their close relatives. They all had straight blond hair and wore kilts, Brooks Brothers sweaters, and penny loafers and carried themselves with an air of confidence that terrified me. To hide my fear, I wore black sweaters and skirts and flats and kept to myself as much as possible.

The other girls quickly made me aware that my pedigree was unacceptable. When, on one tremulous occasion, I admitted that I admired President Kennedy, one supercilious classmate looked over at me and sneered. "Well, *you* would, wouldn't you," she said. "You're Catholic." Being half Catholic and half Jewish at a school overwhelmingly Episcopalian was difficult, especially because the other girls seemed compelled to point out my background at every opportunity. I might have survived if I had been good at field hockey, lacrosse, or tennis, but I wasn't. I was hopelessly awkward. My classmates' faces would fall when I was assigned to their team, and I was always the last person picked if the students were allowed to select their own sides. I felt so left out and miserable that I even tried to talk to my mother about it. She wasn't the least bit sympathetic, and instead of offering support, told me stories about her triumphant career as captain of the hockey team at Sacred Heart. When, on rare occasions, she came to mother-daughter sports days, she loved to grab my hockey stick from me and dash down the field with the team, dribbling the ball expertly the whole way.

Gradually I began to blame the whole city of Boston, instead of this small group of haughty young girls, for my sense of isolation and the feeling that I was unacceptably different. In addition to being half Irish-Catholic and half Jewish, I was the daughter of someone who was famous, and that didn't go over well in the immodestly self-effacing Yankee community.

People in Boston are quick to deny any anti-Semitism or anti-Catholicism and point to the city's long tradition of political liberalism. But I grew up there. The girls in my class at Winsor were open about their attitudes when we were young, and when we got old enough to be more discreet, they patronized me. "Oh," one former classmate said to me years later, "they just felt awkward because you came from a famous family." The sad part about all this was that Winsor was a superb school and I got an excellent and demanding education.

So I was lonely in high school, and at home I barricaded myself in my room with my chihuahua, Bennie. The one member of the family whose approval I yearned for was away or was busy at Symphony Hall. My sister tried to be a companion but finally gave up on me. "You always wanted to be alone," she told me afterward, and she turned to Peter for company. I began to see my brother and sister as allied against me.

One aspect of my childhood that I am still sad about is that Debbie, Peter, and I saw one another as rivals rather than as friends and fellow sufferers. Living in a big house where we each had our own bedroom, and having no exemplars of support and communication in our parents, we learned early to amuse ourselves and not to rely on anyone else. When we grew up, the separateness we felt from each other proved impossible to bridge.

When I looked for pictures to include in this book, I searched for photos of the three of us as adolescents. There is none, except for a not very good picture the three of us arranged to have taken as a gift to our parents on their twenty-fifth wedding anniversary. And, after that picture, there is none at all of the three of us together, except for a few from press coverage of Papa's funeral. I asked both Debbie and Peter if they could remember pictures that I had overlooked. They knew of none. We rarely visit each other, we speak briefly on birthdays and holidays, we often fight, and even at the best times, we are not close. I miss having a connection with my sister and brother, but I don't see how it could have turned out any differently.

Although I had little connection with my siblings, I was pretty sure the people at Symphony Hall liked me, and I liked them. I went out of my way to make friends with the Symphony staff and the musicians. By my late teens, I had a few older friends—my father's secretary, one of his former assistants, one or two of the orchestra's administrators, a couple of the musicians in the Pops. I'm surprised I got as much of a response as I did from these older people. Maybe my loneliness was so apparent that they felt sorry for me.

I had dates with boys my age, but they weren't very successful. One night I came home from a difficult evening and ran into my mother, coming downstairs for one of her midnight rambles. I was feeling so desperate that I tried confiding in her. "Can I talk to you about something?" I asked. It was clear from my face that I had been crying, and I had come in late enough for her to have known I'd been out for the evening.

"Is something wrong?" she asked, sounding a little nervous.

"It's a long story."

"Oh, in that case, I know the best thing for you," she answered. "You go up to your room and get into bed and I'll be up in a moment."

Obediently, I went to my room. Within minutes, my mother knocked, obviously anxious that I not disturb whatever she was doing downstairs. She was carrying a large glass of bourbon and ice —I think a maraschino cherry was floating in it as a frivolous touch because I was so young—and a sleeping pill. "Take the pill and drink this up," my mother commanded, and I did. I don't even remember her leaving the room. I was seventeen and had just learned a valuable lesson, I thought, in how to deal with trouble in my life.

At about this time I was making up my mind about college. The pre-eminent goal I had in continuing my education was to get away from Boston. I think I also knew that the only hope for me emotionally was to get away from home physically.

Sarah Lawrence College, just outside New York City, was one of the most difficult colleges in the country to get into at that time, and this aroused all my determination. I would show my class-mates one last time how intelligent I was by being admitted to a highly competitive school.

There was also the not inconsiderable detail that Papa had inde-pendently picked out Sarah Lawrence as the school for me. He was attracted by the school's liberal attitudes: the lack of rules, the absence of grades, the emphasis on the development of self-reli-ance and self-direction in the students. He thought it would be a good place for me and was delighted when I decided to apply. But his mind was permanently made up about Sarah Lawrence when he sat next to an unknown woman during a flight on one of his trips. "Where is your daughter going to go to college?" the woman asked in the course of their airplane conversation.

"Sarah Lawrence College," Papa replied.

"Goodness," the woman said, "I'm surprised you'd let her go there. That's an evil place."

From that moment on, Papa's mind was defiantly set. I was to go to Sarah Lawrence and nowhere else.

I WAS SEVENTEEN when I left the house on Hyslop Road for my first year at college. Leaving home was an enormous adjust-ment for me; as I learned much later, children from troubled fami-lies almost always have more trouble getting used to new situa-tions than children from happier environments. I had become so accustomed to a perverse family situation that it took a long time for me to get my bearings at Sarah Lawrence.

Once I did, however, things improved immediately. For the first time in my life, I was surrounded by people my own age, and I made friends. Being the child of a famous parent was no stigma at a school filled with children and relatives of other famous people, so I stopped feeling like a curiosity. No one cared who my father was; I could behave almost any way I wanted without hearing the whisper: "Think how this will reflect on your father."

There was one way, though, in which my father did not retreat from my life. He remained a presence in every relationship I had with a man. I was late in getting interested in the male sex, and when my interest began to develop, it did so in the slightly twisted manner of most things that happened to me as I grew up.

From the time I was in my mid-teens, I seemed to appeal to a certain kind of man—older, more interesting to me than boys my own age, and usually from Papa's circle. My mother was horrified by the men I attracted. "What is she doing with men like that?" I overheard her ask my father once. She thought they were too old and too sophisticated for me, and she was probably right.

"She likes them because they're interested in the things she's interested in," my father said, much to my surprise. "Boys her own age aren't interested in opera and chamber music and books. She doesn't have anything in common with them."

Although the people I was friendly with at Symphony Hall were much older than I, there was no problem when I established friendships with women or with gay men. But when I began to spend time with two or three men who were older and heterosexual, the associations proved more complicated. The straight men probably had complex reasons for spending time with me, beyond feeling sorry for a lonely teenager, and I was certainly aware of some sexual attraction toward them. At about that time, I got my driver's license and, with it, more freedom, especially since my father was away most of the time, and my mother appeared not to notice what I was doing.

In addition to the stirrings of my sexual appetite, my relationships with older men had other ramifications. Both my parents appeared to be oblivious of what I was doing, but I certainly knew that they would have been horrified had they been aware. I wonder now whether they didn't know all along—at that age I was not very practiced at being discreet—and chose not to make an issue of it. Maybe I was trying to get them to pay attention to me in the only way I could, but I wasn't successful. My mother fussed a little about some of the more obvious things I did, such as going out on dinner dates with a man twenty years older, but for a long time she never overtly forbade me from doing so; after all, she had done exactly the same thing when she was about my age. By the time she did start banning these meetings, it was too late. I had learned about subterfuge.

My father simply didn't deal with the issue. I assume my mother talked to him about my disgraceful flirtations with older men, but he never spoke to me about any of it. I became even more brazen, meeting musicians from the orchestra during Papa's concerts at Symphony Hall, where my father would have had to be blind and deaf not to have known what was going on. In fact, Papa, who often boasted about being psychic, did indeed have an uncanny ability to sense when any of his children was doing something secretive. He would explode and then try to make us understand that it was the duplicity that angered him more than whatever transgression we were trying to hide. But in the case of my adventures with older men, most of whom were his friends, he never confronted me.

Throughout my adulthood, Papa rarely referred to my involvements with men, and then only obliquely. I remember one night when, in the conductor's dressing room at Carnegie Hall, he told me how concerned he was about Peter's romantic life. He had once feared that Peter would become effeminate, growing up as he did surrounded "only by women who spoiled him." When this dire prediction turned out to be unfounded, Papa progressed to worrying about Peter's showing an inclination to obsessive involvements. It didn't matter how many girlfriends he had; he always was most interested in the one who was unattainable. Papa was appalled. "I keep telling Peter he shouldn't limit himself to one woman," Papa complained to me. "But he doesn't pay any attention."

"You never told *me* that," I said.

"I never had to," Papa answered with a suggestive smirk. Again I wondered how much he knew that he had never let on.

The men who became my friends, all much older, were complete gentlemen. They may have enjoyed my company, but they never took advantage of me sexually or in any other way. Life got more complicated, however, when I met a young musician in the Boston Symphony who was closer to my own age. He was new in the orchestra, wasn't a friend of my father, and had no special respect for him, either. For all these reasons, he had no qualms about a physical relationship with me, and I found in him someone to satisfy my sexual curiosity. I was, as always, careless about hiding the relationship, but this time things were different. Instead of avoiding the subject, my father was openly enraged.

I had heard Papa talk about this musician for months before I actually met him. My father used to come home for lunch and fume about the behavior of the younger musicians in the orchestra. This was the mid-1960s, and as attitudes began to shift in the world outside, changes filtered into the refined atmosphere of Symphony Hall. "We venerated the conductor in Muck's day," Papa said about his own early years in the B.S.O. "Doffed our hats if we met him on the street or backstage." This attitude completely changed by the end of my father's own career, and he disliked it. "You know," he said in 1977, "the other day, as I was leaving Carnegie Hall, a young member of the Pops came charging by. 'Hi, Arthur!' he yelled at me. Damned if I know his name. Imagine what would have happened in the days of Muck or Koussevitzky."

The younger musicians no longer felt compelled to treat their conductors with the exalted respect that had been customary until then. They especially felt no need to treat my father with respect, because they considered the Pops concerts unimportant. Just out of the conservatory, these young musicians held lofty ideals about music. Most of them were in the process of shedding dreams of solo careers and adjusting to the reality of life as an orchestral musician. Angry about having to lower their professional aspirations, some of them saw Papa, who to them symbolized commercialism in the arts, as an easy target. He responded to their contempt with outright fury, which must have strengthened their recalcitrance.

The cellist I became involved with during the mid-1960s was

one of the most rebellious of the younger musicians. He hated playing in an orchestra, hated being in the back of his section, and he took out his rage on anyone older and more established. In addition, his own father was a symphony conductor. Though they try to fight their instincts, orchestral musicians tend to react to their conductors as archetypal authority symbols—fathers, usually —so the cellist had an additional set of negative associations with my father.

Then he met me. I was an easy way to get revenge on one of the conductors he blamed for trapping him in an orchestra instead of giving him the solo career he thought he deserved. For me, uncomfortable in my close relationship with Papa, the cellist was useful in declaring the anger I didn't dare show more directly.

Papa found out about the cellist and me very quickly from his close friends in the orchestra. For a while, he said nothing, hoping that the matter would disappear naturally. But it didn't; even my going off to college didn't interfere, and our involvement deepened. We fought a great deal—I didn't know there was any other way of communicating with someone close. One or the other of us was always ending the affair, and I would get depressed. Papa noticed my growing depressions and decided to talk to me.

He never accused me of being disloyal to him by becoming involved with one of his musicians. This aspect of the situation was the cause of much of my guilt as well as the source of my slight sense of mastery over Papa's stranglehold on my life. "You *can't* do this!" was my father's most frequent argument in the bitter confrontations we had over the cellist. "He's a horrible person!" But this was to be one of the few times that I defied my father; I refused to stop seeing the man, and Papa became frantic.

He tried reasoning with me. "You can't let depression get the best of you," he would say. "Pull yourself up by the bootstraps." Or, "Go out and shovel some snow. That will get rid of your depression." Or, "Don't waste time getting depressed over a man. Men are like buses; there's always another one coming."

He tried yelling at me. This tactic would make me cry uncontrollably, but I would go right back to the man afterward. All of the feuding with my father made my love affair tense, but although my relationship with the musician became more difficult, I stayed with him.

Papa was angry but also concerned. During Christmas vacation, I was home from college for the holidays and began seeing the cellist. One snowy afternoon I went to the Boston Symphony matinee and gave him a ride home after the concert. We sat in the little black Volkswagen outside his apartment and, as we did so often, argued bitterly. Finally, he jumped out of the car, slammed the door, and rushed off. I was left alone, shivering and crying.

Still sobbing, I began driving back home through the rush-hour traffic. At Coolidge Corner, a major intersection in Brookline, just as I was stuck in a long bottleneck, the decrepit car began sputtering. I tried frantically to keep the motor going, but after a few clunks the car broke down completely. I had no idea what to do, and cried all the harder at the honking from surrounding car horns.

Then, to my amazement, I heard the toot of a familiar horn, and looked up to see my father in one of our other cars right next to me. I rolled down the window, as did he. "I was sitting at home, and I had the feeling something was wrong, so I came out to look for you," he said simply. "I'm psychic, you know."

Immediately, a sense of safety filled me, even though I was upset about the fight with the cellist. I had strayed into a dangerous part of life, but my father had rescued me, and this deepened his hold on me. Papa did not ask me where I had been—he probably didn't want to know—and he drove me home and arranged for a tow truck to deal with the Volkswagen. When we got back to Hyslop Road, we walked into the dark and chilly house, and Papa turned to me. "Let's have a drink," he said.

After the cellist and I finally parted, I became more circumspect with my father about my relationships with men. On one rare occasion, my father watched me at a party when I was flirting brazenly with a man he knew. The next morning, as I was driving him to Symphony Hall, he said, after much nervous silence and hesitation, "You know, you shouldn't be too obvious when you're interested in a man. It's not becoming."

I was embarrassed because I knew that I had made a mistake. The mistake wasn't trying to seduce a man my father knew; it was

that I had done it in front of him. I thought I had learned long ago
to be surreptitious.

I didn't know what to say, having broken one of the unspoken
rules that existed between us, so I tried a new tactic. "I know," I
said to him. "You're absolutely right. I won't do it again."

My father gave me an astonished look but didn't say another
word, which in turn astonished me. I smiled to myself; I had
learned another lesson in subterfuge. All I had to do was lie and
then go on doing exactly what I wanted. Apparently this worked,
because he and I never again had a conversation about my personal
life.

I desperately wanted to avoid having such conversations, since
my involvements with men were the one area in which I did something he didn't want me to do. This part of my life was my secret,
my way of not being exactly what he wanted me to be. Men were
important to me, and I clung to my friendships with them, but
always in secret.

Papa gave me lots of generalized advice. "It doesn't take any
brains to get pregnant" was one of his more pungent refrains. He
rarely criticized the few men I dared to introduce to him, whether
I was involved with them or not, but the disdainful expression on
his face was usually enough to dissuade me from seeing them
again. I don't know how I ever had the courage to introduce him to
anyone, but it was probably the only way I had of reminding him
that he wasn't the only man in the world. Unfortunately, this was
mere bravado. To me he was the only man, and no one else was
able to meet the standards he set for me.

That is another problem with having a famous father. When I
was with a "normal" man, I didn't trust my own judgment in
deciding whether he was someone special. I looked to my father to
reinforce my opinion about almost everything in my life, but my
relations with men should have been outside this area.

Occasionally Papa picked out a man for me, usually one of his
acolytes. Most of the time, the hand-picked male was about my
age and was obsessed with classical music. Early on, I had developed a theory that nearly all men who loved classical music had
something seriously wrong with them. They were usually not out-

going, often not good-looking, and they were involved with music to a degree that frightened me. I knew from my own lonely childhood how welcome an outlet a love of music could be, but I had little respect for these men, who seemed to find a similar solution for their loneliness. I even developed a scale of unattractiveness depending on what kind of music the man liked. Men who liked opera tended to be the most acceptable; they were almost normal and could even be glamorous. Men who liked symphonic music were passable; lots of doctors and lawyers, who by and large bored me, went to New York Philharmonic and Boston Symphony concerts, and they were presentable, if not glamorous. But men who liked chamber music were hopeless. And the absolute worst were men who enjoyed solo piano recitals.

Papa's fans were often avid record collectors. Some of them had contacted him because they knew about some of his out-of-print records that dated from the early days of his career, when he had recorded a lot of serious symphonic music. Because he was desperate to be recognized as someone who could conduct "real" music, these compulsive record collectors touched one of his most vulnerable spots. He clung to them and the recognition they provided, and they happily made tapes for him of arcane music they had unearthed and hoped that he would perform someday. I did agree to meet a couple of these people, but they weren't right for me. They answered a need in my father, not in me.

Only once did my own interest and my father's approval coincide. Papa was conducting the Baltimore Symphony, and I went to the concert with a friend of mine, an Iranian conductor named Farhad Mechkat, who was the assistant conductor of the New York Philharmonic. Farhad seemed the epitome of sophistication. He was handsome in an exotic way, elegantly dressed and well turned out, and he smoked French cigarettes, which to me surrounded him with a sensual European aura.

After the concert, I took Farhad backstage, and my father, as always, bridled visibly when I introduced my companion. But Farhad was a practiced charmer. He had grown up in Switzerland and later went back to Iran to conduct the Teheran orchestra, until the Ayatollah Khomeini's ban on classical music forced him to flee the country. Even by the time he met my father, he had been through a lot in his life, and Papa, after his first reaction, spotted a kindred spirit. Also, Farhad was a very funny man. My father loved a partner with whom to trade witticisms, and by the time we sat down to dinner, I knew the two conductors were going to have a wonderful time together. Although there must have been a fifty-year age difference, Farhad and Papa spent the evening swapping stories about orchestras they had both conducted as well as those neither of them had led. They told jokes, made puns, dropped names, and had a collegially good time. I watched in amazement and delight. From then on, I thought, it would be possible to satisfy both my father and myself; I'd just have to keep finding cosmopolitan, successful, articulate, and respectful young conductors. Needless to say, this proved difficult, though I tried my best. My father died too soon afterward to meet any more of my conductor quarries, but the thought that he might have liked and even respected them was almost enough for me.

The men who did interest me were of a very specific type, in any case. It didn't really matter if they were conductors, but the type suited the conducting profession well. Having grown up with a father who demanded and expected full attention all the time, I was uncomfortable around men who were less exacting. When I met a man who was happy to have me be the center of attention, I didn't know what to do. If, on the other hand, the man wanted to dominate every gathering, no matter how small, I knew exactly how to behave. Paradoxically, the more the man needed to be the focal point, the more outgoing I became. The years of being charming and witty for my father's friends had trained me well; I didn't appear to be shy at all when I was with someone outgoing and charismatic. But it was agony for me to go to a large party by myself. When I was alone, with no man to compete with or be protected by, I was overwhelmed by awkwardness and fear.

AFTER MY UNHAPPY RELATIONSHIP with the cellist, I stayed away from Boston Symphony musicians for a long time. But in the early 1970s, I met another B.S.O. player who fitted the mold I found irresistible: rebellious, unavailable, unpresentable in almost every way. I thought him fascinating. Even though I saw how old and sick my father was, I wasn't able to stop myself from another secret involvement with a man I was sure Papa would hate.

I had heard a great deal about this man, whom I'll call Tony, before meeting him; he lived in a particularly lurid style amid the mostly bourgeois B.S.O. musicians. He was known to have had a drug problem, and he was an infamous womanizer; he was even rumored to have seduced a member of the board of trustees. I had seen Tony backstage on several occasions, and we exchanged glances that clearly expressed a mutual attraction. Eventually I manipulated a meeting with him. We became friends and began an involvement that lasted for several years. Since we lived in different cities, we both had serious relationships with other people most of the time we knew each other, but a genuine fondness grew between us.

This time, however, the interplay between my father, the musician, and myself was somewhat more complex. I noticed that Papa, over time, lost his initial animosity toward this boisterous young orchestra member and actually seemed to be growing fonder of him. It helped that Tony loved popular music, unlike his more stuffy colleagues, and he often suggested pieces to my father for Pops arrangements. Papa began summoning him into the Green Room before the concerts to chat, one of the clearest indications that he liked someone. Even my father, who affected a complete lack of interest in the psychological make-up of his musicians, seemed to sense the gentleness that lay under Tony's disreputable exterior. Papa's affection for him persisted through at least one drug arrest and a series of emotional problems. So did my attachment; he was my friend, and I stayed loyal through some difficult times for him, and he did the same for me. I saw him whenever I was in Boston, and we always met when the Boston Symphony was in New York.

On Christmas Eve of 1973, the family gathered as usual at our house for the holiday dinner. Papa was tired because the Boston Symphony had just inaugurated what was to become one of its most lucrative series, Christmas Pops. He had had to rehearse the orchestra and give a series of these extra concerts while doing his annual stint conducting the complete *Nutcracker* with the Boston Ballet.

The cocktail hour was even grimmer than usual. Papa barely sipped his drink and was in one of his silent moods; Mummy came down to dinner at the last possible second; the various Bottomley relations glared at the few Fiedlers present. I sat at the table staring at my plate, praying for the meal to be over, and then I heard a peculiar clanking sound. Looking up, I saw Papa hunched over his plate, his fork banging against the china. He was shivering uncontrollably. Everyone stared in horror, but no one had any idea what to do, because this was our first glimpse of fragility in the person who had always been the strongest of us.

At last we came to our senses, and someone called an ambulance. I sat, immobile, my mind refusing to register what was happening. The ambulance arrived; Papa went off to the hospital with Debbie and Peter. Mummy retired to her room, and other people cleared away the meal. I kept sitting at the table, surrounded by the wreckage of Christmas Eve dinner.

When I managed to rouse myself, I went into the library, picked up the phone, and called Tony. "Come over right away," he said when he heard how upset I was, and I did. He comforted me and was genuinely worried, because he was fond of Papa. I drove myself home at four o'clock in the morning, feeling better able to face what I had come to understand would be a long illness for my father. Once at home and in my room, I started to pull the curtains before turning on the light, a habit I'd carefully cultivated to keep Papa from knowing that I was still up. I stopped, my hand on the curtain cord, and remembered that there was no reason this night to worry about being found out.

Papa recovered from this bout of pneumonia after several months, Tony and I stayed friends, and our relationship continued for a while. My father and Tony became more friendly, and Papa never acknowledged that Tony and I even knew each other. This was a classic example of how I conducted my personal life while my father was alive, both of us careful to avoid confrontations. But in the winter of 1979 there was a bizarre turn of events.

One Sunday night in January, the phone rang in my apartment in New York. It was Tony, whom I hadn't spoken to in at least a year. His drug use had increased to the point where I tried to avoid him, and, hurt, he had stopped calling me. "Guess where I am," he said.

I couldn't.

"I'm at your house in Brookline."

For a few seconds, I couldn't grasp what he was saying. When I realized that he was actually at Hyslop Road, I couldn't imagine what he was doing there. My father was then recovering from brain surgery and was very weak, so it was unlikely that he had invited Tony to visit. My mother, I knew, was away.

"Do you want to say hello to your father?" Tony asked.

"I guess so." I hesitated because this was the first time one of my "secret" friendships had completely escaped from my control, illusory as that control may have been. Papa must be cold with anger, I thought.

"He came to visit me," my father said when he got to the phone. He sounded pleased, and I remembered with sharp guilt how sick he was, and how lonely he must have felt, stuck at home.

"He's a very nice person," I said.

"Where are you?" my father asked, confused. "Are you here?"

"I'm in New York."

"Why did you call?"

"I just wanted to see how you were doing," I lied. "Papa, is Peter there?"

The next voice I heard was my brother's. He sounded terrified. "Yummy," Peter said, "he's got a gun. He came here with a gun."

I was having trouble breathing. No one knew better than I how irrational Tony became when he was high, and I knew that he had been seriously out of control for several months. I told Peter to hang up and call the police or else I would. Peter agreed that he should make the call, and we hung up. I spent the next hour pacing my tiny apartment. I knew that Tony had come to love my father, and I wasn't afraid that he would hurt Papa, but he was so distraught that he couldn't be trusted to know what he was doing.

After what seemed like hours, I made myself dial the number in Brookline.

"He left," my brother reported. "He went away just as suddenly as he came."

"Thank God," I said.

My brother muttered something about hoping that I was satisfied this time, and angry as that remark made me, I felt I deserved it. My secret life had gone too far. My clandestine rebellion, combined with Tony's deteriorating emotional state and my Papa's iconic position, a father figure to both of us, had all collided in what could have been a disaster.

I never spoke to Tony again. Whenever we met at Symphony Hall, I looked away, and so did he. I knew he felt that I had let him down as a friend, but his problems were so gigantic that I didn't know how to help him anymore. And I was terrified of how close he had come to hurting my father.

Two or three years after Papa died, Tony failed to get a promotion in the orchestra that he had desperately wanted. He became even more despondent, and his attendance at rehearsals and performances was so sporadic that it was several days after he missed a concert before the Symphony thought to send someone to his apartment to see if he was all right. He wasn't all right. Alone in his apartment, only a mile from Hyslop Road, he had shot and killed himself, using the gun he had brought to our house that night in January.

# EIGHT

## Part of Papa's World

WHEN I FINISHED Sarah Lawrence, I never considered going back to live in Boston. There were to be difficult times in the coming years when I toyed with the idea of moving back home, but I didn't go through with any plans. If I had a conscious reason, it was that I could not bear the thought of living in a city where my father was a legend. I wanted to make my own mistakes by myself and do so as anonymously as possible. I couldn't live that way in Boston.

The relief I felt at having a geographical and physical distance from my family was powerful. What I didn't realize was that putting miles between my parents and me had no effect on their presence in my mind.

My choice of a career wasn't much help in my struggle to separate. When the time came for me to decide what to do after college, there was no question that I would somehow become a part of the music world. There should have been such a question, but my need to stay close to my father was stronger than the need to choose my own course.

Mummy seemed surprised that both my sister and I were determined to have jobs after we finished school and were, in fact, thinking in terms of careers. I had vehemently rejected a "coming-out" party to celebrate my debutante year and grudgingly went to only a few such festivities given by my classmates before I refused ever to attend another. My mother sourly acquiesced to my resistance because she sensed that this was a fight she was going to lose. My father completely supported my lack of interest in coming out, although I don't think he would have minded a daughter who had higher social aspirations. Two years later, he and my mother did give a coming-out party for Debbie, but he hated it and stayed only for a few minutes before going off to have dinner in a Chinese restaurant with one of his friends. By this time in his life, Papa realized that the social acceptance he had struggled for so diligently as a young man no longer had any relevance. He had become so successful that most of the people he had once wanted to impress were now in awe of him. And his success gave me the freedom to reject the coming-of-age rites prescribed by Boston society.

In high school and college, I had discovered that I loved to write and that, unlike with music, I had some ability in this area. I wrote simple stories about my daily life, and suddenly the teachers were complimenting me and asking me to read my stories aloud at school assemblies. I was surprised but delighted to find there was something I could do, without excruciating and futile effort, that people actually liked.

My father was proud of my interest in music. He respected my musical curiosity, even about opera, which he professed to loathe, and encouraged me to listen to everything and anything. He was also proud of my writing ability, particularly when it was acknowledged by others with occasional prizes and publication, but he carefully made sure I understood that my musical activities were more important.

I gave up early any thought of playing a musical instrument, but in college I earned extra money by working part time for small musical organizations. I worked one summer at WCRB, Boston's leading classical music station, spent another summer writing concert reviews for a small newspaper in Maine, and organized a chamber music series during my last two years at Sarah Lawrence. "You can really go somewhere in this business," Papa told me encouragingly.

He made clear his feelings about a career, however, the summer I was admitted to the Writers' Workshop at Aspen. I showed him my acceptance letter proudly, completely unprepared for his reaction. "No!" he said. "That's not how you're going to spend the summer. Being a writer is no way to make a living, and it's about time you started thinking seriously about what you're going to do after college. You'll never have any security if you're a writer; you'll never know where the next paycheck is coming from; you'll never be sure you can pay the rent. Get a real job!" Those weren't his exact words—I've long since buried them, along with any aspirations I had at the time. Battling Papa while trying to start life away from home was more than I could manage, so I capitulated without much of a fight, and I got another job with the Boston classical music radio station for the summer.

When I finished college, I took a real job. By now, I had acquiesced to Papa's desire that I follow him into music, although not as a performer. I went to work as a management intern at the National Symphony Orchestra in Washington, D.C., and this delighted my father. He told me frequently that he heard from other people how hard I worked and how much I was accomplishing, and I was happy to please him. His ambitions for me and mine for myself began to merge, and I started to achieve some success.

Papa's troubled affiliation with the Boston Symphony briefly affected my own career. As I became more aware of the high regard in which Papa was held by the world beyond Boston, I grew resentful on his behalf. I was most angered by the fact that he had only rarely been invited to conduct the regular Boston Symphony since the aborted engagement in 1944. Then, in 1969, the National Symphony in Washington, where I was working, invited Papa to conduct a purely serious symphonic concert to celebrate his seventy-fifth birthday.

The National Symphony sent out a press release in February 1969 to announce Papa's Washington concert and noted that the

Boston Symphony would be honoring his birthday at Symphony Hall with a similar concert. The press release was picked up and run by the *Boston Globe*. The only problem was that the Boston Symphony had not yet announced Papa's B.S.O. concert, and they were furious at being upstaged, especially at the *Globe*'s making a special point that the news came from Washington. "The National Symphony takes a special interest in Mr. Fiedler's activities," the *Globe* remarked and then pointed out that I worked with the Washington orchestra.

I was bewildered and upset. The job with the National Symphony was my first after college, and within months I was in trouble with my father's Boston Symphony. In fact, I had not written the press release, and the manager of the National Symphony was kind enough to point this out to the B.S.O. Thomas Perry, the B.S.O.'s manager, replied, "I was admittedly a bit chagrined at first because the *Globe* picked it up . . . but now I have nothing but benign thoughts about our distinguished colleague in the nation's capital."

Mr. Perry sent a blind carbon copy of this letter to the B.S.O.'s artistic administrator with the comment "The draft of the letter to Yummy Fiedler that you saw was never sent to her." I imagine that the unsent letter must have been pretty nasty, the implication being that, out of loyalty to my father, I had purposely scooped the Boston Symphony press office. The Symphony certainly was quick to react to any fractious behavior by the Fiedler family; had I actually done this unthinkable thing, I would have been openly challenging the Boston Symphony hierarchy more directly than my father ever had.

Having started to make a world for myself, my own feelings about the Boston Symphony Orchestra, Inc., began to change. Although I continued to see my father as an omnipotent figure, I became aware of how fragile he was, especially around the orchestra where he had spent most of his life. He roared at his wife and children, he sniped at his friends and musicians, but in dealings with the institution of the Boston Symphony Orchestra, Papa seemed powerless.

As I became experienced in the music business, and Symphony Hall became less the center of my fantasy life, I could see with some clarity what went on there. Despite what I had thought when I was younger, my father's other family—the B.S.O.—had been of no more comfort to him than his own unhappy family. It had simply been the more important family.

The job I took with the New York Philharmonic in 1972 included editing the house program and occasionally writing a program note or two, so I clung to the faint remains of my writing ambitions. But then a position completely unconnected with writing came along, and it was too tempting to pass up. I went to the Metropolitan Opera in 1975 as press representative and stayed in variations of that position for the next fourteen years. The days and nights were long at the Met, and I had no time to write.

My sister made different decisions in planning her life. I was well launched in the music world when Debbie decided to go to law school. My father saw law school for a woman as a ridiculous waste of time and money. "I could never understand why a woman would want to go into law," he told a *Washington Post* reporter in 1970, Debbie's first year at Harvard Law School. But Debbie refused to change her plans, and Papa, with much grumbling, agreed to pay her tuition. I watched with awe as my sister stood her ground against my father and won the battle.

Then Papa noticed that people were impressed by Debbie's studies at such a prestigious law school and her zeal in pursuing an ambitious career. He began to warm to the idea, and soon was boasting to everyone about Debbie's career in law. I was exasperated. Here I was, docilely following the route he had picked out for me, and all he could talk about was Debbie's going to law school. I got even angrier later, when his boasting was tinged by reverence as he discovered how much money Debbie was making.

I was certainly not making much money at the Metropolitan Opera, but I was contented. Perhaps I had originally gone into music to maintain my closeness to my father, but I had stumbled into a fascinating world. I was happier at the Met than I had ever been in any job. The people were talented and, for the most part, friendly, and the work was varied and interesting.

The most seductive aspect of the fourteen years I spent at the Met was the tangible sense of belonging. I had never felt as though I belonged, even in my family, except for the few rare moments with my father. But at the Met, I found a home. I could have eaten all my meals in the cafeteria, which was open from eight in the morning until well into the performance at night. My job easily filled the hours between ten A.M. and midnight. There were well over a thousand people working in the opera house, so I had an endless source of companionship. There was a daily supply of stress, drama, and crisis, which reminded me distinctly of Hyslop Road, but at the Met it was stimulating, not draining.

I understood more keenly than before my father's attachment to the Boston Symphony and his world at Symphony Hall. Belonging to a big artistic institution provides a cushion against the disruptions of life. A sense of security comes along with the weekly paycheck. This security is, of course, ephemeral, but while it lasts, the feeling of being taken care of is comforting. The paternalism of a cultural institution also allows its people to think of themselves indefinitely as children. Artists often have a childlike quality —it may be part of the personality mix required of creative people —so they easily become addicted to the quasi-familial atmosphere of a theater, an orchestra, or an opera company.

I don't believe that my father, joining the Boston Symphony at twenty and at a time in his life when he was very much alone, was any more immune to the "orchestra as family" fantasy than I was to be fifty years later. My need to find a family was surely different from his—there was no war that separated me from my actual family—but apparently we were both comforted by belonging to this kind of institution.

I HAD LEFT BOSTON for New York and yet through my choice of work was still strongly connected to my father. Also, staying in the world of music let me continue to view my father as larger than life, which, in that milieu, he was. Every little girl, at least for a short time, thinks her father is God. But a little girl whose father is well known has a unique set of problems; she's not the only one who idolizes him. Other people, too, think he is a hero, and the daughter of a famous man quickly comes to believe that her assessment of her father's godliness is correct.

Most daughters reach the stage fairly early where they understand that Daddy isn't perfect, and they begin to move away from their idolization. But as I reached the age when I should have realized this, when I should have begun to move away, all the evidence seemed to point in another direction. My father, as I got older, was becoming more famous by the moment.

When I was seized with a moment's doubt about my father's superiority—when Papa was cruel to me or seemed not to notice my existence or disappointed me by his remoteness—all I had to do to banish my doubt was look around me. Every time we went out, someone asked for his autograph or told him how wonderful he was or congratulated me on having him for my father. At concerts people stood up when he came onstage and clapped feverishly at the end of every piece. Other adults seemed frightened by him when he yelled; almost everyone quickly agreed with him when he made an outrageous statement. The rest of the world behaved toward my father the way I did myself. Moving to another city didn't change this.

Despite my hero worship, I tried not to allow my expectations of my father to get too high, and living in another city helped in this effort. Life was much safer that way. I had seen my mother, sister, and brother become disillusioned with my father's self-absorption, and I didn't want that to happen to me. "You were the only one who loved him," one of his friends told me after he died. "The others just used him." I'm not sure about the using part, but certainly I was the only one in the family who wasn't mortally disappointed by him.

At the same time, I felt as if I couldn't get away from him. When I first went to the Metropolitan Opera, I was surrounded by people whose world was circumscribed by opera, and many of them had no idea who my father was and, after they knew, couldn't have cared less. An enormous load lifted off me; for the first time, I felt free of the burden of comparison.

Meanwhile, Papa's television series, "Evening at Pops," materialized on the screen every Sunday night. In the beginning I didn't watch. I didn't have a television set, my job was so demanding that I rarely had a free evening, and in any case I had never acquired the habit of watching much television. But soon people started to ask me whether I'd seen that week's show or liked last week's soloist, and I felt the first stirrings of guilt about neglecting "Evening at Pops." And then my father gave me my first television set, and all my excuses vanished. In the middle of Manhattan, Papa had arrived in my living room.

There had never really been a possibility of escaping Papa's fame, because he understood the power of the electronic media and had used them to expand his audiences way beyond the limits of Symphony Hall. He had participated in the very first recordings the B.S.O. ever made in 1917, and, from the moment he became conductor of the Pops, had encouraged RCA to make records with the Pops as well.

Papa loved to record throughout his career, frankly admitting that he preferred recording to live performances. Radio was also vital to him in the early days; in the 1930s and 1940s the national networks broadcast symphony concerts on a regular basis, and actually maintained their own orchestras, like Arturo Toscanini's NBC Symphony. Papa commuted regularly to New York to do live broadcasts, and made sure that the Pops concerts from Boston were aired nationally. He was very aware of the exposure he got from being on the air, just as he understood the powerful RCA publicity machine that made his name, along with the names of Toscanini, Caruso, and Heifetz, familiar to people all over the world.

But nothing prepared him for the impact that television would have on his life. Tom Morris, the Boston Symphony's manager at the time my father died, theorized that Papa's career had three major turning points. The first was the formation of the Boston Pops Tour Orchestra, which started his national career. Then, the uproar and controversy that had made headlines over his symphonic arrangements of music by the Beatles ensured his world-wide fame (or infamy). But it was television that pushed his career into the stratosphere.

Yet he was surprisingly unenthusiastic when the proposal for "Evening at Pops" came along during the first year of the Public Broadcasting Service, in 1970. The program had been conceived, along with "Sesame Street," to make the new network attractive to a national audience. "Watching a symphony orchestra for an hour can be boring," Papa protested. "Sure, the TV director can switch from the harpist to the men blowing their horns, but there isn't very much to see."

The series, though, quickly became the most highly rated program distributed by PBS and was regularly nominated for Emmy Awards. Not that it was greeted with universal enthusiasm. "On one level, somewhere around the gut, the reaction to the orchestra and its bubbly fare borders on acute revulsion," *The New York Times* stated. "On another, struggling for Olympian objectivity, it tends to get a bit mushy over the argument that the orchestra is bringing an awful lot of entertainment and cultural-broadening to an awful lot of people. The key word, I suspect, is awful."

Papa always vehemently denied that he had any educational motive in programming his concerts. When a reporter once credited him with creating a whole new generation of music lovers, his response was "I didn't do it on purpose." But he couldn't deny that his fame had taken a quantum leap once "Evening at Pops" went on the air. "I don't want to sound boastful," he said, "but I have been on millions of record jackets for a long time, yet even so, I notice that more people stop me on the street than ever before and the fan mail is terrific."

I tried to see Papa's continually expanding renown through the new lens of my own professional involvement in his field, and I gained a perspective I couldn't have had at home in Boston. Outside Boston, Papa certainly wasn't revered as a walking myth, as ordinary Bostonians were accustomed to regard him. But I did learn that certain cornerstones of the music business were laid on ideas that he had either created or popularized: chamber orchestras, symphony orchestras playing popular music, outdoor concerts, and performances of operatic music without singing. He felt he never received appropriate credit for establishing these traditions, and he resented other musicians who went on to make a lot of money from what he considered his innovations. But I gradually saw that this was partly his fault. Despite his reputation as a showman and a natural genius at publicity, Papa was helpless at promoting himself.

Reporters wrote articles analyzing his shrewdness in spotting trends and his innate sense about what antics he could perform that would inspire a wire-service story or a photograph circulated around the world.

"Your father never planned anything in his career," an agent once told me. "He just went on to what he saw as the next step, and the whole thing happened naturally." Maybe he did lie in bed on one of his many sleepless nights and plot his next public relations coup. Maybe he did groom himself to look like the archetypal maestro in order to set up a vivid contrast to the crowd-pleasing music he programmed. But I doubt it. "I don't try to look like a conductor, you know," he once pointed out in frustration. He was the way he was. "Some accuse me of being a showman," he said. "I resent that, because a showman is a show-off and I never show off." Whatever he was doing, conscious or unconscious, it was working. I could have lived in Bangkok, and I'm sure I could not have escaped his renown.

The telecasts exacerbated the fame problem for all of us. Just as I was trying to establish myself in a new city, escaping the claustrophobia of living in Boston as the child of "Mr. Boston," Papa seemed destined to become "Mr. USA" to a certain segment of the population. He dealt with the same pressures. "Being in the public eye has many advantages. However, there is a price. You can't be yourself the way you'd like to be; it is a matter of self-preservation. I may be interested and like people—there is something interesting in everyone—but I must restrain myself; otherwise they make so many demands on me that they monopolize my privacy."

My burdens were different. One evening, friends invited me out to dinner with a well-known musician who had a reputation as a womanizer. There was a good deal of salacious chortling from my friends about how the man would approach me, but after several courses had been served and eaten, the man was no more than polite to me. Then, inevitably, my father's name came up in conversation. The musician's eyes brightened; his entire expression changed. "You're *his* daughter?" he said. "How interesting." He turned his complete attention to me for the rest of the meal, and when we were finished he stopped me as I got ready to leave. "Here's my phone number," he said, handing me a business card. "If you don't call me first thing tomorrow morning, I'll call you." I took the card and said good night, but now I was the one being polite. This had happened to me too many times: a man had discovered who my father was and at the same time miraculously succumbed to my beauty and charm, assets that had been invisible to him only moments before. In the taxi on the way home I tore up the musician's card, and I didn't take his calls at the office the next morning. This time I hadn't been interested back. The problem was more complicated when I was.

AS I SPENT less and less time in Boston, I was surprised when I went home and found that my father, whom I thought I knew so well and to whom I felt so close, still seemed involved with my mother. No one could ever have described their marriage as happy, but there remained an attachment between them.

My move to New York had been more successful in separating me from my mother than from my father. Mummy and I rarely had a conversation on my trips to Boston. She seemed delighted that I was gone and she had Papa all to herself. And he made an occasional effort to get closer to her.

In the late 1960s, he somehow came up with the idea of having my mother narrate Aaron Copland's *A Lincoln Portrait* at the Pops and again at the Esplanade. My mother loved to point out to people that she had studied acting and singing before marrying my father, and she was proud of her resonant speaking voice. On a daily basis, her dramatic personal style irritated my father, but he was quite capable of taking advantage of it at the right moments, and the *Lincoln Portrait* project was one of these.

Mummy got a record of the work, and everyone in the house soon became accustomed to hearing the Copland music booming from her room. My initial doubts were soon proven completely wrong, because she learned the piece thoroughly, and before we realized what was happening Mummy was onstage at Symphony Hall narrating Copland. "She was really very good," Papa was quoted by the *Boston Herald* as saying. "Perhaps one shouldn't boast about his wife, but the audience really seemed pleased." So was he, and so was Mummy, who had a wonderful time resurrecting her theatrical fantasies.

But Papa had a diabolical streak. About five years later, again seemingly out of the blue, he decided that I should join the family troupe of players and start narrating concerts. Being onstage and getting attention was as appealing to me as it was to my mother, so I agreed. I did a children's concert with him with the National Symphony both in Washington and at Lincoln Center, and it went so well that he decided my national television debut was the only possible next career step. He scheduled me to narrate *Peter and the Wolf* with the Pops during the first season of "Evening at Pops." Again I agreed, though I had serious fears that I was going too far, too fast.

Somehow I got through the performances, despite missing at least one lighting cue and almost falling off the tall stool that was my perch on the Symphony Hall stage, but the new career as an actress never did materialize. At the end of the performance, my father turned to me and, instead of giving me the expected kiss, solemnly shook my hand.

Now he had two narrators in the family who also happened to be undying rivals for his affection and attention on every possible occasion. Papa must have enjoyed setting up that particular conflict; it was almost as if Mummy and I didn't already dislike each other enough; Papa had to introduce a little theatrical competition into the mix.

"You're just like your mother," Papa used to say to me. "You're nice to everyone the same way she is." I had some pretty mixed feelings about such comparisons. Papa had married my mother, so he must have liked things about her, and therefore it must be good that he thought I was similar to her. But I knew her, and once I had outgrown my pain over the way she had rejected me as a small child, I became dismissive of her. Being like her could only be bad. For one thing, I was beginning to suspect that I had adopted her use of alcohol as an easy medicine for pain.

In 1972 I was in my office at the New York Philharmonic when I got a phone call from my father. He rarely called me at work unless he was in New York, but this call came from Boston. "It's your mother," he said, sounding uncharacteristically frantic. "Something's happened to her and it's very serious. The doctors don't think she's going to make it."

I couldn't get any more details from him, so I got on the first plane to Boston and went directly to the hospital. My father, sister, and brother were all there, as was my mother's sister, May, who had also flown up from New York. Peter had come home late the preceding night and found Mummy lying unconscious on the floor of her bedroom. No one knew what the problem was, but it was clear that she was very sick.

Now, several grim-looking doctors met with us, and they had only bad news. I stared at their somber faces and tried to figure out what I was feeling. I realized that, apart from a vague medical curiosity, I wasn't feeling very much except bewilderment. I had given up on my mother years before; if she was in a coma, she was no more unreachable than she had been to me for a long, long time.

The doctors shrugged their shoulders in bafflement one last time, we left the conference room, and I glanced at my father. To my utter astonishment, he was in tears. That was when I got truly upset, and my primary emotion was mostly anger. I was horrified later to realize that my strongest reaction had been fury at Papa for still caring about Mummy. I didn't actually want her to die, but I didn't particularly want her around, either.

A few years earlier, I had asked my father why, since he was patently unhappy with my mother, he didn't leave. He looked at me with a puzzled little frown. He didn't say, "After all these years?" or "What would she do without me?" He asked, "What would I do with all my music?" obviously thinking about the thousands of orchestral scores that lined his study and the upstairs hall. So one reason my parents stayed together was a combination of inertia and convenience. I decided that this was one more inexplicable situation I would have to accept.

Mummy's illness was eventually diagnosed as a stroke. This was just before Thanksgiving, and since we had already planned the usual funereal family gathering, Papa decided to go ahead with it. The show-must-go-on-and-curtain-must-go-up philosophy was one of his ways of getting through the crises in his life. So Celie cooked Thanksgiving dinner, and assorted Bottomleys and Fiedlers assembled at Hyslop Road. Just before dinner, Papa, who had been making drinks in the pantry, came into the dining room, where I was putting out some hideous porcelain turkeys on the table, relics of long-ago holiday dinners on Beacon Street. He checked the silver placecard holders to see who was sitting next to him, rearranged some of the seating, and then took a long look at my mother's chair at the opposite end of the table from his. His eyes moved to me. "Yummy," he said, "you take your mother's place." I nodded and moved my placecard to cover hers.

Papa continued to work steadily throughout Mummy's long illness, much to the dismay of the Bottomley family. They thought his place was at his wife's bedside, but his code of behavior made his profession his salvation. For weeks, the doctors attributed Mummy's stroke to an inoperable brain tumor, and we all assumed that she was dying. I took the bus back and forth to Boston on weekends in another futile attempt to be a dutiful daughter and make up for the lost years with my mother. But if she noticed, she never commented on my unusually frequent trips. She began to get better, and Papa, who had been more unapproachable than usual during her illness, grew cheerful. The doctors threw out the brain tumor theory and attributed the episode to alcohol withdrawal, and the crisis passed. My mother continued to improve and was able to function in some way close to normal—whatever normal was. I hadn't known that for years.

LIVING ON MY OWN and working helped my self-esteem but didn't make me rich. Yet I would never have considered turning to Papa for financial help. In our family, money seemed to be equated with love a lot of the time, so that being given money became almost as good as being given love. But in fact neither money nor love changed hands very much. My mother gave Peter money behind my father's back; my father grudgingly and complainingly gave Debbie more money than he had ever given me to help her through law school; I suffered in silence, resenting every penny my brother and sister were given while clinging fiercely to my pride in not asking anything for myself. I was so caught up in the family's financial craziness that I never understood how disturbed we all were on the subject.

Any mention of money by any of the three of us children was apt to inspire a lecture from Papa that started with "I was supporting myself completely from the time I was nineteen." He tended to regard a request for funds as an emotional shakedown and a betrayal of the family honor code—even if the money was for tuition or music lessons. The first of the two times I ever asked him for money after I finished college was when I needed a new car after the wreck I'd been driving died on a traffic circle in Washington, D.C. Papa lent me $1500 for a second-hand Volkswagen, and I signed an agreement outlining my repayments. "Take your time on all this commercial transaction," Papa wrote to me. "I don't want to discomfort you in any way." The weekend I moved to New York to work for the New York Philharmonic, I met Papa in the bar at the St. Regis and gave him a check for all I still owed him. "I never expected to see this," he admitted as he put it in his pocket, and I felt hurt.

In the spring of 1978, both Debbie and I underwent emotional crises on practically the same day. My sister was then an associate at a big corporate law firm and was earning more money than I would ever earn in the performing arts. She had been sharing an apartment with another lawyer, whom she later married, but when the relationship seemed about to end, she called my father in a panic because she was afraid that she would not be able to support herself on her own. Papa made plans to send Debbie a monthly supplement so that she could live in her own apartment. "I have to do it," he explained to me when he noticed my expression on hearing him make this promise. "She's in a very delicate condition." By then, I had made such a production of being able to take care of myself that everyone believed my fiction.

I was in a fairly delicate condition myself just then, although he didn't know it. I was living in my tiny apartment on the Upper West Side, which had no doorman or security arrangement, and my salary was under $20,000 a year, about a quarter of my sister's. The very weekend Debbie's relationship ended, I came home late one night and was confronted in the lobby of my building by a man with a knife who sexually assaulted me.

I have only myself to blame that my father didn't know what had happened to me; I never told him. He was old and sick, and I didn't want to upset him. Being sexually attacked in the lobby of one's apartment house is not what happens to the perfect child of a famous person. I didn't think it would "reflect well on Papa."

I may have chosen not to tell him what happened, but I couldn't choose not to be angry with him. I had spent my life trying to win his approval and respect, and when the worst thing I could imagine had happened to me, I wasn't even able to tell him about it. In the weeks after the assault, I was so frightened that I could barely walk down the streets of New York, and going into my apartment building took all my courage each time I walked in the door. I would have done anything to be able to move, but I couldn't afford a better apartment. Every time I thought about my father sending my sister a monthly stipend, my fury would be renewed. I would go home to Boston, planning to tell him everything, but then I'd arrive at Symphony Hall and see the condition he was in. This was only a year before he died, and he was becoming forgetful and disoriented. How could I add to his burdens? I asked myself, but I was still angry.

By the winter, my sister was back with her boyfriend and making wedding plans. I was still afraid to walk down Broadway and was still living in the same apartment. I felt I had no choice but to go on in silence. And then, the following summer, Papa died. Finally I was able to move because I had inherited a little money.

It was only a little, despite all the talk about Papa's being the richest American musician. First of all, he died before the days when well-known musicians began earning enormous fees; the amounts paid to most famous classical musicians started to climb about 1980, and Papa died in 1979. In any case, I doubt he would have felt entitled to ask for those Olympian fees even if he had lived. Also, he had invested his money stupidly, so there wasn't much to leave. And, then, one of his financial advisers had convinced him that the responsible thing to do was to leave his small fortune in a "skip a generation" trust, in which the principal is preserved for the children of his children. Debbie, Peter, and I can never touch the money. For me, this was the ultimate outrage. I had always been careful—overly careful—about money. Yet Papa planned his estate according to what he saw as his children's potential profligacy, not on my conscientiousness. To add insult to injury, I am the only one of Papa's offspring not to have children.

But again I had only myself to blame. Several years earlier, Papa had asked Debbie and me if we wanted to be trustees of his estate. Debbie immediately said yes; I said no. To say yes would have been to admit to myself and to my father that he was going to die, and I was not prepared to do that. So I overlooked my own best interests and tried to reassure Papa that he was immortal. I thought it was a way to show him how much I loved him.

THE SECOND and last time I approached my father for financial help was when I asked for some assistance in paying for psychotherapy. He and I reached an agreement that afternoon: I was to write him a letter every month asking for the money, and he would decide whether or not to send it. The arrangement lasted exactly one month; the humiliation of having to write every month to say I was still shaky enough to need a doctor's help was more than I could stand. For a few months, my father's sister Rosa, who loved me and who knew about my deal with Papa, sent me the money for the doctor, although she barely had enough for herself. But I couldn't carry the guilt of taking my aunt's money and the mortifi-

cation of having asked my father for money. I gave up the psychia-
trist I was seeing and went to a clinic to continue my treatment.

It wasn't that Papa had never experienced the debilitating ef-
fects of depression. He told me that the period after Pearl left him
had been the blackest of his life. It was the only time he had
seriously considered suicide, he said, and, even more extraordinary
in some ways, the only time he had considered psychological coun-
seling. His cousin Siegfried Bernfeld, who had fled the Nazis and
settled in Los Angeles, was a psychoanalyst who had been a student of Sigmund Freud. When Papa approached Sigi about the
possibility of treatment, his cousin responded by saying Papa
would make a fascinating and challenging subject for the analytic
process. But Papa eventually decided against this course and went
on with his life without any kind of therapy.

Instead, he chose to maintain that his psychological disabilities
did not exist, no matter how great the evidence to the contrary. He
had had his own kind of breakdown years earlier. He had begun
the 1929–30 Boston Symphony season triumphant but exhausted
after the first season of his Esplanade Concerts. They had been
successful, but nightly concerts on top of all the fund raising he
was forced to do to subsidize the series had worn him out. In
October, the stock market crashed, and Papa, who had been buying irresponsibly on margin, lost everything he had saved over the
past fifteen years. In addition, the inflation in Germany was so bad
that he had to support his mother, father, unmarried sister, and
married sister and her husband. The financial strain on him was
tremendous.

Then, in 1930, he was named conductor of the Boston Pops. He
was thrilled, but once again was under pressure to prove himself
quickly. By the spring of 1930, when the full impact of the Depression was being felt in the United States, concerts began to
seem a little frivolous and irrelevant. Papa went directly from his
first eight-week season with the Pops into the nightly schedule of
the Esplanade series. Up to this point in his career, he had never
had to cope with this kind of accumulated pressure, although later,
ironically, he would rely on such nonstop activity to relieve more

personal pressures. But in 1930 he had reached a state of physical exhaustion that paralleled his mental fatigue.

He would sit in his dressing room before concerts that summer, wondering how he was going to get onstage. On some evenings, he would bring his doctor to the concert with him, and the doctor would stay in the Green Room, reassuring Papa that he would be able to get through the concert, both physically and mentally.

On July 31, 1930, my father did get through the first half of the concert, but collapsed at intermission. He was so incapacitated that he had to be helped from the concert shell. FIEDLER TAKEN ILL AT CONCERT read the inevitable headline the next morning.

Papa joked in later years that of course people said he had been intoxicated that evening, and by the next night he was back on-stage, conducting in what the newspapers described as his usual crisp fashion. Two weeks later, however, he canceled the remaining Esplanade Concerts and retreated to the country estate of a friend, where he spent several weeks recuperating.

I think this episode must have frightened him profoundly. He always maintained to me that obsessing about emotions was an unhealthy way to live. The most important thing in life, he said over and over, was work; it was the cure for everything. "He who rests, rots" was his famous life motto. "I like to work. I find release in my work," he said, and believed that this had to be true for everyone.

When I was in my early twenties, I was overcome by a depression so intense that I stopped working for several weeks. Papa made up his mind to re-awaken my interest in being alive, and that, in part, is what inspired him to suggest my *Peter and the Wolf* narration for "Evening at Pops."

I was feeling very shaky, and the thought of pulling myself together for something so public seemed impossible. But Papa refused to listen to my objections; he was consistently supportive and encouraging. He gave me a score of the Prokofieff work, and we spent hours at the piano in his study going over the music. Unlike the behavior at the dreadful piano lessons in my childhood, my father was kind and, more amazingly, patient. I learned the piece so well that my self-confidence began to return, and I started to feel better in general. I believe that my father did more to chase away that episode of depression than any medication or doctor, and I'm sure he would have agreed.

My sister watched the whole process with distrust. "That was a real Fiedler nervous breakdown," she said. "Suicidal one week and on the stage of Symphony Hall doing a live national telecast the next."

# NINE

---

# The Last Concert

---

I N THE WINTER of 1977, my father came to New York to
receive the Musician of the Year Award from *Stereo Review*
magazine. The party was held on an icy January afternoon at
the St. Regis Hotel on Fifth Avenue, and the room was jammed
with people from all facets of the music business: classical, musical
comedy, jazz, rock, and country. By the time I arrived, it was so
crowded that I had trouble finding my father.

Papa, who had been at the party for some time, was clearly
enjoying himself. Years later I looked at pictures from the event
and was shocked at how gaunt and thin he looked. Why hadn't I
noticed it on that day?

He and I posed for a few pictures, and I became worried about
the state he was in. He always had a bit too much to drink at
parties, but this time the effect was greater than I had seen before.
I also knew that there was an added problem. Because he hadn't
left time in his schedule to spend the night in New York, he was
going back to Boston on the shuttle flight that evening. And there
was no little black Volkswagen waiting for us outside, so I couldn't
just bundle him into the car and drive him home.

Soon he began to stagger, although by then I realized that he hadn't had all that much to drink. He was eighty-two that winter, and the years were showing. At one point, he leaned over to me. "You know, Yummy," he said confidingly, "I'm very drunk. I don't know how I'm going to get home."

The sponsors of the party assured me that someone would be with him every minute on the trip to the airport and someone else would make sure he got safely on the plane. A car was to pick him up in Boston, so he'd be all right once he reached Logan Airport.

I got Papa's coat, unclenched his fingers from around his final glass of gin, and went down with him to the waiting limousine. I was fighting back tears as I settled him in the back seat, where he promptly fell asleep. Having been convinced that there was no need for me to go all the way to the airport, I futilely waved goodbye to the departing car and my dozing father, and began to walk back to my apartment near Lincoln Center.

I would have gone to the airport, but I had been too afraid of falling apart in front of him. Suddenly he was no longer the familiar and all-powerful father, the tyrant who could alternate affection and terror with no warning. He was a frail old man who could no longer hold his liquor and was terrified about getting home. It was freezing cold that night, but I walked slowly up Fifth Avenue and along Central Park South, tears streaming down my face in the wind. That evening I knew for the first time that he was dying.

NINETEEN SEVENTY-SIX had started off horribly for Papa. He had caught a cold in January but, naturally, refused to consider canceling any concerts, although he got sicker and sicker. During one of his guest-conducting stints in February in Vancouver, he came down with another bad case of pneumonia, and my mother dispatched Peter to bring him home.

His recovery took several months. After every illness, it seemed to take him longer to get his strength back, and this bout was particularly difficult. He had to cancel weeks of concerts, which always upset him. He seemed to think that if he missed one concert, he would never be able to go onstage again. He struggled for a positive attitude over the final three years of his life, but this was a hard lesson for a man whose motto was "He who rests, rots."

On the occasions when he was forced to stop, he experienced actual symptoms of terror.

Last weekend I was in Pittsburgh, where I conducted four concerts plus rehearsals. When I came home, there were no concerts for the next week and I experienced a terrific let-down. Even though I seldom feel my years, there are a few times that I do. When I do, I suddenly think about these let-downs I experience after a lot of hectic activity and then I think I simply couldn't take retirement. When the time comes to pitch out the excitement of my life, I'm afraid the bottom will drop out.

The disappointments resulting from his illnesses began to cause as much pain as the illnesses themselves. The Boston Symphony had scheduled a tour of Europe for March 1976 and planned to include a Boston Pops concert in London. Papa was absolutely determined to conduct this concert, but as the weeks passed even he began to doubt that he could tolerate the transatlantic flight plus the rigors of conducting a full-length concert. The orchestra left for Europe without him, and three days before the date of the concert, he admitted at last that he couldn't do it. "Although I am feeling better every day, I have decided on the advice of my physician to forgo the London concert," his statement to the press read. "I am heartbroken that I cannot be with my orchestra in London. Within a short time, I will again be fit as a Fiedler." Under normal circumstances, *heartbroken* was a word my father rarely used in private and never in public.

The press interest in his condition was gradually spreading beyond Boston. He was still conducting in so many places that his cancelation of eight weeks of concerts affected all parts of the country. In addition, the image of the stalwart old man fending off retirement and death had an immediate poignancy. From early 1976 on, each of Papa's illnesses would be covered extensively. To me, this interest felt almost unseemly; it was as though my private anguish was available to the whole country. I couldn't open up a newspaper, listen to the radio, or watch the news on television without being reminded that my father was sick, probably dying.

Everyone, kindly, constantly, asked me how he was doing. "He's doing much better," or "He's doing a little better," or "About the same," I'd say, and my stomach would tighten. There was no escape from the pall of Papa's illness.

Without the press coverage, though, I would have hardly known he was sick at all. Beginning with the pneumonia attack in 1976, my mother established the habit of not telling me when my father was having a crisis. I did not know he had pneumonia until I saw in the papers the frightening pictures of him, emaciated and haggard, as he was transported through Logan Airport on the way home from Vancouver. The wire-service photos were all captioned with a quote from my mother: "I think I have a very, very sick boy on my hands." When I demanded to know why she hadn't called me, Mummy said simply, "What could you have done?" I began to telephone her regularly for updates, but all she ever said was that he "seemed depressed."

There was the time I was in Atlanta on the Metropolitan Opera's 1979 spring tour. I had seen my father a few days before, and although he was weak, he had seemed in good spirits. But that morning, when I came down to breakfast in the hotel, one of the Met stage managers leaned over to me from a nearby table. "I was sorry to hear about your father's collapse," he said.

"What collapse?" I asked, although I already knew the answer.

The stage manager looked at me in bewilderment and, I think, with a little pity. "I heard it on the news this morning," he said, and I raced up to my room to call my mother.

It turned out that Papa had been rushed to the hospital after his performance the night before. Mummy was in one of her most regal moods. When I asked why she hadn't called me—I had posted the Met tour schedule prominently on the kitchen bulletin board—she had no answer. Nor was there any answer except the truth: I had interfered too much in her life with my father, and she was going to do everything she could to exclude me from his death.

I was enraged. She hadn't let me know that he was sick, and I didn't like the increasing number of quotes I read along the lines of "a very, very sick boy." As he became more frail, she seemed to grow more venomous, sensing a new power in the fact that she was twenty years younger than he. It was almost as if she were compensating for forty years of rage at him. In public, she played a new benevolent role in those last three years; at home, I saw her miss few opportunities to lash out at Papa. He ignored her most of the time, saving his energy for his work.

None of this family turbulence was evident in the stream of cheerful personality profiles that appeared about my father in his last few years. He never ceased to be astonished by the continuing interest in him and in his life. "I'm sometimes very mystified that so many people know about me and recognize me," he told *The New York Times* in 1972. "It comes so gradually, you're not aware of it, and you wonder how it happened." He loathed one aspect of being old and well known, however. All of a sudden people, especially women, seemed to be referring to him as "cute," quite a shock to a man who had relished his reputation as a lady-killer. "It's sort of a combination Santa Claus grandfather thing. People say, 'Can I kiss you? I'd love to kiss you.' I should say no more often."

Sometimes he felt as though people wanted to interview him only because he was old. "They all want to get you before you kick the bucket," he confided to the *Berkshire Eagle*, and they all wanted the secret of a long life. He was happy to oblige. "Work hard, drink hard, and have a lot of love," he said over and over.

Whatever the reason, the public wanted more of my father, and gradually I began to resent the constant intrusions made by the press and the public. Maybe this was because I sensed I didn't have much time left to spend with him. Or maybe it was because I had never had his full interest, no matter how hard I tried.

I drove up from New York to meet my father at Tanglewood one summer in the mid-1970s. After checking in, I took a shower in my room, next door to his, before going out to sit with Papa by the pool. I had washed my hair and was brushing it dry in the sun while we chatted and caught up.

After we had been talking for only a few minutes, a pair of strangers came over to us. "Mr. Fiedler?" the woman said hesitantly, and I immediately recognized the tentative tone of an autograph seeker. "We just want to tell you how much happiness you have brought to us and our family over the years."

I had heard this remark made to my father at least five thousand times, and usually I thought it was touching of people to come over and thank him. But this time, to my astonishment, a wave of intense anger flooded through me. Papa, meanwhile, was being gracious to the couple and then introduced me. I could barely manage a civil hello to them before jumping up and stamping off to my room, where I finished drying my hair.

I was horrified by my behavior. The couple had not been rude; they had even apologized for intruding on our conversation. But I was sick of not being able to have, outside a locked room, a simple father-daughter chat that wasn't interrupted by some reminder of his public life—even when I was doing something as intimate as drying my hair. His career had eaten up too much of my relationship with him, and what was left over for me no longer seemed enough.

We were both seeking attention: I from him, he from his public. In the last years of his life, after "Evening at Pops" began, he became more famous than he could ever have imagined. But every morning he seemed to get up with the goal of proving to himself all over again that he really was Arthur Fiedler. The autograph seekers and well-wishers helped with that quest in a way I never could.

PAPA NEEDED all the support he could gather, because most of his own strength was put to battling the illnesses that constantly sapped his vitality in his last couple of years. He had been sick over and over again for much of his adult life, and he had fought his way back so often that he couldn't believe he wasn't going to be able to do so indefinitely. Papa's doctors were frustrated by his refusal to give in to illness, but they also saw the good side of his attitude: once he was sick, Papa fought the disease with everything in him and often got better faster than another patient might have. I sometimes wondered whether he didn't regard his incapacities as periodic tests of his iron will. "These doctors still tell me what to do," he complained when he was eighty-two. "So I listen carefully. I nod my head yes, and then I do what I want."

One problem he had when being forced to rest was that he had no hobbies. He was an avid reader, particularly of biographies and history, but he did all his reading in the hours at night when he couldn't sleep. Reading fitted well into his schedule without his having to cut back on other activities, so he couldn't imagine trying to fill a life without conducting by reading more. He also collected musical scores and biographies of conductors, but, again, this was something he did by perusing catalogues at night or visiting music shops to fill in time when he was traveling. Performances and rehearsals were his real life.

Whenever a serious illness prevented him from working, he was impossible to be around. He had pneumonia frequently in the last five years of his life, and each attack weakened him a little more. "I would imagine you are the crankiest and most disagreeable patient imaginable," a friend wrote after reading that Papa had been sick. "I trust Ellen's care of you will have you back in business soon."

"You can't imagine how cranky and disagreeable I am at this stage," Papa wrote back. "Much more so than usual, if that were possible. I have had to cancel quite a few concerts, but *I* am trying to get *myself* back in shape quickly."

Papa worried more about his legs than anything else. He knew that often the first thing to trouble a conductor was his legs. A doctor explained to me that conductors usually have overdeveloped shoulders and upper bodies from all the exercise they get by waving their arms. The weight may be too much for their delicate body frames, since most conductors for some reason tend to be short. This fact, added to the enormous amount of time they spend on their feet, often literally causes their legs to collapse under them. Papa had seen this many times during his long life, and he lived in near terror of this particular debilitation. Although he sneered at any kind of formal exercise routine, he religiously followed a rigorous walking regimen from the time he was in his thirties up to the very end. He stayed in shape, he said:

by conducting and walking. Conductors do seem to have a durability. One reason, I believe, is that as you conduct, you perspire terribly. Conducting is like a healthful Turkish bath, beginning with the downbeat.

From the waist up, I'm built like a prizefighter. A conductor gets very developed in the arms and shoulders. Try waving a baton for a couple of hours and you will see what it does. But one must watch the legs. I walk a lot. I shun elevators. I don't walk up Bunker Hill or the Empire State Building, but I'll always walk up four or five flights.

"Poor Pierre Monteux," Papa said in 1970. "Near the end he could hardly get on the stand, and his legs were frozen during a concert." Only a year or two later, my father began having trouble with his own legs, the fate he had been predicting for himself for years. His walking and balance got so bad that he could barely lift his feet off the floor, and we had to install a stair elevator at Hyslop Road.

But at concert times, I would see his will transform his physical condition. Just before a concert, Papa would shuffle out from his dressing room to the door leading to the stage. At the appropriate moment, the stage manager would swing open the door, and Papa would clap his hands sharply just once in a private ritual only he understood. Then he would prance out onto the stage—no shuffling, no hunched shoulders, no frown of effort as he marched through the orchestra to the podium.

IN JUNE of 1976, one of Papa's most cherished dreams came true: he received an honorary doctorate from Harvard University. After all the years during which he had felt deprived of his chance to go to Harvard because of his father's decision to return to Europe, at last he had his degree. Of course, had he graduated sixty years earlier he probably wouldn't have been on the front page of the Boston newspapers, so even Papa thought it was worth the wait. "Look," he said proudly to me at breakfast the day after Harvard commencement, waving the *Boston Globe* in my coffee. "They listed me first."

Life began to proceed triumphantly again after the bad start to 1976. Papa was still rejoicing over his honorary degree from Harvard and a similar honor received a few days later from Dartmouth, when, only three weeks afterward, he gave the Bicentennial Concert on the Esplanade. His life seemed back on an upward swing, and only the death of his dear friend John Cahill marred that summer for him.

At the very end of 1976, Papa learned that he was going to be awarded the Presidential Medal of Freedom by President Ford that coming January. The news that he would receive the nation's highest civilian honor was a fitting conclusion to 1976; the tumultuous year had contained all the elements that were to mark the next thirty-three months: celebrations of achievement interspersed with battles against illness.

Papa's name was inadvertently left off the list of honorees when the White House first announced the Medal of Freedom ceremony. Once the omission was fixed, he ended up getting twice as much publicity as a result of the mistake. "Lucky for the country," the A.P. reported, "the White House got its invitation list straightened out. It wouldn't be much of a party without that grand old music maker. The oversight didn't faze the Maestro. 'They called to say it was a clerical error. I hope that the President wasn't embarrassed. I wasn't.' "

Papa even managed to make his own news the day of the awards by nearly missing the occasion. "Gerald Ford invited twenty-two distinguished Americans to the White House yesterday to receive the Medal of Freedom," the U.P.I. story began. "Eighteen came and their names read like a history of America for the last fifty years. Foul weather in Boston made conductor Arthur Fiedler late for his award, but he managed to arrive at the end of the ceremonies."

My mother, sister, and I went to the White House that day, but I sat with the Boston Symphony's manager at the ceremony, my relationship with Mummy and Debbie having deteriorated to the point where there was no communication at all. We did go through the receiving line together; Mrs. Ford stopped Debbie and me and said, "Sisters . . ." in a reflective manner I couldn't quite comprehend. "She knows," I thought; "it's obvious how much everyone in this family hates each other." At lunch, we all sat at different tables, Papa of course being with the President, and afterward I was too busy gaping at the politicians to notice when my mother and sister left. I had to tear myself away from all these figures who had real power, not conductor-type fantasy power, to kiss my father goodbye as he went off through the snow to wherever he was going next. The B.S.O. manager and I took the train back to New York, and it crossed my mind that for me, as for my father, the orchestra had become real family.

DESPITE THE JOYS of 1976, my father knew that he was failing. He reacted stoically. He never wasted a moment of his life fooling himself, and dying was to be no exception. Sometimes he responded with defiance when people asked him about his health, but there was a growing sense of resignation in the last year or two. When asked just after the Bicentennial Concert how it felt to be an institution, he thought for a minute and then answered, "It feels old."

He was also asked about retirement. "I haven't come to any conclusion about it," he said in 1977. "I'm thinking yes and I'm thinking no. It will have to come some time. I don't want to stay until they kick me out; I'd rather kick myself out."

Early that year, Papa was asked, during an interview, "What's next?"

"Death," he answered firmly. And the remainder of the year did nothing to change his mind. He canceled his season in San Francisco for the first time in almost thirty years and took most of the summer off to rest. When he started traveling again in the fall, my mother accompanied him everywhere, for the first time since the early years of their marriage. "He travels fastest who travels alone" had always been one of Papa's slogans, but he couldn't travel alone anymore. Or not very often. Because of my mother's illness, there were times she was also unable to travel, so he had to go without her. He did, but the fun was gone. It had all become too much of a struggle.

Then, in the first months of 1978, there were more ominous signs. In January, Papa did an interview with a Delaware newspaper. The reporter came to the house on Hyslop Road, and my father appeared, looking exactly as he was supposed to—white hair flowing, gray suit from Savile Row perfectly in place—so it came as a surprise when the first words out of his mouth were "Just exactly what are we here for?"

The reporter explained that the Boston Pops was going to play in Wilmington, and that this interview was advance publicity for the engagement, certainly a sequence of events Papa had experienced before.

My father shook his head firmly. "No, no. I have already been south. I am not going again."

The reporter must have been a gentle man, because he convinced Papa to look at his calendar. I picture Papa pulling out the dog-eared sheets of paper he carried around with him which contained all the information he needed for every stop on his complicated trips. When he located the Wilmington concert, he conceded that the Pops was indeed going there and settled back to be interviewed. He explained to the reporter that he was tired because he had conducted in West Virginia the night before and had another concert that very night.

At about the same time, we began to notice slight slips in Papa's usually unrelenting concentration. There was nothing yet as obvious as what happened during the interview, but there were certain gaps in his conversation, and activities that had once been natural to him became labored, such as his walking.

Because he shuffled everywhere—except, of course, onstage—people in Symphony Hall would hear him coming yards down the marble corridors before he actually peeked around the doorways. Once, he would have strode into any office where he had business; now, unsteady on his feet, he would peer around the door to see who was there. At home, we got used to being sent on errands around the house, hunting for the score Papa wanted or the reading glasses he needed to study the music.

He didn't talk about his legs anymore, because that would have been terrifying, but he complained about almost everything else. People on the street would call out to him, "Hey, Arthur, how are you doing?" Instead of his usual jaunty wave, he would mutter, "No good."

Mostly he talked about how tired he was. "I'm dead" was the

unfortunate phrase he often used, but it's certainly an accurate indication of his state of mind. "Everyone slows down as they get older," he told Bill Cosel when they were making the documentary *Just Call Me Maestro*, which was about Papa's late career. "It's nothing to be ashamed of. But I hate to admit defeat."

Even the orchestra began to feel bad for my father. During his last complete season at the Pops in 1978, he didn't leave the stage during breaks in rehearsals. Instead, he stayed at the podium, and not just because his legs were too shaky to take him to his dressing room. He would stay up there, surrounded by his music, and practice his conducting, beating his way through the pieces still left to be rehearsed. This must have been devastating to his pride, but perhaps he no longer cared.

There were other blows to his considerable pride. "I can't get used to people helping me on with my coat, women even," he complained in one interview with a writer he knew well. "When we go downstairs, they take my arm. I like to be independent. I also like niceties, to be chivalrous to a certain extent. Of course, you don't have to make a damned fool of yourself."

His relationships with women must have preyed on his mind during this period in a way none of us understood. With his life-long habit of discretion in this area, it was the last thing he would ever have mentioned, especially to the family. But he had always been sure of his attractiveness to women, and he derived great satisfaction that this, at least, had lasted as he had grown old. The writer asked whether his legendary amorous encounters had suffered from his exhaustion. "That's automatic," he answered. "You have the desire to do it; you try. But it's very awkward." He quickly added, "I drink as much as I want, though."

One source of satisfaction and affection did prevail to the very end, and that was my father's great love of dogs. By 1978, my mother had managed to rid the house of all dogs except one ancient chihuahua named Sweetie. Sweetie had been born crippled, so the dog breeder–harpist had been happy to find a home for her with us; and then, as a puppy, the poor dog had been more disabled by an accident.

But to my father she was a great beauty. When Bill Cosel made

*Just Call Me Maestro,* he deliberately left out all scenes involving members of the family, not wanting to open up this infinitely complicated area of Papa's life. The only personal scene in the ninety-minute documentary showed Papa arriving at Hyslop Road one day after a rehearsal. Sweetie was sleeping in the sun on the front lawn when the car drew up. As Papa dragged himself out of the car with difficulty, Sweetie struggled to her feet to greet him. The two old personages tested their balance, and then slowly began making their way toward each other. "Hello, girl," my father said, crouching down as far as he could to pet the tiny dog. "How are you doing?"

"He poured out all his feelings on Sweetie," one of his secretaries said to me in amazement years after Papa died. "I saw a side to him when he was around that dog that I never knew was there."

MEANTIME, the Boston Symphony, sensing the inevitable, had decided to find a new Pops conductor. Because I was friendly with people in the management, I was aware of adjunct activity in a way the rest of the family wasn't, although Tom Morris and Bill Cosel were certainly too sensitive ever to discuss the subject openly in front of me.

As early as 1969, during the negotiations with Deutsche Grammophon, the Boston Symphony management introduced into the discussions the possibility of having to find a new Pops conductor. By 1976, the management was seriously concerned. They were worried about "Evening at Pops" in particular, especially if Papa should become incapacitated in the middle of a season—which is what happened in the end. The management memos pondered all kinds of questions, including what to do about shows already produced that were scheduled for reruns.

As Papa's health failed, the orchestra began to bring in a series of guest conductors, something my father would never have tolerated when he was feeling better. For most of his career, he usually conducted every night—except for the one or two nights a week allotted to his long-suffering associate, Harry Ellis Dickson—so there weren't many opportunities for the Symphony to slide in a guest conductor. In his later years, Papa fought the B.S.O. management more fiercely about guest conductors than about any other issue. When his strength began to desert him, he had to give in a little, but he quickly discovered a new battle strategy.

Papa was aware that the Pops musicians were not impressed with the caliber of guest conductors. In the words of the *Boston Globe*'s music critic, Richard Dyer, there was "lively debate among the players about which of these conductors was the worst." Since Papa had maintained through his friends a direct pipeline to the feelings of the musicians, he knew far better than the management just how much the orchestra disliked most of his possible replacements. Therefore, when the management came to him and said that Mr. So-and-So had had a success as a Pops guest conductor, Papa would bow graciously and suggest he immediately be invited back. Not only would the unsuspecting victim hang himself more thoroughly the second time, but Papa could sense that his own status with the musicians rose with every such disaster.

The press caught wind of the search for Papa's successor. The article in the *Globe* was entitled "The Irreplaceable Arthur Fiedler," and started off, "Arthur Fiedler doesn't have to worry—no one is ever going to replace him." It went on, "Not only does Fiedler not have to worry, he doesn't."

Of course he did, but he was determined that no one would know, even though his deterioration was becoming obvious. There were more episodes of his being uncharacteristically vague and forgetful. Jim Christie, an organist, was invited to play as soloist with several other faculty members at the New England Conservatory of Music's night at the Pops in May 1978. By this point, my father was having so much trouble walking that it was clear even to the audience how disabled he was. He would stay on the podium and have the soloists come and go by themselves.

When Jim walked out at the appointed time to play the Poulenc Organ Concerto and reached the front of the stage, my father gave him one of the ferocious looks he could still summon up. "What are you doing here?" he demanded.

Jim, disconcerted, quickly realized that one of the librarians must have put Papa's music in the wrong order so that he was expecting a flutist to appear to perform Griffes's *Poème.* Jim quietly explained the situation to my father. Papa shrugged, cracked his baton across the score as he always did to signal the start of a piece, and proceeded to conduct the organ concerto from memory.

By the summer, everyone who knew Papa was seriously concerned. There was obviously something wrong with him, though he himself didn't seem to realize it. My father always dealt with his physical problems by pretending they didn't exist, but this time he seemed unaware of the mental shortcomings that were becoming evident. Although he had begun, grudgingly, to acknowledge his physical problems, I never heard him admit to any mental failings. He was so determined to die "with his boots on" that he couldn't bear the idea of having his mind fail before his body and his spirit did. He had seen this happen with other conductors, and it terrified him.

His idol was Arturo Toscanini, "the finest conductor that ever lived and perhaps that the world will ever know." When he was in New York in the 1940s and early 1950s, Papa went to as many of Toscanini's rehearsals with the NBC Symphony as he could, and shyly approached the old maestro to say hello in the breaks. He often said that one of the proudest moments of his career was when Toscanini invited him to guest-conduct the NBC Symphony, and his most precious possession was a gold medallion that Toscanini had given him for Christmas in 1949. The Italian conductor had had the medal inscribed, "To Arthur Fiedler, from his old colleague, Arturo Toscanini." My father strung the medallion on two gold chains as insurance against the possibility of one breaking, and wore it around his neck every day for thirty years. He never took it off, except when he was showering or sleeping, and it was nestled on his bureau top the morning he died.

On top of the huge television set in our rarely used living room was a large autographed portrait of Toscanini that the maestro had given to my father. On Sunday afternoons, my father would sit by himself in the living room and listen to Toscanini's NBC Symphony broadcasts from Studio 8H in New York. He would follow along with his own scores, into which he had carefully copied Toscanini's markings, specially collected for him by a friend at NBC. I would sit huddled in a nearby chair, trying to make myself as inconspicuous as possible—not that my father would have noticed in his reverential trance.

On the afternoon of April 4, 1954, Toscanini, on his last NBC broadcast, suffered a memory lapse during the Bacchanale from Wagner's *Tannhäuser*. The broadcast was briefly interrupted until Toscanini could pull himself together and resume conducting. My father was devastated. "I was listening to that last broadcast," he wrote to his friend at NBC, "with the score of the Bacchanale in my hands, and believe me, I sweated blood. Someday I want to know what happened."

Toscanini never conducted again. The horror of his idol's incapacitation was overridden in my father's mind only by the thirty-three months that Toscanini lingered in miserable retirement between his last concert and his death, on January 19, 1957.

In 1974, five years before his own death, my father received a letter from an admirer asking with whom he would most like to be reunited after death. It never occurred to me that Papa would mention anyone from the family, and he didn't. "If there should be a life after death (which I firmly disbelieve)," he wrote, "I would like to shake hands with Arturo Toscanini, who was always an outstanding man and artist in my estimation. I suppose we would converse mostly about music."

IN 1978, PAPA CANCELED San Francisco for the second year in a row, but did conduct his annual concerts at Tanglewood. He then went to Toronto for a concert, which he barely managed to finish. At the end, there were no encores, and Papa had to be helped off the stage. He canceled more concerts and took another rest.

Lydia Fuller Bottomley, who had known Papa longer than anyone else in the family, invited him to come for a recuperative visit to her beautiful home on the ocean in New Hampshire. He wrote back to thank her. "I know it would be heavenly to be in Rye, but I am really only in the mood for trying to get on with myself. My physician claimed that I needed complete rest with very little activity, so I am just sitting around boring myself and doing some reading."

Those of us who saw Papa every day were incapable of pointing out to him that he was too old and tired for the schedule he was trying to meet; we didn't want to demoralize him further. I spent my vacation in France that summer, but went home to Boston for a few days before the start of the Met season in September. I had last seen my father during the spring and was appalled to see how much he had deteriorated in just a month or two. He could hardly walk at all, and instead of showing brief lapses in concentration, he would sometimes be incoherent for long stretches, when he would stare fixedly at a wall or at the ceiling.

No one knew what to do; I think we were all terrified by what was happening—the family, Papa's few close friends, the Boston Symphony management. I had never been able to spend much time in Boston during the busy Met winter season, but in the fall of 1978 I began a pattern that was to continue until my father died. I became afraid to go home at all.

Finally, Papa became so sick that he couldn't get out of bed, and his doctors hospitalized him to try to find out exactly what was going on. It was December, just before the beginning of Christmas Pops, but by this point Papa wasn't even aware of the concerts he was giving up.

He had congestive heart failure, it turned out, which had led to a build-up of fluid on his brain. The neurosurgeon-in-chief at Tufts New England Medical Center, in describing Papa's illness to the Associated Press, described it as a "well-recognized, not exotic condition known as normal pressure hydrocephalus." He said it had caused a slowing of Papa's physical situation and had produced a "not quite as sharp mental condition."

On December 11, the doctors at the medical center operated on Papa and installed a shunt designed to drain the fluid from his brain. It was an awesome operation for an old man, and I woke up in New York the morning of the surgery fully aware that, because of Papa's grave heart condition, he might not survive the operation. "It's not dangerous surgery in younger patients," one of the doctors explained, but when a hospital spokesman was pressed about whether the operation was normally performed on a frail, elderly person, all he said was "It's been done before." I made the decision not to go to Boston on the day of the surgery and instead planned to go while Papa was convalescing.

I remember that day as one of the longest of my life. I worked all day at the Met in a state of almost intolerable tenseness. One of the singers stopped me in the hall and asked how my father was doing, and accustomed as I was growing to the question, this time I burst into tears. I had to work fairly late; when I got home I sat and waited for news.

Needless to say, my mother didn't call, so I called her, although I assumed she was at the hospital. When I reached her, the news she gave was fairly good. At least Papa had survived the operation, though no one knew what the prognosis was—whether he would regain his mobility and his mental capacities, and whether he would ever be able to conduct again.

One of the doctors told me later that when Papa awoke in the recovery room after the surgery, the doctor had asked him if he knew where he was. Papa looked at him and said, "In China-town." The hospital in fact is located in Boston's Asian community, so after that response, everyone felt much more hopeful.

Four days later Papa was out of intensive care, and a week after the operation he was sitting up and even taking a few steps. On December 17, Papa celebrated his eighty-fourth birthday from his hospital bed. Anthony Athanas, a long-time pal of my father's who owned a popular Boston restaurant, Anthony's Pier Four, provided food: fish chowder, finnan haddie, Scotch salmon, caviar, and fresh strawberries. There was wine and of course beer, and even a tiny bottle of Tanqueray gin. His closest friends were there—David Mugar, the Symphony trustee to whom my father was closest and who loved the Esplanade Concerts, Harry Dickson, Tom Morris, Bill Cosel, and Bill Shisler, along with my mother and Peter. Papa tasted the soup, ate a little of the fish, and drank some of the beer. At the end of the meal, everyone sang "Happy Birthday" to Papa, and in response he clapped his hands over his ears.

In the midst of the hospitalization, Debbie got married. Papa obviously couldn't attend the wedding, but Mummy didn't appear either, which must have been hard for my sister. Most of my mother's family refused to come to the ceremony because Debbie was marrying a man who had been divorced, but the small group of us who were there somehow managed to have an enjoyable time.

At Christmas, with Papa still in the hospital, Debbie and I went to Boston, and again I found Papa looking far worse than I had expected. His hair had been partly shaved off for the operation and was never to grow back fully, and he weighed under a hundred pounds. He was weak and grouchy, but we celebrated Christmas in his hospital room with the doctors and nurses. It was far more festive than the usual Christmas Eve dinner at Hyslop Road, which my mother insisted on having despite Papa's absence.

Much of this period is a blur in my mind. I simply could not accept what was happening: my father was old and sick and was going to die soon. I threw myself into my work and into my relationship with a young conductor I had been seeing for several months, almost as if I were preparing an understudy for the role of chief conductor in my life. I could barely eat or sleep, but I kept myself from thinking by frenetic activity, and my brain began its own kind of malfunctioning. It absolutely refused to accept clear evidence of reality. I couldn't bear the idea of losing my father.

Papa was far from done fighting, however. After a long stay in the hospital, he returned to Hyslop Road and gave in to the process of recuperation. When he made his first public appearance, choosing for some reason a party given by the Armenian Assembly, he actually looked better than he would a couple of months later, after returning to work.

He suffered a bitter disappointment when the Boston Symphony made a historic tour of China in March 1979. He had been scheduled to go and share the conducting with Ozawa, but he wasn't well enough to undertake the trip. Still, when the orchestra returned to Boston, Papa was right at Logan Airport to welcome them back. He had wanted to go on that trip as badly as I have ever seen him want to do anything—China was one of the few countries he had never visited—but a small consolation must have been that it was his picture that ran with the wire-service stories about the orchestra's return.

----

ON MARCH 26, a headline on the front page of the *Boston Globe* read: "Arthur Fiedler conducts for First Time since December Surgery: A Comeback at 84." The occasion was a "welcome home" concert and fund-raising television show for the B.S.O. in Symphony Hall. Seiji Ozawa, with his usual kindness, talked to the audience about the tour and added, "We were all sorry, Arthur, that you could not come." Papa then conducted "The Stars and Stripes Forever" and cheerfully told the reporters, "There will be lots of Pops concerts both here and at the Esplanade this spring and summer, and I will be back at the head."

In the few weeks remaining before the opening of the 1979 Pops season he did another couple of concerts to test his strength, but he was careful not to overdo anything. The goal of his life became very precise: he wanted to conduct the first night of the Pops, because it was to be a concert celebrating his fiftieth year as the orchestra's conductor.

I had missed the Bicentennial Concert and had been too frightened to be in Boston the day of my father's brain surgery, but I was not about to miss Papa's golden anniversary. I went to Boston a few days early to spend some time with him, and found him fragile but lucid.

He was up in his bedroom when I got to Hyslop Road, but certainly not the invalid I had expected to see. Dressed in his Chinese dressing gown embroidered with silver dragons, Papa was sitting in bed surrounded by scores. He was getting ready for his concert, and Tom Morris and Bill Cosel were there, as they always seemed to be in those last weeks, to provide moral support. Papa was in an extremely good mood; he now knew that he would be able to do the concert. There was almost an air of jubilation in the house.

My mother and I immediately had a fight because Papa told me that she was coming into his room every hour during the night to check on him and was driving him crazy. Mummy, who by now was the one completely exhausted, was more than a little irritated by my telling her to stop annoying Papa. Everything began to seem familiar again, after the months of fear and dread. Papa was back at work; Mummy was being impossible. Celie was still keeping the household together, and Sweetie was standing guard in her bed under the kitchen radiator, waiting patiently for Papa to come downstairs for his next meal.

Saturday morning was the traditional dress rehearsal for opening night. My mother and I both went, and we maintained an uneasy truce as much as possible. At ten o'clock precisely Papa walked gingerly out onto the stage, and I went up to the first balcony, to my usual seat for rehearsals and recording sessions.

That's when the shock hit me. Seeing Papa in his traditional, familiar place in front of his orchestra, I recognized just how sick he really was. In front of all those healthy, energetic musicians, my father looked like a ghost. He was pathetically thin, with his cheekbones carved out of his face and his brown eyes looking huge. He was also frightened. He had grave doubts about his ability to conduct some of the trickier pieces on the program, as Bill, Tom, and I had realized the preceding afternoon, watching him go over and over the music for each piece.

I prayed the orchestra wouldn't be too nice to him, because that would be so out of character that it would only upset him more. I needn't have worried—they weren't. The musicians weren't unkind out of thoughtlessness; it was almost as if they understood how insulted he would be if they treated him differently from the way they always had. They weren't cruel; they were just professional. That's what he was and that's what he always wanted them to be.

There was no rehearsal on the day of the anniversary concert, Tuesday, May 1, 1979. Papa spent the morning in bed, going over his scores again. The phone rang constantly, but he had the extension in his bedroom unplugged so that his concentration wouldn't be disturbed. I ran downstairs every few minutes to answer the doorbell; lavish arrangements of flowers were being delivered to the house one after another. My mother went out to get her hair done, but I barely noticed, since she and I were still circling each other warily. Back in the winter, she and my father had finally become convinced that she needed some psychiatric help because her physical condition was deteriorating. To the amazement of them both, Mummy was much better; she was really making great progress despite all the stress of Papa's illness. But our relationship had not improved, much to my disappointment. The ingrained lack of trust on both our parts couldn't be changed in a few weeks.

That afternoon, Mummy, Papa, and I had lunch together in the kitchen. He was so weak that even the slight formality of a dining room meal was a strain on him, so we now ate our meals in the kitchen, with Celie perched at the counter next to us.

Everyone was nervous about that evening, for different reasons, and my mother betrayed her tenseness by nagging Papa to conserve his strength. He became increasingly irritated, and I finally lost my patience. "Mummy, he has a concert tonight," I pointed out unnecessarily. I wanted her to know that I was as conscious as ever of what Papa and I considered the priorities.

She gave me one of her most poisonous glances. "The concert, always the goddamned concert," she snapped. "That's not the be-all and the end-all for everyone in the world. Did you ever stop to think, Popie, of how ridiculous you look, standing up there shaking a stick at a bunch of men?" I cringed at hearing her use her favorite nickname for my father.

Papa took a sip of his beer and stared pointedly out the window over his right shoulder.

"Music, that's all that matters to the two of you." She was becoming more enraged now, since no one was picking up the gauntlet for battle. "Well, I hope both of you die lonely old people!" She slammed down her napkin as I concentrated on trying not to remember how many millions of times this had happened before. On this occasion, however, she didn't storm out and run up the front stairs.

My father looked at me. "And they call these the golden years," he said grimly, and then he got up and shuffled toward his elevator. I wanted to run after him, but I knew he was going upstairs to rest and that he wouldn't want to be disturbed.

My mother then turned to me. "You see what I've been telling you? You see how depressed he is?"

"I didn't think he was all that depressed until you started picking at him," I said.

"No, he wasn't," she replied, and I saw her upper lip begin to curl. *"You're* here, and that's all that matters to him."

THAT EVENING Celie and I rode in the Boston Symphony car with Papa. When we got to Symphony Hall, the stage door was surrounded by photographers and television crews, and for a minute my father shrank back in the seat. He was so thin that he had had to have new tails made for the occasion; they had been made by Brooks Brothers, since Papa hadn't been able to get to his usual tailor in London, and he went so far as to invest in a new vest and white tie, as well. But even armored in his elegant new clothing, he didn't feel strong enough to plow into the rowdy bunch of photographers. I knew he was worried about losing his balance on those undependable legs.

Paul, the driver, cleared a path through the throng, and Papa picked his way through to the entrance, where the freight elevator was waiting to take him up to his dressing room. Richard Dyer rode with us in the elevator. "I feel pretty good," Papa told him. "In fact I feel about the same way I did fifty years ago—I'm just as nervous. You have the right to get nervous once every fifty years. I had doubts that night fifty years ago—everybody has doubts. But I did the best I could."

Papa did the best he could at the Fiftieth Anniversary Concert, too. He had designed the program to be rather like the first concert, on May 7, 1930. "Something new, something old, something of our own," he said to Richard Dyer. "There's even a bit of disco. I don't think it's the greatest music, but it's fun to dance to. Am I going to dance? No."

The audience was adulatory for the whole evening, and I heard the word *indomitable* passed back and forth. The combination of the occasion, the obvious ill health of the central participant, and the sense that this was a uniquely Bostonian event brought out a warmth and affection toward my father that he had always received from the man in the street in his native city but rarely from the people he tried so hard to please—the people who ran the Boston Symphony Orchestra. That night, however, everybody was full of love for him and, much more meaningful to him, full of respect for his courage and determination, those very Bostonian virtues.

*The New York Times* commented the next day, "In a way that would not be readily understandable to New Yorkers or residents of some other, more worldly city where no one star can shine alone, no matter how brightly, Mr. Fiedler is 'Mr. Boston.' He is the city's trademark, its most famous and most recognizable resident, the local man who has honored his city." Maybe Papa had sensed this all those years before; maybe that's why he never left Boston.

THERE WAS A BIG PARTY after the concert, but, for one of the only times in his life, my father didn't want to go. We had a brief family discussion, and it was decided that someone should represent the Fiedlers, so my mother went on to the party, accompanied by Debbie and Peter. Papa and I went home.

When we got to Hyslop Road, we had barely got in the door before his adrenaline-boosted strength deserted him. There were two couches in the large front hall, so Papa and I plopped down on them and talked for a long time. He was too weak even to walk the few feet to the stairway elevator, but I also sensed that he wasn't ready to go to bed just yet.

I don't remember what we talked about that night; I'm sure it was about the concert and the people who had come to see him and the usual things that fascinated my father—who had been there and what they had said and done. Finally he was revived enough to walk to the elevator and tired enough to contemplate going to sleep after all the excitement. We went upstairs together. I was leaving early the next morning for Atlanta to join the Met tour, so I reassured him, "I won't wake you in the morning before I leave," and he didn't protest.

I kissed him good night and said congratulations one last time, and he went into his room and closed the door, the dressing room sign reading MR. FIEDLER banging as it always did. The next morning, very early, I left the house in Brookline and flew back to what I thought of as my own life. I never saw my father again.

———

PAPA GAVE UP after his last concert, the Saturday night after the fiftieth-anniversary gala. He had not conducted since, but he wanted to do the weekend concert because James Galway was the flute soloist and part of the concert was to be taped for "Evening at Pops." Although everyone knew that Papa would never give up a telecast, the B.S.O. had arranged for Harry Dickson to lead the untelevised section, and no one expected my father to conduct the whole performance. But Papa refused to stop after the taped part of the performance was over.

After the concert, Papa went backstage to the Green Room and collapsed. Harry sat with my father before the paramedics arrived, and asked him why he had insisted on doing the whole concert. "Because I'm here and because it's my job." Harry was not surprised at this remark; in many ways it summed up Papa's philosophy of life. As he was wheeled out, Papa looked up at Harry. "Don't steal my batons," he said in farewell as he left Symphony Hall for the last time.

THE REST went very fast. After the last concert, Papa was in such bad shape that many people thought he had died on the way to the hospital. He hadn't, although he probably would have preferred that to the misery of the next two months.

He was in the hospital for a few days, and then went home. Almost exactly a month later, he suffered what was described as a "mild heart attack" and again spent a couple of weeks at Tufts New England Medical Center. He was discharged just in time not to conduct the opening of the Esplanade's fifty-first season. But he did arrange for my mother to narrate *A Lincoln Portrait* once more, at the July Fourth concert. Harry Dickson conducted the concert and my father listened on the radio by his bed.

He was feeling so ignored that night that he agreed to have a reporter from the *Boston Globe* come to Hyslop Road and listen to the concert with him. How sad, how pathetic, I thought, reading over the clippings from that occasion. "America's beloved, bed-ridden Maestro was feeling very alone in his ivy-covered Brookline home as tens of thousands of Bostonians swarmed to the Esplanade concert." And again I ask myself the question: Where was I?

" 'I feel a little melancholy,' he said. 'I regret I'm not with them all. I was not asked to play; they were making plans without me. I'm not strong enough anyway.' "

He was sitting up in bed surrounded by the scores for the concert. The reporter asked where the rest of the family was. Some family members were in New York, my father answered. Others were "somewhere else." He went on, "I'm a little old, in more ways than one. You can't force nature. It just has to take its course."

The writer asked him about his position as one of Boston's most beloved figures, and my father brightened for a few minutes. Then his modesty took over. "I'm a born Bostonian. I don't think I've got any hold on this dear place." He began to concentrate on listening to the concert, and within a few minutes he was too tired to talk anymore. The reporter left, Papa's thanks-for-coming echoing behind him, and my father's last interview came to an end.

I remember very well what I was doing that Fourth of July in New York. I had wanted to spend a last few days in New York with a conductor I was seeing at the time, before he left on a long tour of the summer festivals. I put off my trip home until the next week. An easy excuse would be that I had spent too much of my life waiting for my father to come home from trips, and I had decided that I couldn't allow that to happen in my grown-up life. But there really isn't any excuse for why I wasn't in Boston those early days in July 1979.

Somewhere around this time, I had my last conversation on the phone with him, so at least he knew I was on my way to Boston. But a week after the July Fourth concert, he just couldn't wait for me any longer.

Papa had several visitors on Monday, July 9, and he seemed alert and determined to convince them his idleness was purely temporary. I remember, though, what he said on the phone to me a day or so earlier: "There doesn't seem much point in going on." He knew, whether he admitted it or not, that there were no more concerts ahead. Tom Mowrey, his record producer from Deutsche Grammophon, called during those last couple of days to tell Papa that he'd be sure to be at his next concert. "No, Tom," Papa said. "It's too late for me now."

"I'm back, aren't I?" he had said on the evening of his last concert. "I'm always coming back." For years he had been making remarkable recoveries from one serious illness after another, and he counted on the strength of his survival instinct. But since his last concert, the days had passed slowly, just a waiting period before the release he almost welcomed from a life with no music. On the morning of Tuesday, July 10, my mother made her usual hourly check on Papa at seven-thirty and found him, lifeless, on the floor of his bedroom.

My mother called Debbie to tell her that Papa was gone; in keeping with tradition, she did not call me. Debbie did, and together we set off for Boston. By the time we arrived, the city's flags were already flying at half-staff, and special editions of the newspapers were announcing his death. The sense of unreality that had hung over me for months became even more pronounced. When we got to Hyslop Road, it didn't seem strange to us that he wasn't there; after all, normally he was gone most of the time. The press was there, however, camped outside the hedges that bordered the front lawn, along with several police cars and, I think, at least one fire truck.

That night, the Pops concert at Symphony Hall went on as usual. I watched on television, sitting by myself in the library, where I had watched so many of Papa's television shows. "We'll miss him enormously," Harry Dickson told the audience, "but he would want the show to go on." Then Harry turned to the orchestra, gave a cue, and the Boston Pops started playing "The Stars and Stripes Forever" very softly. Harry stepped down from the podium, and the orchestra played on, leaderless.

# T E N

---

# After Papa

---

WHEN SOMEONE FAMOUS dies, so much of the survivors' time is taken up by the public aspect of grieving that the far more difficult and private coming-to-terms with the loss is postponed. I remember only a few vivid details from the days right after my father died; the rest is a hazy amalgam of a lot of people, a lot of phone calls, a lot of flowers and telegrams, and a lot of frantic activity.

Whenever I came into the front hall during those days, there seemed to be a reception line waiting for me—Papa's friends, B.S.O. administrators, members of my mother's family. Mummy, Debbie, Peter, and I picked out Papa's coffin in a benumbed visit to the funeral home; Bill Cosel, Tom Morris, and I began planning a memorial service to be held two weeks later at Harvard; we met with lawyers to talk about the will; we met with a Unitarian minister about the funeral. I'm still not sure who found him, but we all liked him so much that later on he married my brother, baptized his children, and spoke at Mummy's funeral.

The Boston Symphony performed a memorial concert at the Esplanade on the Sunday after Papa died. The program duplicated the Bicentennial Concert and was telecast in Boston. I watched the broadcast, thinking back to July Fourth in 1976, reminded again of how much I had missed of my father's last years.

Peter worked on details of the memorial concert, Debbie dealt with the lawyers, and I planned the memorial service. We all had our duties, except my mother. She floated around the edges of things, a lost soul. None of us paid very much attention to her. She made only one request—to have "Ave Maria" played at the memorial service because it had been performed at her wedding to Papa.

There was no music at the funeral itself. The Unitarian minister read excerpts from Shakespeare, the Bible, and even the blessing Papa had been given when he was made an honorary chief of the Otoe tribe.

For me, the most poignant moment of the day came at the end. The Boston Fire Department had named two fire trucks after Papa in honor of his eightieth birthday—Fiedler One and Fiedler Two. He loved these engines even more than his own, because they were up-to-date equipment and were still in use. They kept going to fires when he was too exhausted and frail to go any longer himself.

When I came out of the funeral services, the two Fiedler fire trucks were parked quietly by the curb. There were no flashing lights or sirens that day, just the firefighters Papa had loved and respected so much standing in silent tribute by Fiedler One and Fiedler Two.

THE BOSTON SYMPHONY administration was helpful to us in planning and producing Papa's memorial service at Memorial Church, Harvard University. Seiji Ozawa spoke, and Senator Edward M. Kennedy quoted Pindar. "A graceful and honorable old age is the childhood of immortality," he said, and I remember thinking that I was not sure I would describe Papa's old age as graceful. It had certainly been honorable, but the strongest emotion had been, at first, rage and, at the very end, profound sadness.

My father's troubled relationship with the musicians in the Boston Symphony continued after his death. Only three members of the Pops offered to play in the chamber orchestra that provided the music. The other ninety-odd musicians stayed away.

The Boston Symphony trustees convened and voted to name the new west wing of Symphony Hall the Arthur Fiedler Memorial Wing. All the Boston newspapers reported the decision. "This will be a tangible and enduring memorial to an extraordinary man," the board's chairman said. My mother donated all my father's thousands of scores to the orchestra, which immediately promised to build a library where music students and musicians from all over the world could come and study the collection of which my father had been so proud.

The Arthur Fiedler Music Library is now part of the Mugar Memorial Library at Boston University, and his scores and papers are part of that university's Special Collections. My mother waited several years for the Symphony to act on its plans to establish a library, but she finally gave up. The condition of the scores and papers was endangered, since they were not securely packed and stored, so when Boston University repeated its earlier offer to house the collection, Mummy agreed, and the material is now beautifully displayed, maintained, and preserved at the school where my father taught for so many years early in his career.

When I was doing research for this book, I used the archives at Symphony Hall. Frequently I would go into the building through the new west wing. It is called the Cohen Wing; I have no idea what happened to the trustees' decision to name the building after my father, and there comes a time when there is no longer any point in asking. The only sign that my father ever worked at Symphony Hall, aside from a few pictures in the music library, is in the archives, where his Symphony correspondence and official photographs are kept. And in a few fading pictures of the orchestra from the early part of this century, I could still make out the dark-haired violist who was carefully labeled "Fiedler, A."

MY FATHER, at his own request, was cremated on the day of his funeral, so there was no burial after the ceremony. Papa had asked to be buried with his family in a Jewish cemetery in West Roxbury outside Boston, but my mother remained mysteriously undecided about Papa's interment. Only much later did I learn that she arranged a secret burial service for my father, which she alone attended. She had him buried in her own family's grave in St. Joseph's, a Catholic cemetery, where he lies surrounded by Kenneys and Bottomleys. Mummy told no one at all about the burial—I'm sure she knew that I would have tried to have Papa's wishes carried out. But it was too late when I finally discovered what had happened.

The house on Hyslop Road was sold almost immediately after Papa died, and my mother moved to Cambridge with Celie. She hated her apartment there, and spent most of her time reliving the past as she imagined it had happened, re-creating her marriage to my father as the happiest union two people had ever shared. She also continued to have a surprisingly large number of gentlemen friends, because, bereaved as she was, my mother remained to the very end the charming woman who had once intrigued my father.

I saw her rarely, and our relationship was as troubled as ever. She frequently expressed her frustration over my personal life, because I stayed stubbornly single while my brother and sister both married and had children. I did my best to ignore her, but her stinging remarks about my "way of life" hurt more and more, and I tried to avoid her.

I did visit Mummy one afternoon in 1983 while the Met was on tour in Boston. She looked terrible and I was concerned enough to give her a lecture about going to see her doctor. I even picked up the phone to make an appointment, but she came over and took the receiver out of my hand. There was nothing more that I could do, I decided. She was living comfortably in a beautiful apartment, surrounded by the trappings of her life with my father, and I could not make her feel happy there.

As always, Papa's name came up often that afternoon as she reminisced about Hyslop Road. "You thought you could take him away from me," she said, looking at me spitefully, "but you couldn't."

I stared at her. After all the years the two of us had fought over my father, it still amazed me that she saw the struggle so vividly and could speak about it so openly.

"No," she went on, her tone firm, paying no attention to the fact that I hadn't responded, "in the end, I won."

There was no point in saying anything, so a few minutes later I said goodbye and went back to my hotel. There was never another chance to respond. Mummy had a stroke a few days later and died in a nursing home in October 1984.

AFTER MY FATHER DIED, I was lost for a very long time. An old boyfriend sent me a note when he first heard about Papa. "I hope," he wrote, "that now you'll be able to find some peace." People tossed around words like *resolution* and *closure*. I had a busy life, a close romantic relationship, and financial security. But I felt mostly emptiness.

My job at the Met was exciting and demanding, and I was never bored. My position involved working long hours in the office during the day, followed by long hours at the evening performance. I would come home late at night, exhausted, fall into bed, and sleep until it was time to go back to work early the next morning. It was a great job for someone who didn't want to have time to think.

By having a career, I also was saving myself from being like my mother. I went even further to differentiate myself from her: I chose not to get married. There were several men I could have married, but as soon as the man made it obvious that marriage was his goal, I would leave. On the other hand, if the man wasn't interested in something permanent, he had me for as long as he wanted; if there was no danger of marriage, I thought there was no danger at all. The man could be cold, remote, unable to form a close relationship, and, in some cases, physically abusive—and I would stay with him. Only when someone gave signs of wanting something close would I decide that things weren't going to work out. I had seen enough of marriage to convince me that I wanted none of it.

The closest I came was with the young conductor I had been seeing during my father's last year. He had come to Boston for my father's funeral and stayed with me for a few days before going off to conduct at a summer music festival. I remained in Boston to plan Papa's memorial service. But almost immediately I began to fight bitterly with my mother, sister, and brother; it was as if we were trying to establish familiar routines in this strange new life without Papa. Frustrated by the anger with my family, I temporarily abandoned the preparations for the memorial service and went to join the conductor at his summer festival.

It was a strange few days. I stayed in our hotel room while he rehearsed. The PBS stations all over the United States were rebroadcasting several of Papa's recent television shows as a memorial, and I often sat by myself in the hotel room and watched concert after concert. I would see my father on the screen, frail and tottering, and I would sob away the afternoons. When the young conductor bounded in after his rehearsals, full of spirit and verve, everything seemed even more surreal.

In the evenings, I went to the conductor's performances. These were held outdoors and of course reminded me of the Esplanade Concerts and Pops concerts at Tanglewood. There were the same warm evenings, the crowds gathering early to picnic before the performance, the musicians relaxing or tuning up in the fresh air outside the stage entrance. The past and the present began to merge. "Thank God I don't have to give all of this up," I thought. "I couldn't have endured that, but I don't have to. It's still happening." Just with a different conductor.

Of course it didn't go on indefinitely, and of course the relationship didn't work out. The fact was that the young conductor was a different conductor and a different man from my father, and this became impossible for me to accept. He had been born in the suburbs of New York City and was only in his late twenties. Despite all the traveling and concertizing he had done at an early age, not much sophistication had rubbed off. He was largely self-educated and loved to show off the languages he had taught himself to speak—the "languages of the great composers," as he described them—and the books he had read. "I keep expecting him to pull out a reading list," a friend of mine said after one tedious dinner. Papa, who had grown up speaking German, English, and French, never would have thought it something to brag about. He had lived both in the United States and Europe from the time he was an infant, and sophistication seemed bred in him. The contrasts I made between him and the young conductor were as vivid as they were unfair—and my feelings slowly became clear. I wanted my father.

But in the middle of wanting my father, I resented the same things with the young conductor that I had disliked about coping with the demands of my father's career. At the beginning, I loved having people recognize my boyfriend on the street and in restaurants. I was used to this with Papa, and it seemed perfectly normal to me. But gradually I began to hate the constant interruptions by eager fans. I didn't like being pushed aside by people who were paying attention to him and mostly ignoring me. He rarely introduced me, which made me feel even worse. We would fight after almost every one of those episodes, and he would accuse me of being resentful and jealous of his celebrity and the prestige it brought him. He was probably right.

I also hated his long absences on guest-conducting trips and complained about how rarely he was in New York. When he tried to please me by coming home more often, I would resent his concession, which seemed like an intrusion. I claimed that his constant departures and reappearances were interfering with my life.

He suggested that our lives would be easier if I gave up my job at the Met and traveled with him. "My career should be enough for both of us," he said, much to my dismay. He amended that to "You could write; it's what you've always wanted to do." But I refused to give up my job, and it became clear that our days together were coming to an end.

I accused him of being unfaithful while he was away, which he sometimes was, though I too strayed during his absences. I missed him when he was off on one of his trips, but felt smothered by him when he was in New York. There was no way to make me happy, though he certainly tried and for much longer than I should have expected. When I realized that I couldn't scare him away by my mood swings and vacillations, I did the necessary thing and found somebody else. The new man was, as I suspected from the start, a monster. But somehow anything seemed better to me than a man who truly cared about me and wanted a full and close relationship.

My terror was overwhelming. I knew what could happen if things worked out; I had seen it all before.

IN TIME my work in the music field helped me lay some of my ghosts to rest. As my first grief over my father's death began to die away, two fundamental questions emerged that I started to brood about: what kind of a musician had my father been, and what could I do about the way he had been treated by the Boston Symphony?

The question of Papa as a musician was one that had also haunted him, I suspect. I started grilling everyone who had worked with him or played under him. The answers that came back were all similar. Papa had been extraordinarily well trained, a painstaking and hard-working musician, and had had a legendary ear and an efficient rehearsal technique. He had been a thorough professional.

Many people I asked avoided saying anything negative because they didn't want to hurt my feelings, but occasionally one would be honest. A former Boston Symphony administrator admitted to me that the Symphony's reluctance to engage Papa on the regular subscription series partly sprang from doubts about whether his concerts would be musically interesting. "He was efficient and reliable," said a soloist who played with him many times. "He had a tendency to push tempos, but a lot of people do that. At least he didn't drag."

"He didn't have all the grace in the world in his music making," a B.S.O. musician told me, "but he overcame that by his vitality." "Fiedler could conduct six nuns playing the cello, and it would be a sell-out," another musician said, and I began to think that my search for the truth about Papa as a musician was unattainable.

The composer and conductor Morton Gould, a good friend of my father's, noted, "Arthur had charisma before there was such a word."

Papa knew that audiences loved him. He was fond of quoting Liberace's famous remark about music critics: "No one loves me except the American public." But Papa never pandered to public taste. "I do not perform for the audience; I make music for myself, not for the audience. When we play for television, we do not know who is listening—maybe no one. I do not care how many are listening. You make each performance the best performance you can."

In the obituary about Papa that he wrote for the Boston Symphony's program book, Michael Steinberg made an important point. "There was at one time a real serious musician in him, and that's a part of him that everyone lost sight of, including himself. And I don't think he was ever completely at peace with himself because of that."

What I eventually had to accept was that all my questions about Papa's musicianship would in the end accomplish nothing. His life had been primarily that of a musician, and a gifted one at that, but his career was based on something beyond his skills. People didn't love him because he was a great conductor; they loved him because he was a simple, honest human being who brought them a vast amount of pleasure. I stopped hoping that the world would view him as a peer of Toscanini's or Koussevitzky's; in any case, it wasn't my battle.

Nor was Papa's struggle with the Boston Symphony my battle either. For a while I thought that I might be able to make up for having failed Papa in his last days by getting the B.S.O. to acknowledge him as somebody important. I believed that the Boston Symphony had never fully appreciated him. But eventually I understood that Papa had learned to live with the Boston Symphony, and I would have to, too. It wasn't my struggle; it had been his, and for me to continue the conflict was just another way to keep Papa in my life.

WHEN I TURNED FORTY, I began to feel that something was wrong with the way I was living. I loved everything about my job at the Met—the familial atmosphere, the travel, the constant excitement and stimulation. But I didn't love the rest of my life, what little else there was. "You *sleep* in your apartment," one friend said to me, "but you *live* at the Met." She was right.

I couldn't understand why I was so restless and dissatisfied when I had such an interesting life; why, when I had an evening off, I passed the time drinking at home alone instead of being with other people or writing; why my romantic relationships were more infrequent and more crazy when they did happen.

Then I thought about how I had ended up working in music in the first place. I remembered those long conversations with my father about what I was going to do when I grew up. I remembered how he had disparaged my idea of becoming a writer and urged me toward the music world. I began to wonder which of us had chosen my career.

Certainly it had been satisfying to do what was important to my father. My jobs made the musical world something only we two in the family shared. I would come home for the weekend and go right up to his bedroom. Sitting on the edge of the bed, I would tell him the latest New York gossip, and I knew that it was almost a relief for him to have someone at home to talk to about what mattered to him.

My mother, sister, and brother would always accuse my father and me of "talking about all those people *we* don't know." But no one seemed curious about what we were discussing, and by that time, I think, my father and I were quite happy to be left alone to converse about what fascinated both of us. We spoke a musical shorthand to each other that no one else understood.

My career had brought me closer to my father, but suddenly, years later, I wasn't sure whether that had been such a good thing. After all, I had moved to New York to separate myself from my family, and yet here I was, even more enmeshed. To complicate things, the Met had become a kind of new family to me.

When I told people that I worked for the Metropolitan Opera, I could see their eyes light up with interest—interest that wasn't there when they first met me, any more than it had been there before someone found out who my father was. Again, my sense of myself depended on something outside me, and though my connection with an important person and an important institution was an easy counterweight to how little I thought of myself, it was not a solution.

In 1989, after much unhappiness and much soul searching, I left the Met. I first ran a performing arts series and managed a chamber orchestra, but that job turned out not to be the answer, either. Even having my own little orchestra couldn't make up for my still living my father's life. I had to leave the music world and all its comforting familiarity and do something that had direct meaning for me.

About the same time that I decided to leave the Met, I faced the inevitable fact that I was also reliving my mother's life: I was drinking too much. As I grew more unhappy, I turned more and more to alcohol as a way of dulling my misery. Of course, I was also dulling all the pleasant and satisfying parts of my life, but I was so depressed and angry that I no longer acknowledged that there *were* any good parts. I became very frightened.

Leaving the Met, my adopted family, threw me into more confusion and loneliness. My new job had none of the sense of community I had come to cherish. When I talked of missing my old job, one friend said reassuringly, "It's like a divorce." But I wasn't comforted. I drank to find comfort—and became more miserable. I couldn't do anything, and I didn't want to do anything.

Then another friend confronted me—with gentleness and understanding. I didn't have to share my mother's destiny; there was help to be found.

Alcohol had been the family cure-all. "Let's have a drink" was the reaction to any occasion, and I had to accept that the ancestral panacea no longer worked for me. So, with the help and patience of a kind doctor and faithful friends, I understood. It is a long battle, one I saw my mother lose, and one my father refused to acknowledge he was fighting.

Severing this connection with my mother, and relinquishing the music world and all its comforting connections to my father, was an attempt to do what I wish I had been brave enough to try half a lifetime ago. In changing my life so that I would have the time and energy to write this book about my father, I had to leave music and, at long last, mourn for my father.

While Papa was alive, I felt as though I were living life in Technicolor. He died, and the screen flickered and became black and white. Things got worse when I left the Met and the familiarity of a world that had become home to me. I feared that everything would be a monochrome forever. But gradually the colors are beginning to filter back, and this time they are colors that I have chosen.

At times while I was writing the book, I felt as though my father still spoke to me from wherever he had gone. "I've made all my plans for the future based on the fact that I'm here to stay," he had said in one of the clippings I found. "After I finally pop off, my ashes will be scattered into the wind. It delights me to think that, one way or another, I'll be around hundreds of years from now. Like my music. It never ends, you know. Often I think of it—the vibrations going out into infinity. It goes on forever, you know."

When I went back to Boston to do the research for this book, it was almost as if Papa had been right about going on forever; he seemed to be present. If I made an airline reservation or a dinner reservation or gave my name under any set of circumstances, I would hear the familiar quickening of interest in the other person's voice, see that familiar flicker in their eyes. I knew what the next question would be: "Any relation?" Only at Symphony Hall did Papa seem far away. But people outside the orchestra remembered.

Patsy Cardillo tells a story that, though it certainly sounds apocryphal, he swears is true. He had picked Papa up at Hyslop Road one night to drive to Symphony Hall, as he frequently did. For some reason, that evening they decided to try a new route (there were constant arguments in our family over whose route to Symphony Hall was the fastest and the least plagued by Boston's traffic jams), and they got lost. They ended up in a rough and unfamiliar part of the city, and when they had to stop at a traffic light, both of them felt some apprehension. Several children playing ball in the street looked into the car with great curiosity. Suddenly the eyes of one little boy widened. "Look!" he called out to his friends. "Come over here! It's Beethoven!"

That was how Bostonians felt about Papa, and it seemed to me that his death had changed very little. "It never ends, you know."

Returning to Boston for the first time in years, I was lonely. I had few friends left—in fact, I had had few friends there in the first place—and felt as desolate as when I was a child. Worst of all, there was no more tie to Symphony Hall to make life exciting. I was all grown up, and my father was dead.

One dreary, cold, rainy Sunday afternoon in February, I couldn't stand my cramped sublet apartment on Beacon Hill for another minute, so I took my dog, Lily, for a walk on the nearby Esplanade.

We went down the hill of Mount Vernon Street and across Storrow Drive on the Arthur Fiedler Bridge, a pedestrian span built to honor the twenty-fifth anniversary of the Esplanade Concerts. A plaque with Papa's profile adorned each end of the bridge, and I glanced at them cursorily. My dog and I, shivering in the damp wind off the river, walked by the deserted Hatch Shell, where I had gone to my first concert, and over the spot where my father had dreamed of starting his free concerts, more than sixty years earlier.

A statue of Papa now overlooks the Charles River Basin. All this time I had been in Boston, I had avoided going to see the statue and the concert shell just as I had avoided going to Symphony Hall unless I absolutely had to. Those were the sacred places of my childhood, and I didn't want to see them completely changed. Even when I took the T train over the Longfellow Bridge to Cambridge, I would turn my head as we passed the Esplanade so that I wouldn't catch even a glimpse of my father's statue.

But that Sunday, I went back. Lily and I wandered along the trails by the river, the same pathways where my father had taken his daily walks when he was a young man in Boston. The park was almost deserted in the chilly weather, and it was beginning to rain harder. We made our way to the back of the lawn that spread out from the shell.

I came face to face with Papa's statue almost without warning. It loomed up, huge and stony, from the wintry brown grass in front of me. His giant granite head is turned to face the concert shell, as though he will be there forever, listening. Thinking how pleased

Papa would have been at the way he was remembered here, I went as close as I could and looked at the plaque on the statue.

It was then that I began to cry, my first tears since I had come back to Boston. The inscription was exactly right.

ARTHUR FIEDLER, it read. MUSICIAN.

# Notes

ONE  "You're a *Fiedler*"

p. 19 Birth announcement—Associated Press wire copy, Sept. 17, 1945
p. 19 Why Fiedlers had children: Interview with Arthur Fiedler by the syndicated columnist Heloise, Dec. 1974
p. 21 Home situation at Brookline apartment: Interview with William Berenberg, M.D., Children's Hospital, Boston, Feb. 1991
p. 29 Return of Fiedlers to Europe: Unpublished oral history given to Columbia University, 1962, and subsequently withdrawn by AF
p. 30 Arthur's early education: Interview in the Boston Herald American, May 1977
p. 30 Visits to the firehouse: Interview with Irving Kolodin, *Stereo Review*, Feb. 1977
p. 30 Visits to the firehouse: Interview in the *St. Louis Globe Democrat*, Nov. 1974
p. 31 AF gets his own fire engine: Interview in the *San Diego Union Register*, Aug. 1970

TWO  The House on Hyslop Road

p. 44 AF not a family man: Interview in Arts & Leisure, *The New York Times*, Winter 1972
p. 44 AF as an old-fashioned father: Interview in the *San Francisco Chronicle*, Aug. 1963

p. 44 AF much older than his offspring: Interview in the *Bergen Record*, Nov. 1971

pp. 49–50 AF's views on religion: Interview in the *Boston Herald*, May 1977

p. 50 AF's life philosophy: "Words I Live By" in the *Boston Globe*, 1975

p. 58 AF and animals: *Boston Globe*, July 1945

p. 58 25th anniversary of Esplanade: *Boston Globe*, July 1953

p. 62 AF on drinking: *San Francisco Chronicle*, July 1967

p. 65 AF on 1953 tour: *Boston Herald*, Jan. 1953

p. 65 AF on tour orchestra: *Boston Herald*, Jan. 1953

p. 68 AF on Argentina: *Boston Globe*, 1957

p. 69 AF on vacations: Associated Press, Feb. 1965

pp. 69–70 AF on his schedule: Letter to Richard Mohr, June 1975

Three   Papa

pp. 71–72 AF's reluctance to resume his education: Unpublished oral history given to Columbia University, 1962

pp. 73–74 AF's growing interest in conducting and musical education in Berlin: Ibid.

p. 74 AF's early experience as a conductor: Ibid.

p. 75 AF on attractive women: Interview in the *Boston Globe*, June 1971

p. 75 AF on his career plans: Columbia University oral history

p. 76 AF on start of World War I: Ibid.

p. 77 AF decides to leave Berlin: Ibid.

p. 78 AF's loneliness in Boston: Ibid.

p. 79 AF invited to join B.S.O.: Ibid.

p. 80 AF on why he admired Karl Muck: Ibid.

pp. 89–90 AF on his early days in B.S.O.: *Boston Herald-American*, May 1977

p. 91 AF on his revived interest in conducting: Columbia University oral history

p. 91 AF on founding Fiedler Sinfonietta: Ibid.

pp. 92–93 Letter from George E. Judd to AF, May 19, 1926

pp. 93–94 Letter from AF to William Brennan, Dec. 27, 1926

p. 96 AF on founding Esplanade Concerts: Columbia University oral history

p. 96 AF on conducting ambition: *Coronet* magazine, May 1953

p. 97 Review of AF's first Esplanade season: *Time* magazine, July 9, 1929

p. 98 AF named Pops conductor: Columbia University oral history

p. 98 AF as matinee idol: *Boston Post*, 1934

p. 99 AF on his label as Pops conductor: Interview in the *Miami Herald*, Aug. 1972

p. 100 AF on Koussevitzky: Retrospective by Richard Dyer, *Boston Globe*, July 15, 1979

p. 102 Letter from Serge Koussevitzky to AF, Nov. 20, 1944

pp. 102–103 Letter from AF to Serge Koussevitzky, Dec. 2, 1944

p. 103 Letter from Koussevitzky to AF, Dec. 15, 1944

p. 103 Letter from AF to Koussevitzky, Dec. 17, 1944

pp. 103–104 Koussevitzky's last concert: Interview with AF in *The New York Times*, March 1972

p. 104 AF's last experience with Koussevitzky: Interview with AF, Ibid.

pp. 104–105 AF's attitude toward public: *Birmingham* (Ala.) *News*, July 1972

FOUR  Mummy

pp. 106–107 How Mummy met AF: *Boston Globe*, Sept. 1978

p. 107 AF on decision to marry: *San Francisco Chronicle*, Aug. 1963

p. 111 AF on life as a bachelor: *Honolulu Advertiser*, Nov. 1974

p. 114 AF as a bachelor: Interview with William Berenberg, M.D., Feb. 1992

p. 115 AF on courting Ellen Bottomley: *Good Housekeeping*, 1954

p. 116 AF on courting Ellen Bottomley: *San Francisco Examiner*, July 1962

p. 117 AF on his engagement: *Honolulu Advertiser*, Nov. 1974

FIVE  Sinfonia Domestica

p. 132 AF on childhood: Columbia University oral history

p. 136 Morton Gould on AF: Gould interview in *Boston Globe*, Jan. 1978

p. 136 AF on programming: *St. Louis Globe-Democrat*, Feb. 1958

p. 138 AF on programming: Ibid.

p. 139 AF on the Beatles: *Boston Monthly*, Sept. 1979

pp. 140–41 AF on playing light music: *Dallas Times-Herald*, Sept. 1978

p. 141 Leonard Bernstein remembers AF: From memorial broadcast, WGBH–FM, Boston, July 1979

p. 143 AF on parties: *Lancaster* (Pa.) *News*, Sept. 1973

p. 144 AF on sleeping: New Zealand Broadcast Guide, Feb. 1968

SIX  Backstage at Symphony Hall

p. 154–55 Rehearsal anecdote: Interview with Pasquale Cardillo, Feb. 1992

p. 156 AF on orchestra snobbery: AP story by Jules Lohr, undated

p. 156 AF on staying with B.S.O., *The New York Times*, March 1972

p. 156 AF on leaving Boston: *Stereo Review*, Feb. 1977

p. 157 B.S.O. attitude toward AF: *Boston* magazine, 1973

p. 157 Boston Pops finances: *Wall Street Journal*, July 1976

p. 159 AF on B.S.O. attitude toward Pops: *The New York Times*, March 1972

pp. 160–61 Letter from AF to William Brennan, June 1932

p. 162 Letter to AF from George Judd, Aug. 1944

p. 163 B.S.O. internal memo from Thomas D. Perry, Jr., to James J. Brosnahan, March 1960

p. 165 B.S.O. internal memo from James J. Brosnahan to Thomas D. Perry, Jr., June 1962

p. 165 B.S.O. internal memo, ibid.

p. 166 B.S.O. memo from Thomas D. Perry, Jr., to Henry Cabot, June 1962

p. 166 B.S.O. memo from Henry Cabot to Thomas D. Perry, Jr., June 1962

p. 166 B.S.O. memo from James J. Brosnahan to Henry Cabot, March 1963

p. 166 Letter from Thomas D. Perry, Jr., to AF, Feb. 1969
p. 170 AF on B.S.O. quality: *St. Louis Globe-Democrat*, Feb. 1958
p. 170 AF on B.S.O. policy in regard to conductors: AP, Dec. 1964

SEVEN   Papa and the Other Men in My Life

p. 183 AF on attitude toward conductors: *Stereo Review*, Feb. 1977

EIGHT   Part of Papa's World

p. 196 Letter from Thomas D. Perry, Jr., to M. Robert Rogers, June 1969
p. 201 AF on orchestras on TV: *Fort Lauderdale News*, Aug. 1970
p. 201 Review of "Evening at Pops": John O'Connor, *The New York Times*, Aug. 1971
p. 201 AF on being famous: *Jacksonville* (Fla.) *Times-Union*, Feb. 1977
p. 202 AF's career: Interview with David Foster, June 1992
p. 202 AF as showman: AF interview by Gene Shalit, *Ladies' Home Journal*, Nov. 1977
p. 202 AF on fame: *San Francisco Chronicle*, Aug. 1963

NINE   The Last Concert

p. 215 AF on fear of retirement: *Lancaster* (Pa.) *News*, Sept. 1973
p. 219 Correspondence between AF and Harry Beall, March 1976
pp. 219–20 AF worries about his legs: *San Diego Register*, Aug. 1970
p. 220 AF on Pierre Monteux: *San Francisco Examiner*, July 1970
p. 221 AF invited to White House: AP dispatch, Jan. 1977
pp. 221–22 White House ceremony: UPI dispatch, Jan. 1977
p. 222 AF on age: *San Francisco Chronicle*, July 1976
p. 224 AF on aging: *Boston Globe* magazine, July 1978
p. 224 AF on aging and sex: Ibid.
p. 226 Replacing AF: Ibid.
pp. 226–27 Concert anecdote: Interview with Jim Christie, Feb. 1992
p. 227 AF on Toscanini: *Greensboro* (N.C.) *Journal*, March 1967
p. 228 AF letter to Lydia Bottomley, July 1978

TEN   After Papa

p. 247 Morton Gould on AF: *Boston Globe*, Jan. 1978
p. 251 AF on immortality: *San Francisco Examiner*, Summer 1961

# Selected Discography

The following is a list of recordings conducted by Arthur Fiedler currently available on compact disc or audiocassette as of May 1994. Check your local record store for more information.

100 Fiedler Favorites (RCA Victor Gold Seal, 09026-62698-2)
3-CD Box (RCA Victor Gold Seal, 09026-68011-2)
An American Salute (RCA Victor Gold Seal, 6806-2-RG)
A Christmas Festival (RCA Victor Gold Seal, 6428-2-RG)
Christmas Treasures (RCA Living Stereo, 09026-61867-2)
Classics for Children (RCA Victor, 6718-2-RG)
Fiedler and Friends (RCA Victor Gold Seal, 09026-62578-2)
Fiedler on the Roof (RCA Victor, 3201-2-RG)
Fiedler's Favorite Marches (RCA Victor, 09026-60700-2)
Fiedler's Greatest Hits (RCA Victor Greatest Hits, 09026-60835-2)
Gaite Parisienne (RCA Living Stereo, 09026-61847-2)
Gershwin: Rhapsody in Blue (RCA Victor Gold Seal, 6519-2-RG)
Hi-Fi Fiedler (RCA Living Stereo, 09026-61497-2)
Irish Night at the Pops (RCA Victor, 09026-60746-2)

Leroy Anderson's Greatest Hits (RCA Victor Greatest Hits, 09026-61237-2)

Little Drummer Boy (RCA Victor, 09026-61837-2)

Living Stereo Pops Christmas (RCA Living Stereo, 09026-61685-2)

Lullaby (RCA Victor Greatest Hits, 09026-60876-2)

Marches (Victrola, 7881-2-RV)

Marches in Hi-Fi (RCA Living Stereo, 09026-61249-2)

Motion Picture Classics I (RCA Victor, 60392-2-RG)

Motion Picture Classics II (RCA Victor, 60393-2-RG)

Pops Around the World (RCA Victor Greatest Hits, 09026-61544-2)

Pops Roundup (RCA Living Stereo, 09026-61666-2)

Rimsky-Korsakov: Russian Easter Overture (Victrola, 7813-2-RV)

Stars and Stripes (RCA Living Stereo, 09026-61501-2)

Tchaikovsky: Suite from *The Nutcracker* (RCA Victor Gold Seal, 07863-55233-2)

Tchaikovsky: *Swan Lake* (Excerpts) (Victrola, 7879-2-RV)

Themes to Academy Award Winners (RCA Victor, 09026-60966-2)

White Christmas (Deutsche Grammophon Galleria, 419 414-2)

# Index

Arthur Fiedler Bridge, 252
Arthur Fiedler Memorial at
    Symphony Hall, proposed,
    242
Arthur Fiedler Music Library,
    242
Athanas, Anthony, 230
Atkins, Chet, 139

Bailey, Pearl, 139
Baltimore Symphony Orchestra,
    67
Bambi (chihuahua), 129
Beatles, the 139–40
Bennett, Tony, 139
Bennie (chihuahua), 129–30
Berenberg, William, 114
Berliner String Quartet, 74
Berlin Philharmonic Orchestra, 72
Bernfeld, Siegfried, 210
Bernstein, Leonard, 50, 141

Blake, Eubie, 139
*Blue Danube, The,* 137
*Bolero,* 137
Boston Pops Orchestra
    all-request concerts, 137
    arrangements for, 140, 164
    booking of outside
        engagements, 167
    Boston Symphony, financial
        relationship with, 157
    Christmas Pops series, 155,
        189–90
    encores by, 137
    Fiedler family's attendance at
        concerts, 132–34
    Fiedler hired as conductor
        (1930), 97–98
    Fiedler's application for
        conductor position (1926),
        93–95
    Fiedler's final concert, 237

Fiedler's golden anniversary
    concert, 232–36
Fiedler's lighthearted moments,
    154
Fiedler's relationship with
    musicians, 146–48, 150–56,
    183
Fiedler's successor as
    conductor, 225–26
E. Fiedler's performances with,
    203–4, 237
J. Fiedler's performances with,
    211–12
guest conductors, 225–26
impersonal demeanor at
    performances, 135–36
playing in tune, 148
popular music and, 139–40
pranks by musicians, 151–53,
    154–55
principal players, 156
program format, 136–41
radio broadcasts, 200
rare works, performance of, 138
"runout" engagements, 174–75
season of, 68
sexual infidelity of, 126–27
snobbery among musicians,
    155–56
soloists and, 137–38
televised performances, 39, 139,
    200–1
tribute to Fiedler, 239
See also Esplanade Concerts
Boston Pops Tour Orchestra, 65–
    67, 158, 165
Boston Sinfonietta, 91–92, 152
Boston Symphony Orchestra, 28,
    29
    anti-German feelings of World
        War I and, 82–84

Boston Pops, financial
    relationship with, 157
China tour, 231
Fiedler hired by, 79
Fiedler's conducting, 93, 101–3
Fiedler's decision to remain
    with, 169–71
Fiedler's expulsion and
    reinstatement, 92–93
as Fiedler's "family," 81–82,
    198
Fiedler's playing career, 82, 89–
    90
Fiedler's relationship with
    management, 87, 157–67,
    170–71, 196–97
Fiedler's salary, 98, 159–64,
    165–66
Koussevitzky's directorship, 90–
    91
Koussevitzky's resignation, 164
memorial concert for Fiedler,
    240–41
memorial to Fiedler at
    Symphony Hall, proposed,
    242
Monteux honored by, 88–89
Monteux's directorship, 86–87
music library, 164
record companies and, 168–69
wildcat strike of 1920, 87–88
Boston University, 162, 242
Bottomley, John Taylor, 108
Bottomley, Lydia Fuller, 106–7,
    110, 114, 115, 228
Bottomley, Mary Kenney (May)
    (mother), 108–9, 133, 134
Bottomley, May (daughter), 22,
    110, 205
Brennan, William, 160
Brosnahan, James J., 163, 165, 166

Buffalo Philharmonic Orchestra, 67

Cabot, Henry, 166
Cahill, John, 20, 142, 174–75, 221
Cardillo, Pasquale, 142, 251
Casella, Alfredo, 95, 97
Chicago Symphony Orchestra, 68, 148
Christie, Jim, 226–27
Christmas holidays, 54–57, 189–90, 231
Christmas Pops series, 155, 189–90
Columbia Artists Management, 167
conductor-orchestra relationship, 146–47
Cosel, Bill, 142, 168, 224–25, 230, 232, 240

Dartmouth College, 220
Delabeque, Pearl, 112–14, 115
Dellheim, Peter, 168
Denver Symphony Orchestra, 56, 67
Deutsche Grammophon, 168–69
Dickson, Harry Ellis, 68, 140, 142, 225, 230, 237, 239
Dohnányi, Ernst von, 74
Dyer, Richard, 104, 226, 235

Eagels, Jeanne, 111–12, 114
*1812 Overture*, 14, 15
Ellington, Duke, 139
Emery Nippon Symphony Orchestra, 67
Esplanade Concerts, 158
    dogs and, 58
    first season, 95–97

Fourth of July concert (1976), 13–16
    popularity of, 97
"Evening at Pops" (television series), 39, 139, 200–1

Fiedler, Arthur (Papa)
    birthday gifts given by, 39
    birth of, 29
    Boston Sinfonietta, 91–92, 152
    boxing, interest in, 40
    brain surgery, 229–30
    Broadway theatre work, 90
    burial of, 242–43
    childhood of, 29–30, 32–33, 34, 71, 131–32
    children's careers and, 194, 195, 197
    chores for children, insistence on, 39–40
    clothing preferences, 80–81
    code of behavior, 50–51
    conducting career, decision on, 73, 74–75
    conducting style, 133–34
    daily routine, 13
    death of, 237–39
    debut as conductor, 74
    decline in later years, 213–20, 222–25, 226–27, 228–31, 233
    displays of affection, distaste for, 32
    documentary about, 224–25
    dogs, passion for, 58, 224–25
    drinking habit, 55, 62
    driving lessons by, 61–63
    eighty-fourth birthday, 230
    electronic media, use of, 200
    empty time, intolerance of, 61–62, 68, 215, 219

estate of, 209

European years, 71–78

exercise regimen, 219–20

J. Fiedler's romantic
involvements and, 181,
182, 183, 184–88, 189–92

Fiftieth Anniversary Concert,
232–36

firefighting, interest in, 30–32,
241

forgiving nature, 154

funeral of, 240, 241

going on forever, 251

guest conducting, 69–70, 103,
148–50, 166–68, 195–96

health problems, 20, 46–49,
190, 191, 210–11, 214–17,
218–20, 229–31

hearing loss, 149

hobbies of, 219

honorary degrees, 220

humor of, 142

income of, 98, 159–64, 165–67,
168

innovations by, 201–2

insecurities of, 72, 77–78

insomnia of, 144

intonation, concern with, 148

Jewish heritage, impact on
professional life, 170

"light" music, association with,
98–99

memorial service for, 240, 241–
42

mental failings, 223, 227, 229

military career, 84–86

miserliness of, 37–39

musical education, 30, 73–74,
76–77

musical taste, 139–40

Musician of the Year Award
(1977), 213

musicians, relations with, 146–
56, 183

musicianship of, 247–48

music lessons for his children,
45

namesake of, 72–73

papers and scores of, 242

parenthood, attitude toward,
19–21, 25, 27, 44–45

parties, love for, 142–44

personality change in middle
age, 104–5

physical appearance, 75, 110

politics of, 84–85

postconcert routine, 141–45

precision, passion for, 80, 136

prejudice, victim of, 83–84

Presidential Medal of Freedom,
221–22

psychic ability, 185

psychological problems, 210–11

publicity, desire for, 158–59

public's interest in, 217–18

reading preferences, 72, 112

record collectors and, 187

record companies and, 67, 168–
69

religious beliefs, 50

royalties from record sales, 168

San Francisco, love for, 63–64

secretiveness about personal
life, 84

self-promotion, attitude toward,
94, 202

self-respect problem, 159–60

seventy-fifth birthday, 169, 195–
96

social standing, 113, 116, 194

statue of, 252–53

Symphony Hall persona, 131,
134–35
touring by, 65–68
wallpaper incident, 36–37
women, passion for, 75, 111–15,
224
"writings" of, 54–55
*See also* Boston Pops Orchestra;
Boston Symphony
Orchestra; Esplanade
Concerts, Fiedler family;
*specific persons*
Fiedler, Bernhard (uncle), 29, 78,
86
Fiedler, Deborah (daughter), 22,
88, 123, 212, 221
birth of, 25
coming-out party, 194
emotional crisis, 207–8
law career, 197
schooling, 52–53
sibling relations, 25, 26, 43–44,
125, 178–79
wedding of, 230–31
withdrawal from family, 125–26
*See also* Fiedler family
Fiedler, Ellen Bottomley
(Mummy) (wife), 99, 103
childhood of, 108–9
concert narrations, 203–4, 237
cooking by, 59, 122–23
death of, 244
debut into society, 109
drinking habit, 110, 123–25, 206
eccentric behavior, 120–22
Fiedler's affairs prior to
marriage and, 115
Fiedler's health problems and,
48, 216–17
Fiedler's relationship with
closeness in later years, 203

courtship, 115–17
first meeting, 106–7
happiness of early married
life, 118–19
marital strains, 121, 134
music's impact on, 172
separate lives, 37
Spanish dance incident, 110
staying together despite
problems, 205–6
wedding, 49–50, 107, 117–18
D. Fiedler's wedding, 230
J. Fiedler's relationship with,
26–27, 173, 177–78, 179–
80, 221, 233–35, 243–44
J. Fiedler's romantic
involvements and, 181, 182
final years, 243–44
forebears of, 107–8
health problems, 205–6
parenthood, attitude toward,
19–22, 27
physical appearance, 175
psychiatric help for, 233–34
religious beliefs, 51
social life, 109–10
viciousness of, 52
*See also* Fiedler family
Fiedler, Elsa (sister), 47, 133, 134
Fiedler, Emanuel (father), 28–30,
32, 33, 57, 71, 72–73, 88,
100, 101, 131
Fiedler, Fredericka (sister), 133,
134
Fiedler, Gustav (uncle), 29, 57,
78, 86, 110
Fiedler, Isaac (grandfather), 28
Fiedler, Johanna (daughter), 88,
123
as "bad baby," 26–27
birth of, 19, 20–21

Boston, abandonment of, 193
as Boston Symphony brat, 131–
    32, 134–35
career in music, 193–98, 199,
    244, 249–50
college years, 180–81
concert narrations, 204, 211–12
dogs for, 128–30
drinking habit, 205, 250
driving lessons, 61–63
early childhood, 22–27
Fiedler's fame, impact of,
    202–3
Fiedler's relationship with, 27,
    33–34, 185
  boxing matches and, 40
  final goodbye, 16
  final time together, 236
  flirtations, 176–77
  idolization of Fiedler by
      Johanna, 198–99
  sharing of music, 23, 45–46,
      172–73, 211–12, 249
  traveling together, 173–75
Fiedler's statue, confrontation
    with, 252–53
E. Fiedler's relationship with,
    26–27, 173, 177–78, 179–
    80, 221, 233–35, 243–44
Fourth of July (1976), 13–16
friendless periods, 177–78
money problems, 208–10
musical education, 45–46
musical talents, 23
physical appearance, 175–77
pitch, sense of, 23
psychological problems, 209–10,
    211–12
rebellions by, 23, 53
romantic involvements, 179,
    181–92, 244–47

schooling, 24, 52–53
search for herself, 248–51
self-control of, 24
sexual assault incident, 208
shyness of, 173–74, 176
sibling relations, 25, 26, 43–
    44, 125, 178–79
single life, decision on, 244
stuttering problem, 24–25
writing talent, 194, 195
"Yummy" nickname, 20–21
*See also* Fiedler family
Fiedler, Johanna Bernfeld
    (mother), 29–30, 32–33, 34,
    72
Fiedler, Peter (son), 22
  bicycle accident, 41–42
  birth of, 25
  Fiedler's relationship with, 41–
    42
  romantic involvements, 182
  sibling relations, 178–79
  television watching, 126
  "Tony with a gun" incident,
    191–92
  *See also* Fiedler family
Fiedler, Rosa (sister), 33, 52, 56,
    133, 134, 209
Fiedler family
  anger and resentment in, 43–44
  Christmas holidays, 54–57, 189–
    90, 231
  Fiedler's death and aftermath,
    239, 240–43
  Fiedler's time at home, 68–69,
    70
  financial matters, 37, 207–10
  lunch ritual, 122
  pets, 57–61, 128–31
  Pops concerts together, 132–34

public image of happy family, 42–43
  religious life, 49–54
  sense of doom, 46–49
  traveling together, 63–65
  vacations at home, 70
Fiedler home (Hyslop Road), 26, 35–37, 40, 243
Fiedler name, origin of, 28
Fitzgerald, Ella, 139
Flack, Roberta, 139
Ford, Betty, 221
Ford, Gerald R., 221
Fourth of July (1976), 13–16
Fuller, Alvin T., 106, 113
Fuller, Viola, 110, 113

Galway, James, 237
Gericke, Wilhelm, 28
Gervais, Cécile (Celie), 26, 27, 36, 59, 64, 122, 232–33, 235, 243
Gillespie, Dizzy, 139
Gould, Morton, 136, 247

Harvard University, 220
Hess, Willy, 74
Higginson, Maj. Henry Lee, 81, 82, 83, 84, 86
Hindemith, Paul, 92
Hirsch, Kurt, 76, 77

"I Want to Hold Your Hand," 139

Jacchia, Alfredo, 92, 93
*Jaws* theme, 154
Judd, George, 92–93, 162
*Just Call Me Maestro* (documentary), 224–25

Kennedy, Edward M., 241
Kennedy, Joseph P., 108, 109
Kenney, Ellen O'Rourke, 108
Kenney, Grandpa, 107–8
Kleffel, Arno, 74
Kneisel Quartet, 29
Komische Oper, 72
Koussevitzky, Serge, 50, 86, 89, 92, 97
  directorship of Boston Symphony, 90–91
  Fiedler's relationship with, 99–104
  resignation from Boston Symphony, 164
Kreisler, Fritz, 28

Liberace, 247
*Lincoln Portrait, A,* 203–4, 237
London Symphony Orchestra, 148–50
Los Angeles Philharmonic Orchestra, 68
Louise (housekeeper), 21, 59, 116–17

Massachusetts Institute of Technology (MIT), 72
Maugham, W. Somerset, 112
McCartney, Paul, 139
McCormack, John, 108
Mechkat, Farhad, 187–88
Metropolitan Opera, 127, 197–98, 199, 249–50
Milnes, Sherrill, 69
Mohr, Richard, 69
Monteux, Doris, 88
Monteux, Pierre, 63, 86–87, 88–89, 220
Morris, Thomas, 158, 159, 163–64, 171, 200, 225, 230, 232, 240

Mowrey, Tom, 238
Muck, Karl, 79–80, 83, 84
Mugar, David, 230
Musician of the Year Award, 213

National Symphony Orchestra, 67, 195–96
NBC Symphony Orchestra, 227–28
New Orleans Philharmonic Orchestra, 67
New York Philharmonic Orchestra, 127, 197
Nicky (fox terrier), 57–58
Nikisch, Artur, 72–73

*Of Human Bondage* (Maugham), 112
Ozawa, Seiji, 171, 231, 232, 241

Paderewski, Ignacy Jan, 148, 149
Perry, Thomas, 196
*Peter and the Wolf,* 204, 211–12
Philadelphia Orchestra, 68
Presidential Medal of Freedom, 221–22
Public Broadcasting Service (PBS), 201

Rabaud, Henri, 86
Randolph, Boots, 139
Ravinia Festival, 68
RCA Victor Company, 67, 168, 169
Royal Academy of Music (Berlin), 73–74, 76
Royal Liverpool Philharmonic Orchestra, 139

Sambor, Ukraine, 28
San Francisco, Fiedler's love for, 63–64
San Francisco Symphony, 63
Sanromá, Jesús María, 110, 115, 149
Sarah Lawrence College, 180
Shisler, Bill, 66, 142, 164, 168, 230
Short, Bobby, 139
Sinatra, Frank, 101–2
Sparky (Dalmatian), 59–61, 122, 128, 130–31
Spotts, Joseph, 35, 141
"Stars and Stripes Forever, The," 15, 141, 155, 239
Steinberg, Michael, 157, 248
*Stereo Review* magazine, 213
Strauss, Johann, III, 74
Sweetie (chihuahua), 224–25
Symphony-Dinner Concert series, 99–100

Tanglewood Festival, 68, 100–1
Thomson, Virgil, 141
Tony (J. Fiedler's friend), 188–92
Toscanini, Arturo, 137, 200, 227–28

Vaughan, Sarah, 139
Villa Lobos, Hector, 103

Wild, Earl, 148, 149
Wilford, Ronald, 167
*William Tell Overture,* 137
World War I, 76–77, 82–84, 85
World War II, 85–86

Zimbler, Pepi, 152, 156